DRUMS OF MER

ION IDRIESS

ETT IMPRINT

Exile Bay

This 25th Edition published by ETT Imprint, Exile Bay in 2025

First published in Australia in 1933 by Angus & Robertson (reprinted three times); 1934 (twice); 1936, 1938, 1939, 1941, 1942 (twice); 1944, 1947, 1949, 1951 (twice); 1962, 1966, 1967, 1973, 1977

Electronic published by ETT Imprint in 2017

Published by ETT Imprint in 2020. Reprinted 2020.

Copyright © Idriess Enterprises Pty Ltd 2017, 2020

This book is copyright. Apart from any fair dealing for the purposes of private study, research, criticism or review, as permitted under the Copyright Act, no part may be reproduced by any process without written permission.

Inquiries should be addressed to the publishers via ettimprint@hotmail.com

ISBN 978-1-923205-62-8 (pbk)
ISBN 978-1-922384-05-8 (ebk)

Designed by Tom Thompson

FOREWORD

To one who for a good many years has lived among the tropic isles of Torres Strait, and whose constant regret has been that their romantic attractiveness is so little known even to Australians, the *Drums of Mer* comes with very strong appeal. There are some who may think that Mr Idriess is giving us simply an imaginative picture, but the author has travelled the Strait with the discerning eye and contemplative soul of the artist who is satisfied only with first-hand colour, and who, while blending history and romance with subtle skill, at the same time keeps within the region of fact. The records and documents placed at his disposal by those who have patiently collected them in the interests of history, of ethnological and scientific research, and (if one may be allowed to say so) even of missionary theological science also, provide the rich store upon which he has drawn for the thrilling story he has woven round the people of Mer and the other islands of Torres Strait. We have been waiting for someone to catch the charm and appealing mysteriousness of these islands, and to visualize the days, not so very long past, when the great outrigger canoes, with their companies of feather-bedecked headhunters, traversed the opalescent waters a couple of hundred miles down the Barrier, to return perhaps with cowering white captives or grim human trophies for the ceremonies of the "Au-gud-Au-Ai," the "Feast of the Great God." And if it seems that the starkness of tragedy throws a cloud here and there over the dramatic episodes which the author has so well narrated, possibly it is a good thing for present-day tourist-travellers (and others too!), to realize that a trip along the Barrier and through the Strait on the way to China was not always so free from danger.

Although they extend almost right up to the beach of New Guinea, the islands of Torres Strait, with their curious mixture of people, form part of Australia, and are within the boundaries of Queensland. Hydrographic charts reveal how ocean currents seem to chase one another right across the Pacific and up the east coast into the centre of the shoals and reefs which make a network of the Strait; and the strong south-east winds, which blow for the eight or nine months of the year when the nor'-west is not casting its lowering storm-clouds over the islands, may, in combination with the currents, help to account for the migratory canoes of legend. These, setting out for new lands in South America and New Zealand, found themselves cut off from the main body, and, passing through channels of the Great Barrier, landed (possibly four or five hundred years ago) in the group of islands round which the author writes his story. Chinese junks and Malay proas knew these waters, probably also the Dutch and the Japanese; but the honour of discovery has gone to Torres, concerning whose voyage the recently published *Relación* of de Prado has given us much additional light. And when the enterprise of Captain Cook was followed up by those epic-making voyages of the *Bounty* and the *Pandora,* which placed new names on the chart, Torres Strait began to come into prominence as a new sea-highway to the East. White-winged ships, singly, in pairs, or half a dozen at a time, braved the unlighted and unmarked course along the Barrier, facing the dual dangers of concealed coral reefs and the aggressiveness of the headhunting Island "Indians," as they were then called. The treacherous reefs took heavy toll, as witness the long but yet incomplete list of wrecks in the *Australian Encyclopaedia*. The beautiful palm-clad islands became linked with dark tragedy; and so it is that, as one journeys from island to island and listens to native story and legend and song from the lips of the old men, it is possible to piece together the tale of some ship's mystery of earlier days, when the craft herself vanished without trace of passengers or crew. Sometimes it is the discovery of an old inscribed ship's bell that has set one on the track; or some coral-encrusted relic retrieved from the reefs; or perhaps old, quaintly worded documents which have somehow escaped the devastating hand that would consign everything to the flames.

But with the tragedy there is also romance. The Strait teems with it. The anthropologist, who hopes to solve the secrets of the mysterious Bomai-Malu Cult, which had its headquarters at Murray Island (Mer, right up at the top of the Barrier, where so many ship-skeletons lie); the conchologist, who discovers wondrous things of delight in the great marine gardens of the strait – these and many other "ologists" find a lure within its waters; and the seekers of marine wealth in the shape of mother-of-pearl and trochus and trepang, as well as the treasure-hunters who from time to time have come upon rich hoards of Spanish gold (and still hope for more!) realize its potentialities from the utilitarian standpoint.

Ships now pass right alongside the islands of the once dreaded "Indians," whose descendants still hunt the waters, not for human heads but for the store of marine produce which adds to Australia's wealth. But under the palms on shore the old men sit and pass on the stories of the "Drums of Mer." In giving us his latest book, Mr Idriess has helped to preserve a little-known portion of Australia's northern history with a vividness of colouring which makes it extremely realistic and enthralling, and not least so to those who know the place and people well. One looks forward with eagerness to further stories of the Strait from the same pen, for Mr Idriess has by no means exhausted the riches of the historic mine which he has opened up, where, often, truth has proved so strange that as fiction it would provoke the smile of incredulity.

Wm H. MacFarlane
Mission Priest, Torres Strait.
Administrator of the Diocese of Carpentaria.
31 July 1933.

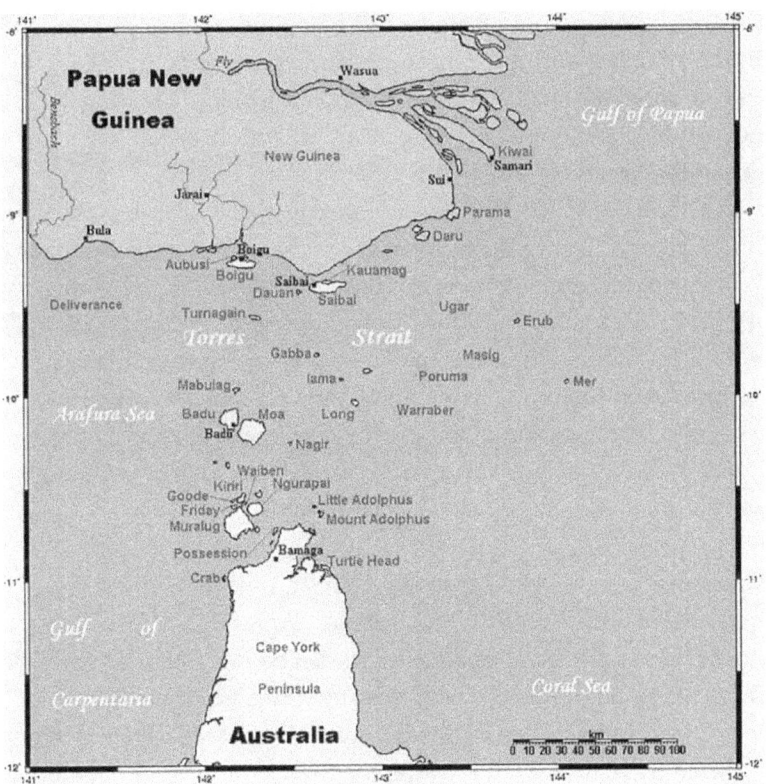

Author's Note

This story is in all essentials historical fact. Almost every chapter contains an incident in the comparatively recent history of a little understood but once remarkable people, told in detail by the last survivors of those best able to know. As to the voyages, the fights and massacres, the mysticism and cruel customs described – well, such were once part of the life of these people; and this book would give a false impression if the few ruddy incidents occurring at the period of this story, were deleted.

Ethnologically, too, the story is correct. Here, I am greatly indebted to the splendid *Reports of the Cambridge Anthropological Expedition to Torres Strait* and to that living mine of Torres Strait ethnological lore the Rev. W. H. MacFarlane (the well-known "Wandering Missionary of the Strait,") who put me in personal touch with the Island historians. Cruising with MacFarlane, landing on out-of-the-way islands, and hearing the story from the lips of the last of the Zogo-le, was fascinating work.

MacFarlane has toiled for many years among these Islanders, but it was only after years of sympathetic friendship that he gained the inner confidence of the old keepers of secrets. These at last, seeing the younger generation fully reconciled to the unconquerable changes which civilization had brought upon them told much of their secret history to MacFarlane just about the time I came along and reaped the benefit of it. A little later and old Maino, son of the great Kebisu, and old Passi of Mer, and other warriors of the grim old days, would have died with their people's secrets unrevealed. (Passi died while this book was going to press.)

The names of native chiefs, especially Kebisu and his club-swinging friend Maros, were quite recently household names from Cape York Peninsula right across the Strait to New Guinea. The few pearling vessels mentioned are ships that helped to make history, lurid and otherwise, at the time when the Strait was growing her "eye-teeth." Practically, the only departure from fact is in a slightly different timing of several chapters, due mainly to the difference between the native calendar and our own; and the difficulty, in what was then a new country and an isolated sea in the throes of its pioneering days, of pinning any episode strictly to date after the lapse of years. There is, also, a departure from the sequence of fact in chapter XXII. Here there were actually two shipwrecks, not one; the incident of the monkey occurred during the looting of one ship, that of the looking-glasses on the other. But to describe each incident separately, would have lengthened an already long book.

My one conscious lapse into fiction is the treasure within the heart of Gelam. Even this may not be entirely fiction, for to this day old Spanish coins of gold and silver are occasionally dug up in the gardens of Mer, of Eroob, and Ugar. Jardine's ill-fated schooner captain, in these same waters, found his coral-encrusted treasure chest of nearly £4000 worth of old-time silver dollars. On various islands of the other Groups, old-time coins are found after nor'-west storms have ravaged the beaches. Jack McNulty, of the Federal Hotel, Thursday Island, has a collection of such relics. An old Spanish coin of gold, dug from Mer, was bought by a resident from a native when I was last in Thursday Island.

As to Mer and the heart of Gelam, well, the old extinct crater is there, the rumour is there, the legend of the Spaniards and Las village is there, and since this story was written Nasana of Mer tells realistically of his trepidation on creeping into an underground cave which apparently runs in far under Gelam. The mummification of bodies of course, is fact, merely the custom, but recently faded into disuse. This treasure story is, so far as I am aware, in no relation to the mysterious English enterprise which searched gloomy Naghir Island some years ago, and so silently stole away. The Islanders tell of precious stones unearthed in years gone past, and the rest of the story seems to fit in rather uncannily.

If ethnologists are incredulous concerning the statement that the forefathers of some of these natives came from "Ekinpad" in northern Queensland, I can only say that the Zogo-le themselves definitely stated that they did.

I have to thank, too, Roddy Bruce, the nephew of that protector and great-hearted friend of the Islanders, John Stewart Bruce, Baba (father) of Mer, for giving me such intimate glimpses into the heart and mind of both the Islander and the aboriginal. Roddy Bruce, the first white baby born on Mer (and born under tragic circumstances) was mothered by a native woman and reared as a child of Mer.

As a guide to incidents from the white man's point of view during the "white invasion of the Strait," I was fortunate in having placed at my disposal while at Somerset House, Albany Pass, Cape York Peninsula, several volumes of Jardine's diary dealing with that period. And later at Thursday Island I was loaned four cobwebby volumes of valuable official records, which had been unearthed from an old lumber-room in the Court House.

Jakara, is to a certain extent, conjecture. A very few white castaways have survived against all odds amongst those once fierce Islanders: Ned Mosby, for instance, who made favourable history on Massig Island, and whose sons are well established there now. And there have been occasional blotches on the white man's escutcheon, such as that renegade Wini, "The Wild White Man of Badu," who attained a power sufficient to terrorize both native and white. A parallel to Jakara's romance is the fate of the four lonely lads, survivors of the wreck of the *Charles Eaton*. The castaways clinging to the rafts were clubbed and their skulls hung round the neck of the great Au-gud of Aureed Island. The boys, D'Oyley brothers, Ireland, and Sexton, were claimed as "Lamars." Baby D'Oyley and young Ireland were the lucky ones, old Duppa of Mer claiming them as Lamars (living spirits) of his sons. Years later, the captain of the *Mangles* reported white castaways living among the savages of Mer. Eventually the New South Wales Government sent out the rescue schooner *Isabella* to rescue them, with the result that the younger D'Oyley and Ireland were bought from Duppa. The two other lads could never be found. MacFarlane and I often speculated as to their fate. On this subject, for some reason or other, the Islanders were very reticent to MacFarlane's inquiries.

As to the mysterious *booya*, the stone which shed the brilliant flame, I can only say that the natives declare it to have been a luminous "stone."

My thanks are due to Father Chester of Sydney, who allowed me access to the records and diaries of his father, Lieutenant Henry M. Chester, who established the seat of government at Thursday Island, and later hoisted the flag on New Guinea. The diaries of this well-known historical figure have helped me considerably in placing as authentically as possible, a number of incidents in this book from the white man's point of view as well as the native's.

As for the few white women mentioned in this story – well, the fate of several as here described is, alas, only too true.

For the photographs in this book my thanks are due to Messrs. G. Bright, N. N. Lyons of Murray Island (Mer); H. Hudson, formerly of Torres Strait; to Frank Pryke, leader of the Sir Rupert Clarke expedition up the Fly River, to John Sandes, Colin Simpson, and to the *Reports of the Cambridge Anthropological Expedition to Torres Strait* (Cambridge University Press).

Ion Idriess.

CONTENTS

The Dance Of Death	11
Preparing For The End	20
Forcing The Secrets Of Heaven	30
The Heart Of The Pretty Lamar	37
The Coming Of Kebisu	43
War Drums Of Mer	53
The Massacre On The Two Brothers	61
The Return	67
Jakara Makes Love	72
When The Blood Lust Calls	78
Velvet Claws	84
The Menace Of The Lamars	90
The Leaden Fist Of The Lamars	96
Within The Crater Of Mer	102
Women	113
The Pearl Ships Of The Lamars	122
The Dance	129
The Trouncing Of Kebisu	137
The Sailing Of The Fleet	143
The Looting Of The Lamar Ship	151
The Raid Of The Tugeri	158
The Peoples Of The Auwo Oromo	166
The Great Trade	172
The Battle On The Fly	179
The Cyclone	188
A Girl's Plan	195
The Duel	202
The Coming Of Gareeb	210
In Which Gareeb Learns There Are Other Peoples, Other Lives	217
Virgins Of Waiat	227
Plans And Counter Plans	238
As Is Written In The Courses Of The Stars	248
Glossary	256

CHAPTER I

The Dance of Deaths

Utter silence, not even the swish of a night bird's wing. The island, towering black, big Gelam with its little hills sloping away down to the indistinct lands. A stone's throw across the water was shadowed the precipitous peak of tiny Dauar with the castellated cliffs of Waiar, isle of evil, beside it; and over all a dome of velvet-blue pierced by a million stars. It seemed that the curtains of heaven were withdrawn, so that angels might gaze upon Mer.

Mer the terrible! Mer the beautiful: chief lodge of the Zogo-le!

Within the Sacred Grove the tenseness was such that the people breathed fear. The sacred Wongais encircled the grove, their massive, twisted branches, their grey-green leaves still and silent.

In the centre loomed a dome-shaped thatch like a mammoth beehive. It was the chief Zogo-house of the Eastern Group, and it housed one of the most powerful gods known to Island peoples. Pressed back upon the sacred trees, as far from the Zogo-house as they could squeeze, waited a thousand men and women.

Not a large meeting, for this was but a local thanksgiving to the Augud for a successful raid, made spectacular by the young son of the Mamoose having brought back a prisoner.

Pregnant silence in the Grove; the captive's ears tingled to the sigh of hostile people breathing around him in the dark. And often at a movement came a gleam half seen and frightening – the eyes of savage people nearly hysterical from an ecstasy of excitement and fear.

Suddenly, as if propelled from a giant's searchlight, a flame of liquid gold shot from the sea towards the sky. It crinkled while it grew, as if the long-drawn "Ah" of the people fanned it to a flame that crept up behind the black summit of Gelam. From flaring silhouette the crater's edge turned into fire of gold as the long grass leapt into view. A bath of silver dashed upon the sea. Hills, trees, villages leapt to form, adorned in silver coats. The hill-crests gleamed, a crimson line.

From somewhere came a rumble that broke into a concerted throb of drums. Those shark-jaw drums of Mer! Throbbing a passion that echoed in the beating hearts of men. Far out across the Strait the leathery snakelike head of a turtle clove the water and floated wonderingly.

A circle tip of molten gold pierced the crimson line. The crowd in frantic accord raised their arms and roared a chant, fierce yet strangely sweet, while the tip swelled to a disk that shot clean above the hill-top to the quickening pulse of the drums.

Burnished gold, swimming in its own brightness, this wonder moon of the Coral Sea! They gloried in its majesty while it sped up, up, up, and strikingly were its beams reflected within the Sacred Grove, until the straws upon the Zogo-house were visible as in the day. Perhaps some property in the ground, or shrewd advantaging of trees and rocks and hills, was responsible for this fierce white reflection.

Bamboo masts (the Sarokag) stood around the Zogo-house, arranged mathematically to form a sign of the Bomai-Malu, each mast capped by a symbol upon which the light was reflected mirror-like. These symbols were skulls. Crowning a coral dais was a gigantic clam-shell of pure white, mothering the Zogo-stone, round and black and glistening, for it had just been anointed with human oil. The moon beams licked upon the living as if by its light imbuing their bodies with life of itself. Warriors and women, youths and maids, of splendid stature with arms upstretched and faces transformed above the meaning of their song. These were the Miriam-le, all the people of the villages of Mer.

The village men of Mer were tall heavily-built savages, dark brown men in colour, strong limbed. Their faces were broad, with features uncompromising under jet-black brows which shadowed keen aggressive eyes. Their hair, in thick ringlets, fell back over the shoulders; their beards were divided into ringlets of three dark coils speckled with ivory of crocodiles' teeth; sharks' teeth gleamed along the double edge of their broad, heavy swords. Among these darker peoples of the Miriam-le, some, men of Las village stood out like the bronzed statues of a sculptor's dream. Their faces were arrestingly pleasing, their black-brown eyes keenly alive, while their finely chiselled features and haughty carriage irresistibly reminded the one white onlooker of the arrogance of Spain. The black eyes of their women flashed merriment and coquetry, while their athletic figures made the onlooker resentful that their skin was not pure white. The single petticoat of fig-tree root, teased into strands of silk, clung from supple waists to just above the knee. The maids not yet initiated into womanhood, however, adorned the many leaved croton, while a hibiscus necklace in scarlet flowers toyed across their breasts. Their hazily pretty hair was a wave of profuse strands, all of minute crinkles. Pridefully cared for, it fringed the forehead in massed waves where every strand lay in place combed back over the head to the nape of the neck, where it was gathered by a gleaming clasp of mother-of-pearl to spread out and up like a peacock's tail, a fan-shaped mass of fine black hair. A brown colour at the tips was due to constant diving and swimming in the sea. Strange that among these people were numbers with the countenance of Jew and Arab!

And upon all the Miriam-le alike there shimmered beautiful ornaments, insignia of office, *dibi-dibi* pendants of warriorhood, leg-bands, brow-combs, breast ornaments of gleaming mother-of-pearl, of sparkling nautilus shell, of mottled tortoise-shell, the armlet-shell rare and carved, necklaces of brilliant corals and tiny vividly-coloured shells; the insignia of the Zogo-le and Mamooses were cut and carved and polished with a highly artistic taste.

Surrounding the chief of each tribal group and holding themselves apart, were arrogant men from whose brows floated the ominous black feathers of one of the most feared societies ever formed, the Bomai-Malu Cult. Standing in cynical isolation, his huge arms haughtily folded, was a giant clad in the dread insignia of Waiat. From his glance all maids trembled away, seeking to hide their faces and figures among the crowd. All the clans of Mer were there, all except one, the Gamard-Bauer, outcasts and ghouls of the night. And joining with the song of the Miriam-le chanted the graceful people of Las, taken out of themselves in adoration of a "Something" which they but dimly realized. "Gesu! Gesu! Gesu!" "Oh Au-gudeem! Oh Au-gudeem! Oh Au-gudeem!"

Among the black warriors of Mer there sang a Las man, or, rather, such he seemed to be for his skin was kissed a deep, rich brown from the sun .and sea. There the resemblance ended. He was not so tall as the Las, but his body, now afire with tense emotions, was as lithely muscular as theirs. He wore the badge of the men of Mer, he shook on high a sword of Mer, his hair was as long as theirs, only his was *brown*. He wore the crescent *mai*, proud insignia of a chief. The square jaw was beardless, unlike some young men around him, numbers of whom too wore the hair cut short. Strangely, among that black-eyed throng, his eyes were *grey*. Once a boyish laughing grey, they had grown cold and steely and cruel, alive with a snaky quickness that registered every happening in the grove, eyes that reacted to some ever-present fear of the mind.

Outwardly he was just like the others as his vibrant voice sang praise of Bomai, of Malu, of Segar, of Kulka, of the Au-gud, and of the Zogo and the Zogo-le.

The drums ceased – silence gripped all as the moon, now satisfied that the men of Mer paid homage, proceeded majestically up into the skies to veil its face with wispy cloud-lace of pink, a wondrous moon, the golden moon of Torres Strait.

With lowered arms the people trembled – fear hushed the grove – the walls of the Zogo-house slid within themselves, the interior opened. A thousand people fell upon their knees, with heads bowed to the earth and crying, "Oh Au-gudeem! Oh Au-gudeem! Oh Au-gudeem!" From deep among the men of Mer the brown man peered up from under his eyebrows, intent upon the chief Zogo, not the fearsome Au-gud. Even at that distance he strove to combat the master mind behind the gigantic mask, to seek out its camouflaged thoughts, its secret intentions towards himself. As the trapped rat stares at the waiting snake so he stared but with his mind alone, never with his eyes when perhaps others might notice.

C'Zarcke the Zogo, the great Au-Zogo-zogo-le and Au-Maid-maid-le, master of hypnotic sorcery, chief and head of the Bomai-Malu, gazed out over the bowed crowd, his strong teeth gritted in an ecstasy of power. Full well he knew that he could, if he wished, call on these people and they would turn and slay until not one man or woman was left alive. And these were merely a handful of the multitude to whom but a thought from him could bring death. Chief Zogo of the most powerful Island group and Geregere-le (the Beizam-boai who had charge of the sacred emblems), of the Bomai-Malu Cult which controlled the three main Island groups and even tribes in distant Dowdai (New Guinea), he was ruler and supreme arbiter in life; and – they believed – after death, of the destiny of many people.

A Tami-le (secondary priest) respectfully removed the mask, disclosing C'Zarcke clad in a magnificent head-dress of plumes of the red bird of paradise, the feathers inset within a curved arch of mother-of-pearl which fitted down over the head to the lower jaw. Encircling the arch, like nails in a horseshoe gleamed iridescent green and pearl. These were of a tiny green coral shell highly prized and rare, but the pearls merely possessed a superstitious value, since they were "Stones of the Sea." Down his back, over massive shoulders, fell blue-black curls which, with the banding of pearl and drooping plumes, framed a savage face mesmeric with mental power.

On his broad chest glittered the Zogo-mai, of which there are only three in the world. About five inches in diameter, this beautiful ornament was of perfect mother-of-pearl, disk-shaped, perforated with fretwork into a series of polished patterns. The art of the work had been lost centuries before at the birth of the Bomai-Malu. In the far-off days of the Ad Giz (the first gods or ancestors) the art had been born. Only the chief Zogo of Mer, of Eroob, and of Ugar, dare wear a Zogo-mai. On one thick arm C'Zarcke wore a Zogo-kadik, a finely-plaited arm-guard of cane from which flaunted metallic plumes of the bird of paradise. Round his body clung a voluptuously thick skirt which appeared like thousands of jet-black threads of hair, curling to the knees. These were selected feathers of the cassowary. The waist-band into which the skirt was gathered scintillated with phosphoric beads of shell and flame-stones, which flashed suspiciously like European jewels. With one hand linking with the base of the Au-gud, so C'Zarcke stood.

Above its dais of coral and shells the Au-gud loomed to a height of six feet; a sitting figure in the form of a man, it was fashioned from picked plates of tortoise-shell, polished to a mottled beauty. As it sat with heavy arms folded and slightly bowed head, its broad face expressed savagery shadowed by a cynical wisdom. To the left and right of the Au-gud stood Ses and Aet, who, with C'Zarcke, composed the Zogo-le of Mer. Farther to the right stood the three Zogo-le of Eroob, and to the left the Zogo-le of Ugar. The chief Zogo of each Zogo-le wore the Zogo-mai, but C'Zarcke alone wore the metallic feathers in his Zogo-kadik. Also the skirt of the lesser Zogo-le as fashioned of silken strands, delicately plaited of Ze-leaves. These men wore, throughout, the fantastic masks of Malu, only partially visible behind a barbaric shield of turtle-shell. The face was broadly barred with white in designs apparently geometrical in pattern, each design representing a secret order of Bomai. The cheeks were marked with a row of red triangles, with central disks of yellow. A drooping busby of coloured grasses tasselled from the top. Around his neck each man wore a necklet of the lower jaws of human beings.

Standing in two semicircles partly enclosing the Au-gud and the Zogo-le, were the barbarically dressed priests, the Tami-le. From the head of each drooped an ominous black feather.

C'Zarcke turned to the Au-gud, and his deep voice boomed within the Zogo-house and was thrown back and far out over the amphitheatre of trees. The Zogo-house had been designed by cunning men who understood the magnifying properties of sound. From the Au-gud's nostrils belched streaks of greenish flame, met by a fiery breath from the god's mouth which carried the intermingling flames straight out towards the centre of the Sacred Grove.

An instant change came over the people who, leaping erect, shouted thrice to the accompaniment of waving arms and a rhythmic, thunderous stamp of feet: "Oh Au-gudeem! Oh Au-gudeem! Oh Au-gudeem!"

Then with martial tread and flashing eyes, stalked forward Bogo, Mamoose of Mer. Behind him came Beizam, his stripling son, filled with a trembling pride at the greatest event of his life. For in a moment he would be a warrior, he would have taken his first head!

Under like circumstances, a boy on getting his first man would not remove the head himself, that would be done by the uncle (maternal), and the head would be brought to the boy's mother to hang on the post near the home. But Beizam was the son of the Mamoose, and now he was nearly dying of dread lest he make a mess of removing his maiden trophy in the presence of all these.

For in the surprise raid Beizam had overpowered a prisoner, and his triumph-flamed mind had borne a great idea. He, the chief's stripling, would slay his prisoner before the Zogo-house in front of all the people! Fitting tableau to the initiation of a chief's son, and quite in accord with the keen dramatic instincts of the Islanders!

Between two warriors was dragged the prisoner.

They stood him upon nerveless feet before the Au-gud. The man was a warrior of the Yardigan tribe, an aboriginal mainlander. He was tall of stature, and the scars crossing his chest and corrugating his back and shoulder muscles were proof positive that he had slain his men. In nakedness he trembled there, just nerveless clay. Sweat glistened upon his body, which was astench with human grease. A strikingly different specimen of humanity, this stone-age man, his animal-like features strongly contrasting with the clean-cut features of the Islanders.

Contemptuously Beizam thrust a warrior's *gaba-gaba* club into the captive's nerveless paw. But he just stood there, thick-lipped mouth sagging, deep-set shaggy eyes staring piteously at the Au-gud. He was no coward, this Australian aboriginal, simply a child of the forest. Fear held him mesmerized; this sudden transition from the sunlit, quiet bush to these undreamt-of happenings benumbed the reasoning of the brain.

Beizam stepped back, transformed. With lips parted and expanded chest he stared a moment at this hairy man as if he were the most wonderful, the most beautiful, the most coveted thing in the world. Then, with a panther step forward, he swung his stone killing-club and with practised flick of the wrist brought it squarely on the temple of the aboriginal. To the "smack" of the blow there roared shouts and shrieks of approval. It had been a perfect blow, exactly on the right spot, not too hard, not too gentle, just sufficient to stun. Beizam leapt on the fallen man, his *gaba-gaba* swinging from a wrist-thong as his left hand flicked loose the *singai* loop from behind his neck while his right whipped out the *upi* head-knife, razor-keen. Grasping the clay-daubed hair in talon-like fingers, Beizam jerked the face toward the skies and slit the throat beneath. Through this he thrust the *singai*, until the cane loop poked out from the mouth; then, thrusting the handle through the loop, he drew the knot tight.

Gaba-gaba / Singai loop.

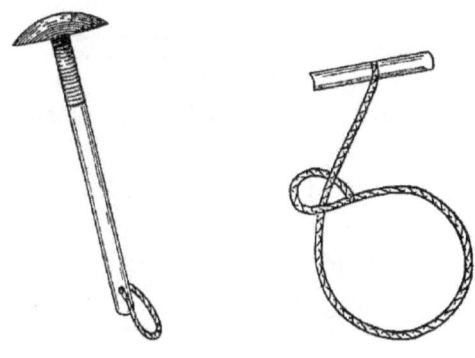

Upi – Head-knife.

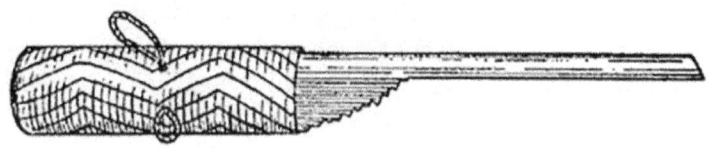

Mai. / Bone dagger.

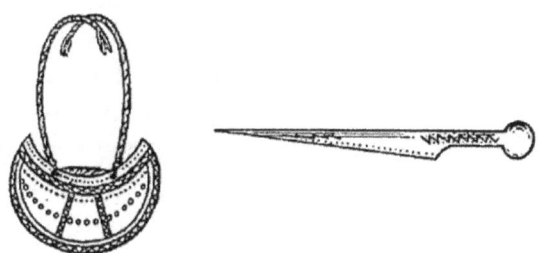

There followed a roar like that of stampeding cattle, as the people, all frenzied at the kill, packed themselves before the Zogo-house.

Grasping the *singai* handle, Beizam jerked up the head so that the throat strained as the reason-cords of the brown man gazing on were straining. One quick slash of the knife cut through the neck to the joint of the spinal cord. With a flick of the wrist the head was jerked sideways, so that the back muscles tautened, and the knife without a jar completed the circle. With left hand stretching the *singai* and right twisting the head, Beizam pulled strongly but evenly upwards. There was a pronounced "click" and sob, the head parted, and, as Beizam raised it on high, a tapering streak of marrow was drawn out with it. Beizam clenched his teeth on the grizzly neck and sucked and chewed. Thus was the courage and strength of the dying man being drawn into himself! The headless body rose on staggering feet and, with grotesquely thrashing limbs, spun round and round like a stunned fowl giddily striving to keep its balance. A screaming roar rent the air to accompany the dance, and the contorting face and kissing lips of the head above Beizam's mouth seemed to be screaming in unison. For several moments the body writhed, then sagged down, but Beizam still danced to the roaring acclamations of the throng.

One among them danced too, but his movements seemed regulated as the dead man's had been; the eyes stared as his had done, the mouth gaped open too, soundlessly.

A sickly feeling touched a sense in his brain. He shouted wild congratulations upon the triumph-intoxicated Beizam and acted more like a human being guided by his own power, for he knew that the eye of C'Zarcke was upon him, that coldly and cruelly C'Zarcke was deciphering his very thoughts and fear. He dare not now even glance towards the Zogo.

Presently the brown man slunk from the Sacred Grove; he was at liberty now to go. Like a shadow he moved among the Wongai-trees, shuddering from their touch. He avoided the village path, though it was broad and deserted and lit up by the moon. Instead, he stole through the banana-trees, emerged on the shadowed hill-track, and crept into his hut. The darkness was a friend. There was no human eye to see. The tense savagery left his face, and he sighed like a tired child. He bowed himself upon his mat, and prayed.

"Dear God, help me, let them not do to me as to the aboriginal, as to all that fall into their hands. Succour me, or kill me, but protect me from the Dance of Death. Death itself would be sweet, but I die a thousand deaths each time I see the Dance of Death. I dance with the dying man, I feel the drawing of life from the body – and C'Zarcke knows! Please God help me!"

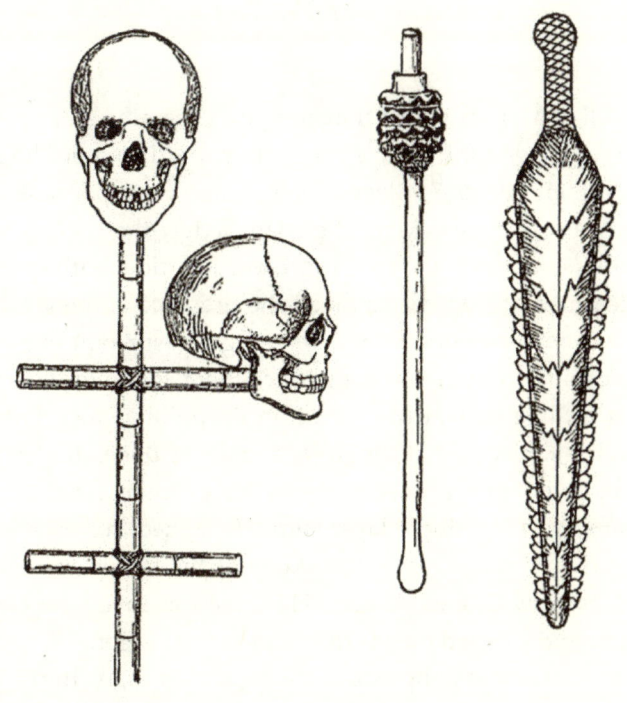

The Sarokag pole / Pineapple club / Shark-tooth sword.

CHAPTER II

Preparing For The End

On the second hill of Mer sat Jakara the Strange – dreaming. His eyes saw the palm-tops that shaded the village roofs; they saw the shore hills and the little jungles, then peeping villages again. Some were palisaded, and each had its golden beach speckling the island edge; the curling waves beyond foamed in song upon the reef, for it was low tide, with spume in the air and a clearness of sky that betrayed the presence of the great reef, which showed as a water-cloud of vivid yellow-green surrounding nearly all the island. Peeping from below the surface there shone up wondrous coral gardens stretching seaward to vanish in deep blue water. From his eyrie on the hill Jakara could distinguish a mile of queer under-water growths. But his mind saw unseen things which caused heart-ache for deep below that coral ledge there lay a ship. He sighed, his eyes misted with tears, for his ship-mates, even the skulls of his father and mother, had been traded to New Guinea savages. He alone was saved, for Gobeda had snatched him and claimed him as the "Lamar" of his son.

Jakara's eyes cleared and he could distinguish Eroob, thirty miles away towards New Guinea, its big hill, Lalour, showing like a rounded pyramid through a haze. And away towards the eastern horizon a peculiar sight; columns of smoke, miles in length, spouting skywards as bursting shells fall on distant trenches. It was the rollers from the open Pacific thundering upon the Great Barrier Reef. Away out there lay the frigate, *Pandora,* with the mutinous bones of some *Bounty* men strewn among the guns.

Jakara glanced down at Dauar and Waiar close inshore, joined fittingly by a treacherous coral reef. Tiny Dauar thrust upward its big and little peaks; Au (big) Dauar must be six hundred feet high, Kebi Dauar about three hundred. On the hummocky ground between the two peaks was a small dull patch of vegetation. Au Dauar was very steep, covered with grass, as if to ape giant Gelam, the extinct crater of Mer.

Waiar stood frowning in a crescent-shaped wall of battlemented rock three hundred feet high, grim and foreboding. In its barren gullies clung scanty tufts of vegetation. Both islets were the remnants of two blown-out craters. Waiar often reminded Jakara of a monstrous decayed tooth thrust up from the coral jawed sea. The islet's associations are as sinister as its fantastic crags. He looked to the skies and found pleasure in their unending beauty.

So far he had done well – preserved his life, his intelligence, and a clean white heart. The rock beside him was scarred with rude marks, his diary of the years. Twelve marks – and he was sixteen when wrecked. Twelve years' study of the native mind – above all, study of C'Zarcke's. By the knowledge gained he had kept his head, which mattered less than the Dance of Death, the dance of the headless body. He had learned intimately the language of the people, their customs, their ceremonies, their ideals, their life-pursuits. He could sail a canoe with the best, throw the heaviest *wawp* (harpoon), shoot an unerring arrow, and laugh and dance to their delight and admiration. He had won initiation step by step as their own youths had done, had fought in battles and killed his men, but – he was not a warrior. The only thing he could not do was to stun a man and —

He understood the native mind so intimately that at a smile and a word he could turn a blood-thirsty animal into a smiling boy. And the women – they were complicated.

As for the Council of the Zogo-le, and their attendant priesthood, he had studied them in the delirium of the ceremonial dances and all alone in the brooding quiet of the night. He had studied them for fear of his head, and later, as the years passed, because of an intense curiosity as to the secret of their undoubted powers. He had gradually realized that the mummery which kept the natives in subjection was merely a means to an end, that behind it all there lay a tangible power hardly realized by civilized man. Jakara knew that the three of the Zogo-le, headed by the dreaded Zogo, C'Zarcke, could and did converse and plan with one another while long distances apart, without the aid of words or written messages or sound. He had often known C'Zarcke to inform the clans, to the very hour, of a happening a hundred miles away. This strange power seemed partly dependent on atmospheric conditions and on the mental state of groups of people at different points. C'Zarcke could read men's minds, too. He could decipher secret thoughts, and could put men to sleep at a glance. Their medicine-men were a degree lower in the cultural scale, but could cure apparently hopeless diseases by mesmerism and hypnotism and some allied mysterious power.

Far below Jakara was a grassy knoll crowning a sheer black cliff, jocularly known now as "Geedee's Lookout," for the girl nursed a broken heart there. From his position on the hill he could see big Maiad village with its nearly mile-long spread of beehive-shaped houses, each protected by its stout outer palisading of bamboo; he could just see pleasant-faced Geedee coming up to sit in her loneliness. "She is stealing away from her work in the gardens," thought Jakara, and his face softened as the distrust eased from his eyes, the wariness from his figure; even the crooked fingers of his right hand straightened a little – fingers that were ever ready to grip the heavy double-edged shark-tooth sword that he carried.

His gaze wandered away again down over the tobacco and banana patches and valleyed gardens towards the dome-shaped house of the Zogo. He hated but feared C'Zarcke, who for years had read his mind and would have had him killed long ago but for Jakara's unfailing shrewdness in planning native warfare. Then came the frightening thought that some day C'Zarcke would cynically command him to plan an attack upon a wrecked ship, and Jakara shuddered, remembering the head-knife. Oh, curse C'Zarcke! Curse him! Curse him! Why would he not die! He understood so well Jakara's secret fear, though he never spoke of it by word of mouth.

From a hiding-place in the rock Jakara reached down a battered ship's telescope. It was his treasure. It showed him ships hours before the natives could see them – except C'Zarcke. C'Zarcke always knew, hours before the telescope could see. Jakara sighted the telescope at the Zogo-house. C'Zarcke stood outside under the crimson flame-tree. Jakara could distinguish the thoughtful lines of that remarkable face. A man of heavy stature, C'Zarcke's personality would have compelled attention among a notable gathering from civilized nations. Few as were the barbaric articles of his clothing, each carelessly worn ornament spelt more power to his people than did the insignia upon a European emperor. His very presence caused instant silence to the most hilarious merriment; men trembled as if with fever. For C'Zarcke held power of life and death without any exception, even though his foe were hundreds of miles away. Far more, every Islander implicitly believed that C'Zarcke could influence a man's spirit after death. His close-shut jaw was covered by a beard divided into three long rolls, each the thickness of a man's fist; his brow was broad and corrugated, his nose almost hooked; his lips close shut and firm. Strangely, there was not a hair on. his chocolate-coloured chest. Body and limbs were massive, the head a leonine thing of dominant mental power. His eyes were large and black, alive with an almost insane urge to learn more – to understand! Like the eyes of all the Zogo-le, they queerly changed when —

As if impelled, C'Zarcke turned his face, and Jakara gazed right into the eyes of his enemy. The savage seemed almost to have an understanding soul! Jakara felt guiltily inclined to put the telescope down, but clenched his teeth, staring hard. How he hated the man! He could count the very eyelashes on the lids that he so much wished would close. What a broad, ruggedly handsome face, a calm face shielding burning thoughts! Those eyes – C'Zarcke's black eyes – turning an intense blue-black, icily staring, growing larger but as if a glaze were obliterating earth-life to enable him to absorb unseen things. A sickly hair-raising sensation touched Jakara's consciousness. Despairingly he covered his face just as C'Zarcke turned and strode thoughtfully into the Zogo-house.

C'Zarcke, the searcher after knowledge, had become aware that Jakara the white Lamar was spying upon him, and with evil wishes. He had *felt* it! And by this, as in years past, C'Zarcke was disturbed, for this Lamar of the seas possessed a power unknown to him. C'Zarcke had watched this alien and learned new things, but this power, apparently similar to his own, the priest had not solved. He knew where Jakara was, and that from the distance, when even his form would be indistinct, Jakara could bring his face to him, and by a different process from his own. C'Zarcke was deeply moved to know how.

Jakara hid the telescope. This was his private ground – "Jakara's Lookout." Here for one day in every week he talked to himself, thinking and arguing of all things he had learned before the shipwreck, lest when he should be rescued his mental state might have sunk to savagery. Here also he pondered over the mysterious learning of the Zogo-le and by disdaining the mummery of the people his brain had grown quick and shrewd, alert with the white man's sense combined with that of the savage. The natives, though curious, seldom troubled him here. One was coming now, a tall young man proudly nodding as he smiled to the salutes called to him while walking through the village. With swinging arms he strode through the manioc gardens and on up the slope of the hill. Beizam, son of Boga the Mamoose of Mer, a bashful smile on his handsome face, coming eagerly to show Jakara the head-mai which flaunted upon his neck.

The friends met with a smile and clasping of hands upon shoulders.

"Beizam is a warrior now, and the head-mai becomes him well," congratulated Jakara warmly.

Beizam's teeth gleamed with pleasure. "It was a perfect stroke," he said quickly, "and in the raid I caught him by myself. He was a warrior too, and had killed his men."

"It behoved the son of a Mamoose to take the head of a warrior as his first kill," replied Jakara gravely. "Bogo, your father, is a noted fighter, but even he did not make such a beginning as you have done. It is a good omen."

Beizam's face shone. "Why don't you become a warrior, Jakara?" he asked quickly. "You are a brave man, and for your wonderful cunning the Zogo-le have made of you a chief. Yet you will not drink of the blood of any that you have slain."

With admiration Beizam raised his sinewy hand and touched the pearl-shell circlet round Jakara's neck. It was of similar design to Beizam's head-mai, except that it lacked the carved skull, the final badge of warriorhood. Instead, Jakara's circlet had little nicks, and each represented the life of a man.

"I cannot," he replied gravely. "My religion forbids, as the men of Mer know, otherwise I would have done so long ago!"

Beizam gazed quizzically seaward. "Truly we call you 'Jakara the Strange,'" he said, "the greatest honour that man can earn has lain before your sword time and again yet you have let it lie there and rot rather than drink. Truly you are 'strange.' And your gods! How can they possibly be greater than our Au-gud, who knows the very courses that the stars take!" Smilingly he faced Jakara. "Only, Jakara, that we know you breathe the cunning of the serpent in the councils of war, I should count you brave; but a fool!"

Jakara laughed heartily. "Only," he said, "that I know I should have no chance against Beizam, I would take the maid."

He pointed downwards to a banana-garden from the broad leaves of which a brown-limbed girl gazed up at the men.

Beizam laughed gleefully, and with joking farewell hurried down the hill. Jakara kept a smiling face until the two met and, waving to him, disappeared among the banana-leaves.

Jakara scowled. His steel-grey eyes, the tight-pressed lips, gave his face an instant savagery. The determined jaw but particularly the slightly hooked nose, made him strikingly like the clean-built men of Las; the likeness would have been more evident if his brown skin had been tinged with the chocolate colour of theirs.

"Murderer," he whispered, "burning to make others dance the Dance. How many will you make quiver? And will there be any poor wretches of whites amongst them? How I should love to slit that big full throat of yours, if only I could keep my own head too."

Gloweringly he leaned against the boulder and gazed towards invisible Tutu. Gradually his face softened to a tender sympathy, for on blood-stained Tutu there dwelt another Lamar, and, a girl!

To these Torres Strait Islanders every white person was believed to be a "Lamar," a human spirit of the dead, to be instantly killed. Shipwrecked people in boats were thought to be Lamars, that is, spirits given up by the sea itself, and were especially feared, for, if they were once allowed to breathe the air of land, they inhaled the power to wreak catastrophe upon all humans. Very rarely, because of some fancied resemblance, an Islander claimed a shipwrecked person as his dead son or daughter returned to earth-life in spirit-form, and such were spared. Thus had Jakara been spared, and also a few, a very few, men and women who had survived shipwreck among the superstitious natives of those islands.[1]

Jakara blamed C'Zarcke that he had never met Eyes of the Sea, as the natives called the Lamar of Tutu. Though he had voyaged to Tutu Island, he had never seen the girl who had been taken from a shipwrecked vessel when five years old. She had been claimed as the Lamar of a Tutu girl. Jakara had often pondered upon the white girl's plight. Reared as a savage, she had been forced to take part in all their dreadful ceremonies. Jakara shuddered as he thought of the Waiat rites, but she had so far escaped the "Wedding of the Virgins." He knew her age; she must be twenty now, just the age at which a white girl would be dreaming of the glories of life.

Jakara sighed, and walked thoughtfully down the slope. Hilly Mer is very pretty. The foliage screened villages below, each facing its own tiny beach, with a fleet of big fighting-canoes drawn right up to the front avenues of palms. Each village was flanked by steep grassy headlands, or deep green of tangled jungle, with the intense green of banana-patches away behind. Behind, and farther back still, were the well-kept vegetable and fruit gardens climbing up the little hills, and towards the centre of the island the green-grey of the Wongais surrounding the Sacred Grove. And, brooding high over all, the sombre mass of Gelam, its dead crater-rim circular and glassy, miles in circumference, its great maw now supporting grassy slopes. The island was so markedly different from the Great South Land; in its people, its rocks, its trees, its birds, its corals and fishes. Seven hundred feet above the sea, in the lava rocks of that old crater, are huge chunks of dead coral, proving how in ages past the volcano pushed Mer right up through the bottom of the sea. The Miriam-le were vastly different from the nomadic Australian aboriginal. They were expert navigators, canny traders, and keen agriculturists, and had conquered, explored, and colonized all Torres Strait.

The village houses were plentiful and neat and clean, adroitly thatched with grasses and mats of plaited palm-leaves. Before every house there stood a Sarokag pole, sometimes adorned with big spiral shells, which showed that the man within was initiated into manhood, but was

---

[1] (*Thus had Mrs Barbara Thompson been spared after the wreck of the cutter America on the distant Prince of Wales Group. She was claimed by the chief of Entrance as the spirit of his deceased daughter, Gi-'om. Boroto, chief of Murralug (Prince of Wales Island), took the white woman to wife. After five years she was rescued by H.M.S. Rattlesnake and restored to her friends in Sydney.)

not yet a warrior. On other poles were skulls, the number of which denoted the fighting-power and honour of the master within.

Over Jakara's house also there stood a pole, and it bore a strange device. This consisted simply of wings of palm-branches topping a bamboo and turned by the wind like a windmill. In answer to questions, in this matter as in numerous others, Jakara had smiled wisely. He had always striven to impress upon these susceptible people that there were things of which he understood more than they. And they had long since accepted him at his own valuation; admitted him as one of themselves, and let him alone, though he was always "Jakara the Strange."

He entered the house, latched the door close, and took down a staff of seasoned ironwood from behind the festoons of bright yellow tobacco-leaf along the walls. Inside, the bamboo pole fastened to the windmill came through the roof and whizzed round. Attached to it by a simple wooden device was a stone killing-club, which whirled round at striking angles at the height of a man's head. Jakara stood before it and struck, and the house rang with wood smacking stone as he warded off the swift blows. With spurts of the breeze outside the club revolved at erratic speed, and, to protect himself, Jakara became a machine of sinew and energy and unerring sight.

For years he had thus practised against the club, though occasionally it had sprawled him senseless on the floor. But practice and fear for his head had set him running the mill faster and faster, until he had long since developed a quickness of eye and foot, body and sword, and above all the lasting of his wind, which had earned him among enemy peoples the title of "Jakara the Unkillable." Leaping back from the vicious club, he took from the wall a small shield which fitted snugly over his left forearm. It was of hardwood, thickly studded with iron bolts hammered from floating spars, and weeks of thought and labour and fear had gone to the making of that buckler. But in several hot fights it had saved him from a cracked skull. Now, setting the mill to its limit, Jakara rushed the whizzing club, while the villagers hushed to listen to ringing blows of stone and wood and iron. Sparks were slow in comparison to the quickness of Jakara's eye.

Though self-defence was one object of this unceasing practice, the chief motive was the fear that at some time he must face the possibility of being forced to perform the Dance of Death. If he could only die fighting, so that they could not possibly stun him! For if they killed him outright he could never Dance!

The practice over, from the wall he took down a long rapier, pulled the shining blade from the scabbard, and balanced the thing, his eyes sparkling with unholy love. This blade was "Lightning," so named by fighting warriors who had seen its gleaming swiftness in action. If he might only fight out the last act in the midst of a ravening crowd with his one earthly love in his hand! But, O Lord above, they were such experts at the stunning stroke. Though he killed and killed, they would strive and strive to stun, and stun only. Sighing, he bent the rapier like a bow, then whirled it around his body until the weapon hummed. Again he examined the steel, tenderly feeling its point and edge, and again, as at many times past, wondered at its history, for it was a Spanish blade. He had seen ear-rings of Spain adorning a girl of Las, and odd men of Mer wore rings heavy with the gold and workmanship of Castille. The Las villagers also used quite a number of Spanish words. What was the story of these relics? Without the slightest doubt, the wreck of a Spanish adventurer in the long ago.

Jakara knew that from the sixteenth century Dutch and Spanish ships had ventured into these treacherous seas, jealously keeping their discoveries secret until the great Cook had sailed through the Strait and claimed Australia for Britain. Jakara knew from the diving natives that the bones of many vessels, mostly unknown, lie among the reefs. What romances of the white man's history C'Zarcke must know! C'Zarcke had given him the blade as a reward for the planning of a highly successful raid.

With the point piercing the floor, he leaned thoughtfully on the hilt. C'Zarcke, always C'Zarcke! Presently he jerked himself straight, with the old terrible feeling at the base of his neck – a feeling such as a man might have when half awake if a spirit breathed upon the back of his neck. He *knew* C'Zarcke was thinking of him. Hurriedly he replaced the weapon and, leaning over the coral hearth, blew the coco-husks into flame.

Within the Zogo-house C'Zarcke sat brooding with the night. Care creased his brow, thought clouded his eyes, his heavy lips drooped with a childlike despondency. C'Zarcke was not worrying about himself – he was dreading the future of his nation. For as a nation the Island people classed themselves.

C'Zarcke feared not the Lamars, but their numbers, the incomprehensible things that were theirs, and above all, their understanding. So far, these strange people had not troubled the Eastern Group and but little of the West, but he knew that at the Central Group of islands, and along the coast of the Great South Land and its islands off shore, wherever the Lamars wished to land, they landed; that whatever the Lamars wanted, they took.

For centuries past the mere existence of the Lamars had been acknowledged as a peril by the Zogo-le of the Strait. Those strange beings had come from they knew not where; they had come like a hurricane, done their damage, and vanished like the storm.

Throughout the centuries they had come in this manner, and the Zogo-le of the day had left on record that the arrows of the Islanders had splintered against the bodies of these beings, their toughest spears had crumpled up, even their stone clubs had bounced shattered from the heads of the Lamars.

After each visitation the people had become more and more convinced that the Lamars were invulnerable, that it was hopeless to fight against them.

The Zogo-le have their legends of our first known navigator of the Strait, Luiz Vaez de Torres, in the Spanish frigate *San Pedro* in 1606. C'Zarcke did not know him by that name, but their legends definitely told C'Zarcke how the Lamars by unbeatable force had taken twenty Islanders, who had vanished from their sight for ever. The Spanish captain had taken these natives to show to His Majesty the King of Spain. Portuguese navigators had done the same. The Lamars, except when caught in distress, had always been invincible. There was but one case in which the Lamars, actually in fighting-ships too, had fled before the Islanders. But C'Zarcke understood full well that this was probably because their ships were in a perilous position due to the sea. Very vividly the legends of the Zogo-le pictured the sack of Eroob by the Lamars. In June 1793 Bampton and Alt in the *Hormuzeer* and *Chesterfield* sent a whale-boat ashore for water. The Erubians attacked the boat, killing five men, and great was the joy to find that at last the Lamars had become vulnerable to spear and club. But next day the crews of both vessels landed, drove off the Islanders with slaughter, burned six villages, destroyed a hundred and seventy huge war-canoes, cut down the gardens, and played general havoc.

There were other instances, all ending in the same result, which the Island history told to the Zogo-le. The Lamars, with their mysterious and unexplainable weapons, were invincible! For centuries past they had but come and gone, leaving to the people only the remembrance of a nightmare.

But now they were coming in great numbers, and staying! C'Zarcke was full of fears; upon him lay the entire responsibility for the Island peoples.

To the Zogo-le on Mer were constantly brought news of the doings of the Lamars over hundreds of miles of waterways. C'Zarcke knew the increasing numbers of these strange beings; he knew that so far they had proved invincible to attack by coloured men. What were their real numbers? What did they want? Would they ultimately overrun all the Islands? Could they not be stopped? Must the Island people eventually perish?

C'Zarcke thought and worried far into the night, but this great question was as insoluble as that of the stars, as indefinite as the Lamars themselves. He did not know what the Lamars were, these strange people who had suddenly invaded the Island world – from the very skies, the Islanders believed.

C'Zarcke did not now believe that Lamars were the spirits of men come to earth again for a season. As he thought of Jakara, he grimly resolved to prove the matter. This Lamar had passions very similar to those of Island men. C'Zarcke would bring Eyes of the Sea, the woman Lamar, to Mer. The priest smiled cynically. He was positive of the result. But he sighed again, thinking deeply on matters more important.

He had dreamed of learning so much from Jakara, as the boy Lamar grew up. He had thought to find out everything that the Lamars really were. But C'Zarcke could not realize the difference of mentality between coloured and white. Also, one was a frightened captive of a totally unknown race of human beings; the other was a great chief hedged round by superstition and savage power. The very environment of the two, not to take into account utterly different racial customs and ideals and the tense distrust between them both, was alone more than enough to intensify the feeling of antagonism between them, and defeat C'Zarcke's hopes.

C'Zarcke had learned little, and that little had but added to his fears – fears for the ultimate fate of his people.

Sighing deeply, the great priest cupped his chin between his hands and stared unseeing at the sacred mats upon the Zogo-house floor.

CHAPTER III

Forcing The Secrets Of Heaven

Evening. A breath from the sea became sweet with scent of flowers whose leaves reflected shy kisses from the stars. Gloaming light spread over the hill-sides, darkened the valleys, and brightened the boulders upon the shore. Myriad diamonds sparkling among the beach sands, their whiteness chequered with a black mosaic which was the distinct outline of shadowed palms.

The happy voices of men and maids as the villages practised the dance; the plaintive music of the *burral,* the flute of reeds; laughter of children tumbling upon the beach, while from sympathetic groups screened by fern and palm came an occasional little laugh which was part of the beauty of the night.

Along a banana-shadowed pathway Jakara strode noiselessly, impelled by the night and loneliness to ascend to his Lookout and commune with the loveliness which the heavens were showering upon the earth. He halted in surprise when from the foliage beside him there stepped a dream from the night. She smiled eagerly, while the shadows of the leaves played upon her alluring body. She was dressed in the clinging skirt of maidenhood, and her rounded arms were prettily girlish in their bracelets of pearl; a circlet of mottled crotons banded her hair, so profuse and wavy, every teasing strand a chain of tiny ringlets. Lithe and tall with strength in her beauty, her face was bright with intelligence, her lips dangerously ripe, her eyes big and black, full of liquid brightness. The velvety softness of her skin was not even as brown as his. Upon her clung an indefinable, a tantalizing scent, the *kerakera* – the girls' love-charm.

Jakara gazed warily, for the Pretty Lamar of Las was a pleasure to look upon, and now her presence breathed a magnetic power. All these years, he had fought against an alliance with a native girl, because of the white man's pride and because of the terrible thought that he might bring others unborn to the killing-club. And he desired to meet Eyes of the Sea. The night murmured with sympathy, and nature smiled, knowing that oft-suppressed desire forgets conscience. He stepped aside to pass, but she laughed softly and held up her face to be kissed. He seized her roughly, and her lips met his swiftly and sweetly. She nestled to him and sighed while her hands caressed his neck; the warmth of her breasts set his heart thumping hotly. Suddenly she thrust him aside, her eyes like those of an animal afraid. "Go!" she whispered tensely. "I hear something! It may be only a snake."

He hurried away, his ever-present fear instantly master as his ears strained to catch the indrawing of a breath, the patter of hurried feet behind. Thus he came to the open hill-slope; and then wheeled round, gripping his shark-tooth sword: he was smiling in friendly inquiry.

Beizam's fine chest was heaving, his eyes menacing. "Jakara," he hissed abruptly, "do you desire the Pretty Lamar?"

"No, Beizam," smiled Jakara with a shake of the head; "she is yours for the taking! I want no maid. As you know, my religion forbids me women, and, besides, I have no desire! Just as well, otherwise what chance should I have against a proven warrior, and he the son of a Mamoose?"

Beizam's body relaxed. He sighed as he smiled, then his eyes widened ominously as he gazed at Jakara's notched *mai*. The wrist-thong of his *gaba-gaba* tightened around his wrist.

"Better hasten after the maid," advised Jakara, "While the night is young! A moment ago she mistook me for you, but only for an instant. She was abashed, and now is the chance for a warrior to comfort her."

Beizam laughed musically as he laid a warm hand upon Jakara's shoulder in genuine friendliness.

" 'Jakara the Strange,' " he smiled, "and 'Jakara the Wise.' What a warrior you would be if you would only drink of the Dance of Death! And not a girl in all the Islands would say you nay." Like a young panther hot on the scent of a promising love affair he bounded down the slope.

Jakara drew a long, long breath, lifting frightened eyes to the stars. It was not because of the recent escape; he had experienced others such, and though the tongue be mightier than the sword, still the sword thrusts only once! No, it was for something else! Those deadly nicks upon the *mai* round his neck, representing the lives of men. What a prize the head of Jakara would be! His noted bravery, his cunning in war, his unbeaten fighting strength! Whoever drank of the head of Jakara – what a famous warrior he would instantly become! He would imbibe all Jakara's qualities to strengthen his own. The killer would become invincible!

And now the idea had dawned in the ambitious mind of Beizam! It was sleeping again, but time would surely bring it to full wakefulness. As likely as not some little unexpected incident would hurry its consummation. Jakara's spinal cord shuddered in sympathy. Mentally he decided to discard his native weapons and never walk without Lightning, nor ever meet the Pretty Lamar again, even by accident. The natives jokingly called her "Lamar" simply because she was the whitest-skinned girl on the island.

Weeks later, and Jakara had whistled as he climbed. He was glad to be away from the Council. For a solid week he, with the chiefs, had listened to a dispute which involved complicated land-laws whose rights went back for centuries.

For a great land-stealing case was before the Council. It had gone past individuals, having implicated the villages of Zerwageed and I'Laid. The island was seething with excitement.

But now Jakara's duties in the case were over. Always he had sought to abstain from meddling with the affairs of the island otherwise than in war. Thus he incurred no man's enmity, ran the risk of no private feuds. He merely took his seat on the Council when his position made it necessary. But he never helped in the voicing of any decision against individuals.

With war the matter was different. There the whole of the island was united, and the men who could plan success were revered as the greatest in the Group.

Jakara reached his Lookout, got his telescope, and searched the sea – searched as if he awaited some dearly beloved thing. But the horizon all around was bare of any sail. Sighing, he trained his telescope down on Mer.

Around the disputed land all the population was gathered in an interested circle, very quiet, however, for C'Zarcke and the Zogo-le were personally examining the boundary line before judgment.

Jakara then directed his glass down upon the snub nose of Gelam-Pit, where the waves rolled lazily against the cliffs. From the south-west end of Mer the island rises steeply in long grassy slopes to culminate in giant Gelam, and Jakara trained the telescope well inland at the main taboo country hidden around its base. The telescope showed plainly the huge training-ground in the centre of the Kwod.

The Kwod was purely a training college, where the island youths were fitted to become men of Mer, to be worthy of its past traditions, to fit themselves to carry on the work begun by the great supermen of the past.

Their training lasted from early boyhood until stripling age. As tender lads, numbers of them were taken from their homes and rarely saw their parents again until they were almost grown to manhood.

Their training was Spartan. Jakara could see squads of them now, while he watched with a reminiscent sympathy as they broke and flew when, with a fearful yell, a crowd of hideously masked men, flourishing shark-tooth swords, rushed on them from the surrounding timber. Thus were the lads trained in quickness of brain, eye, feet, and body. Also for an hour twice daily they were shot at, the severity growing by degrees until finally some of the best bowmen on Mer would fire at them with war-bows. Later still the lads would have to stand in the open and dodge showers of arrows that rained on them from archers hidden among the trees. With the arrows would whizz many sling-stones. Naturally, a number of lads each year never left the Kwod.

Jakara had had to go through all that strenuous training. He had done so willingly enough, and now was very glad. In it he had gained an amazing proficiency in the use of weapons, and had developed his physique in a manner that stood him in good stead when he had to fight in earnest. There he had gained proficiency in harpooning dugong, in turtle capture, in all manner of fishing. There he had learned the religion, the beliefs, the life of all the Island peoples. Step by step he had won his initiation degrees, and at last, most interesting of all, he had been put through their mystic rites relating to the spirit-land, though only to the degree permitted to a fighting chief. The deep secrets and the malevolent magic were for the Maid-le alone, while the "most known by men" was only for the Zogo-le, with their terrible head C'Zarcke, Au-Zogo-zogo-le, Au-Maid-maid-le.

Jakara stayed on his Lookout until the sun went down. It was very lonely then. He climbed down the Lookout to his hut, not whistling. From Maiad village came the plaintive fluting of the *burral,* sweet but sad. The villages slept. The Islands slept. The sea never sleeps: she dreams sometimes, as does the night. Upon their mats the people slept coiled up like tired children, a wealth of resting limbs and tangled tresses abandoned in dreaming repose. Outside, all was utter silence; even Nature dreamed and leased the air and the land and the sea to the spirit folk and the unknown energy that is.

Within the Zogo-house sat C'Zarcke the dreaded, C'Zarcke the all-powerful, C'Zarcke the hungry seeker after knowledge. He communed in silent company, for skulls do not talk, at least, in words that humans hear. Twenty were his company, once men whose individual history was a lifetime spent in acquiring knowledge. Each had its characteristics, and each a personality of its own which grimaced: "Read me now, if you can!" There were two characteristics common to all: their silence, and the roominess of the brain cavities. For his personal souvenirs, C'Zarcke collected only those relics whose bony walls had once held brains that reasoned, that sought to know things.

Though mostly of black and brown people, there were representatives of high civilization there, for a Spanish don leered over one shoulder while C'Zarcke stared straight into the eye-sockets of an English captain.

A blueness illuminated the shadowy room; the light was diffused from the sockets of a box-shaped skull. Other things were in that room, a nameless feeling of presences in the heavy air; the vagueness, and the possibility of what might be, gave to that ghostly, dimly-lighted place a fearfulness that belonged to darkness. Yet something – to the human mind a repellant feeling of uncanny power – would not be denied, and that heavy silence and darkness seemed to be its element. Not nearly so repugnant were the sentinel forms of men stretched mummified. Their appearance was dreadful, so let them stay shrouded in the night. Then there was a "something" from the rafters that stared straight down upon C'Zarcke's head. It had once been a woman. So terrible was it that no stranger would have looked twice, although he would at once have realized that the woman had triumphed over death, for she was still beautiful.

C'Zarcke sat as in a death-like trance, made horrible, however, because his "dead" face was so expressive of life and burning expectancy; inside the massive head all reasoning was concentrated to absorb something coming to him through the air. Presently his eyes clouded as if to dim his vision and focus sight straight back upon the brain within. Then in his eyes appeared that intense, blue-black glitter. He sighed lingeringly, and his splendid chest barely moved, while through his eyes, and possibly his ears, he was drinking in mind-energy sent to him from all the Zogo-le of the Strait, aye, and from every Maid-le priest of the Bomai-Malu Cult far south down the Australian coast, and to north-west right up along the New Guinea shores. Each of these sat in a comfortable position inside his Zogo-house, and, if compass lines had been drawn from every island, the three groups of the Zogo-le and every man of the Maid-le priesthood would have been found staring straight towards C'Zarcke. In a crescent around each man, with his own head as the centre, were evenly-placed skulls, though it is believed that these were kept not because the present Zogo-le believed them to possess a really tangible power, but because their ancestors in dim ages had superstitiously used them in first seeking after knowledge. Each skull grinned on a level with, and at, the priest's head. All else was darkness, a waiting, almost a living silence, and every man of them – some with brutal, but all with intellectual, faces, drawn taut and strained, and their queer, bright eyes with the purple glitter staring inwards and outwards – strove to hypnotize his body and brain and force out towards C'Zarcke that deep inner consciousness which, they firmly believe, quits the body temporarily in sleep, but for ever in death.

Presently, the Zogo of Eroob sighed, his body sagged, his thick brown arms slid down beside him queerly reminiscent of dying snakes. His head settled upon his chest, he fought to control the stream of his consciousness going out, out – and C'Zarcke the receiver awaited with chest expanding and big eyes widening, intensely bright. When the Zogo of Eroob crouched limp as a man dead, C'Zarcke whimpered like a baby in gratification, for within his brain-cells he had stored the reasoning life of his lesser priest.

The Zogo of Ugar was the next to lend tribute of reasoning force. With him, visibly at least, the forcing out of his consciousness was painful. He moaned in sore distress while his legs and arms shot out with the jerky, stiffly-controlled movement of an automaton. His muscles bunched, his sinews stretched the skin like tautened bow-strings. Moaning horribly, he rolled back with open mouth, shrunken in body and with stiffened limbs all crooked.

Then, in quick and urgent succession, as C'Zarcke accumulated each man's power of reasoning, so into trance slipped each one of the Zogo-le and the lesser far-scattered priests of the Bomai-Malu Cult.

C'Zarcke, though trained during many intense years and with the knowledge of others gone before to help him, could not have absorbed more vibratory energy, or else even his great mind would have burst under pressure of the force within. As the last priest surrendered his reason, C'Zarcke stood up, not of his volition, and raised knotted arms to the roof. The physical strength of the man, immense at any time, was now supernatural. Vitality electrified the muscles that appeared straining from the body. His face was radiant as at a vision of deified power. His hands snatched at a salvaged bar; with a smile of intense joy he bent that iron, tied it in knots, and twisted it until the hot metal snapped and clattered to his feet. He fastened his teeth in a hardened beam of Wongai wood, and the timber splintered like a match chewed by a child.

Then something unexplainable happened within C'Zarcke, for that portion of his mind which he had first purposely put to sleep, was endeavouring to control and combine the reasoning individualities which he had absorbed. We know how it is with a man dreaming, who is aware that he is dreaming and determines that he must remember his dream and impress it on his mind for reference in waking hours, and who, on awakening, remembers that he had a dream – remembers perfectly that he tried to impress the vision upon his conscious mind – but now remembers nothing of the dream itself. With C'Zarcke the reverse was the case. In years of study he had striven to impress his conscious mind to take control after he had fallen asleep; for then every physical motion released his surplus power back to the Zogo-le from whence it had come. They were starving for its return, as demagnetized iron might starve for that of which it had been robbed. C'Zarcke was like an engine under terrific pressure, whose dreamy driver hesitates which button to press in order to control its strength so that every atom will be utilized as directed, and this power was attached by invisible threads to those who craved its return. C'Zarcke was quivering to expend his borrowed energy on a mad excess of physical exertion. It had always been so, the fight of the physical to take command, the resolve of the mind to control the physical and also to impress the waking memory with the wondrous things which in these flights he saw.

For C'Zarcke sought to transplant his mind out into the world of space. Such has been a mind-dream of men in many ages.

With but a partly-trained reason directing him, he reached up and, like a child handling a toy, slid back a portion of the roof. Under this was a rude couch; C'Zarcke leaped up, lay flat on his back, settled his body to perfect ease, and then rolling back his tongue attempted to swallow it. As he lost consciousness the glorious star of Kaek smiled down and enveloped the priest in dazzling affinity with existences in space. At long last, after the Zogo-le were deep in exhausted sleep, C'Zarcke's eyes opened vacantly to the risen sun. Long he lay, then covered his face with his arms. C'Zarcke the feared sobbed like a heart-broken child. He had glimpsed the vision splendid and could not remember it – only fantasies of an entrancing dream. And, as time sped on, the Zogo-le and the priests of Bomai would individually, like a flash, on some odd occasion, glimpse a something wonderful, which they would recognize was what C'Zarcke had really seen with a portion of their being when he was seeking among the stars.[2]

MASKS OF THE GREAT AU-GUD

---

[2] As the writer of this story, I would like to explain what the remnants of the Zogo-le have assured me the great priest saw in these "mind" travels of his. Such, however, might only prove of interest to students of the occult. To other readers, such an attempted description might read as a fantasy. I. L. I.

CHAPTER IV

The Heart Of The Pretty Lamar

The sun smiled on Mer. Insects hummed while frail adventurers from overseas flitted in splashes of ethereal beauty among the crotons and hibiscus and flame-striped soos-soos grass. Birds trilled and squawked and squabbled. The wee sunbird with breast of purest gold built her swinging nest with labour and song and love. The waters sparkled. Flying-fish glistened over the waves; fish of wondrous colours played in coral gardens. The big, snake-like head of a turtle rose from the depths to glory in the sunlight. An ominous fin clove the surface. The air was sweet as the laughter that echoed among the groves of Mer and in her valleyed glades and along the sides of grass-grown hills. Old women chuckled under the village palms as they wove their mats and fibre petticoats. Men, practically naked, lazed on the beach making fishing-nets, or loafed under the palms with their *zoobs* (bamboo pipes); often the men did not wear the grass skirt unless on duty. Groups of them squatted among the houses, spinning the *kolap* (the stone top) and wagering keenly on the result. Some men could spin their *kolap* for thirty minutes, and were very jealous of their toys.

The shrill treble of children, the intriguing laughter of girls, and the boisterous greeting of the men carried something exciting in it, something more than the ordinary joy of life.

For Kebisu was coming, Kebisu of Tutu, Kebisu the Conqueror. C'Zarcke had foretold that he would arrive on the third day. And arrive he would, with a handful of his warriors and women, even Eyes of the Sea. Kebisu, invincible Mamoose of Warrior Island – Eyes of the Sea, Lamar of little drowned Sea Maid, prettiest and sauciest girl of all the Western Islands, the wonderful dancer with cornflower eyes.

So the Miriam-le made ready for the feast, and the gardens of Eroob sent tribute.

Down the village path strode Jakara, warmly excited. Eyes of the Sea! He would see her at last, this sea-waif of his own colour, the first he had seen since the ship went down! A countrywoman of his own, perhaps even an Australian! A white girl who would be proud of it and have all the ambitions of the whites, and white desires and hopes, and white love, and the white man's God.

How much would she remember of her home and civilization?

Their mutual remembrances would bring a flood of happiness to both. He would console and sympathize with her, and protect – yes, why not? He was valuable to C'Zarcke. Could he prevail upon this chief demon to allow the girl to remain at Mer under his protection? Certainly he must think of a way, but curse C'Zarcke! Would she be good to look upon? Would she be as pretty as the natives said? Not the slightest difference whether or no; she was a white girl with a white girl's heart and mind. Her companionship would be pure happiness to him.

Near a profusion of flowering creepers, where a track led in from a garden, a bevy of Mer girls passed him bearing baskets of yams and manioc and huge bunches of bananas. Shapely and attractive of face, they were all in merry mood. Geedee was there, and Miriam – the sauciest flirt in all Mer. She giggled among her comrades, then with the happiest smile, raced across Jakara's path and challenged him to deny that she was in every way a more desirable sweetheart than his Lamar girl to come.

But their skin was dark, so he joked with them smilingly, and detested them, taking no thought at all that they had been born to one of God's moulds. With smiling nods and jokes he greeted single warriors and parties of guards on their way to the gardens and the fish-traps. Fine men all, with big chests and fierce independent eyes, armed with shark-tooth sword and stone club, sling, or bow and arrow. The going of a man along those jungle paths made no slightest sound; his tread was noiseless as that of a wary panther; every pert bird twittering upon a creeper made far more noise than he, and often did not hear when man passed directly below. Neither did man cast any betraying shadow within the green gloom.

The track meandered down to a shingly beach, where upon a black rock sat crouched what seemed to be the carving of a witch, only blacker than the stone and as moveless, but alive, with bones like knobs stretching the skin, and breasts like skinny bags sagging to the rock! Scraggy arms clasped bony knees upon which the chin rested. Her hair drooped like the tail of an old grey horse, matted with the neglect of years. Jakara paused. A fellow-feeling made him sorry for old Sasowari, the mad one, lonely in her hopeless mourning. From this spot years ago, on another such sunlit morning, her daughter, Gareeb, fairest of all Las, had laughingly paddled away in a fishing canoe and never returned.

Jakara patted her shoulder. "I wish you comfort for your lonely heart, Sasowari," he said kindly. "Why not go into the village and watch the preparations for the feasting? Forget, in the joy of others."

The face, a maze of wrinkles, turned to him; bleared but shrewd old eyes peered towards his: "Does Jakara forget – in the joy of others?" she added quietly, then patted the man's hand while her eyes smiled. "Jakara has always understood another's troubles and is selfishly lonely in his own. Jakara the Lonely, but Jakara of the Understanding Heart! Friend Jakara, you are luckier than you know, in that you have youth as a comforter. Why not seize the happiness of youth and forget in the arms of joy?" And her trembling hand pointed to the track ahead disappearing among the palms.

Jakara smiled. "Those same arms that would caress my neck might well bring it to the bamboo knife," he answered grimly; "the joys of forgetfulness often forget to awake."

"You are a fool, Jakara the Wise," replied the old woman, sharply. "Joys to the ready come often, death but once, and death can well be the greatest joy of all. Oh, Jakara, *she* is coming back!"

Expectancy quivered upon the shrunken face, so pitiful in its forlorn age. Her eyes grew bright as a snake's. "You do not believe," she hissed; "you think that her spirit has long since flown to Boigu, Isle of the Blest, but I speak truly. Gareeb, my Lily of Las, is coming; even now she flies to me before the wings of death."

Jakara soothed the hot old brow. "I wish you peace, mother," he comforted, "and hope with all my heart that your daughter brings you happiness untold." He walked a little unhappily across the shingly beach; then, shaking off depression, strode more briskly up the path that wound among the shadowed trees. From them the Pretty Lamar stepped before him, and her face was radiant.

Jakara smiled, pleased despite himself. "Why, croton girl, you are as pretty as the sunbird: why such a gay face this morning?"

"And why, Jakara," answered the soft voice, "are you striding with head and shoulders braced? And for whom is your smile this morning?"

Jakara's smile broadened. "Whisper me your secret," he parried, "and I will tell you mine."

"Needless for either to tell," flashed back the answer. "Jakara awaits Eyes of the Sea, and I await Jakara." His smile disappeared. She returned him stare for stare, aggravatingly attractive in her defiant poise, her big dark eyes in startling contrast to the almost olive skin – Jakara could hardly resist touching it.

And she was so obviously his for the taking!

Such, outwardly, was the Pretty Lamar, fairest of the Las girls since the going of Gareeb. And now her movement seemed a caress, as she whispered pleadingly: "Why be angry, Jakara? Am I not fair to look upon? Am I not desirable?"

Jakara's heart thumped. Imperceptibly, she leaned towards him, her lips sweet with invitation. He whispered urgently: "Pretty Lamar, you are lovely, a woman a man might die for; but I am a Lamar proper – we can never love. Stick to Beizam! If you persist in playing with me, we shall lose our heads – on the Sarokag pole!"

All Eve beckoned in the girl's smile, as she twined an arm round his neck, caressing him with touch, and looks and words. Her body was scented with the *kerakera*.

"Nay, Jakara the Wise," she whispered, lingeringly; "Beizam is a mud shark – you are lord of all the Islands, if only you will! Nothing then could say us nay. We—"

He gripped the firm warm shoulders as she clung to him the more. "Pretty Lamar," he hissed, "you are a chief's daughter! Forget not the custom of your people – Death! Or else I must marry you—"

Her hair touched his cheek while her lips came warmly to his. "Would that – be – very hard?"

He crushed her to him and she kissed passionately; she would have given him her life, this fierce wild thing born under an unhappy star. By the banyan-tree they were when C'Zarcke came along and for the first time in his life gazed down into eyes which blazed back hate unabashed – the eyes of the Pretty Lamar. Jakara turned as he felt that awful sensation at the base of his skull, even while his arms clasped the girl. C'Zarcke, giant among big men, walked noiselessly down the path. Softly the seconds passed. The air was heavy with the scent of flowers: the silence shouted tragedy. The girl clung desperately for dread of losing him – but she had lost, the hair was bristling at the base of his skull. He sprang erect, and in cold fear he forced her arms away.

On the third morning after, with his back comfortably warmed against the big black rock of his Lookout, Jakara lazed away time, smoking the *zoob*, and occasionally picking up the telescope to gaze over the deep blue of a tumbling sea. The *zoob* was a bamboo about two feet long, a smoke-cylinder with carvings burnt upon it, simply the native pipe. Jakara loved his *zoob*, and had often wondered that these savages should be growing tobacco and understanding how to cure it, centuries before Sir Walter Raleigh found its solace.

The Zogo-le had developed the knowledge, of course. The great majority of the people lived away their lives in an atmosphere of ignorance and superstition, only those men who of right could cluster around the Zogo-le being taught to understand things. Jakara's musing gaze rested on a flat rock bottom swept clear by the outgoing tide. The sea had churned out little circular pools in that floor-like rock, and in his last bath sat Ramu. Ramu had been a promising young warrior, until his indiscretion outstripped his ambition. Consequently, while he slept, he had been made to breathe of the "Flower of Death." Jakara knew that this was an extraordinarily fine, perfumed powder, blown across a person's nostrils from a long tapering reed. One puff meant everlasting sleep for the body. And now Ramu sat in his salt bath, very quiet, right up to his neck. At long intervals an attendant unceremoniously dipped the warrior's head under water.

For Ramu was undergoing mummification. Jakara often wondered. Some of these people had Egyptian names even. Their huge war canoes, too, with the tall stern and arrogant – often beaked – bow, their barbaric decorations reminded him of prints of old-time galleys of the Nile which in his boyhood days he had seen in books.

Dreamily he turned his eyes away from Ramu, sitting down there in his last bath, picked up his telescope, and gazed away out to sea. He sat up straight, fully alert, stared hard for a while, then hurriedly hid his telescope and with a smile sprang up and ran like a man in the pink of condition down the long winding path that disappeared towards the seashore villages.

So Jakara spread the news that the sail of Kebisu was in sight. Always careful was Jakara not to prophesy himself; he merely confirmed C'Zarcke. There were three vessels, and Jakara added that the great warcanoe of Kebisu sported a new sail.

C'Zarcke, sitting, thinking within the Zogo-house, was told all. To each message he said nothing, but merely looked wise; but he was wise, too, and puzzled himself again as he had done for years past to understand this power of Jakara. Although he knew that the vessels were coming, C'Zarcke could not visibly see any sail, much less three, nor could he see that the canoe of Kebisu possessed a new mat sail! Yet Jakara never told falsely. Often he had raised the cry, "Lamar-Nar! Lamar-Nar!" (A spirit ship! A spirit ship!) Throughout the years, often long before the ships were in sight, he had foretold their passing, distinguishing between the fighting-ships of the Lamars, those other vessels which were like fat pigeons ready for the plucking when haply they struck the reefs, and those little hornets of the seas that Jakara called "blackbirders," filled with fighting-men – little ships always looking for fight and always a fury to tackle. Also there were distant sails growing ominously frequent of late when the fool Lamars searched for pearl-shell and combed the ocean-floor for slugs of the sea; and occasionally the clumsy, queerly-shaped boats of those sea-nomads, the little brown Malay men, who always made great sport in fighting to the death, but luckily were not armed with such deadly fire-weapons as the white Lamars.

But Jakara had never told of a Lamar ship in distress, or of one obviously slewed among the many reefs, and C'Zarcke knew full well that he must have seen numbers in that plight. What was this power that Jakara possessed, and what other knowledge did he possess? C'Zarcke had watched him for years in the effort to learn. In his younger days C'Zarcke had really believed that white men were spirits of the dead, until he had thought over the strange fact that they and their women fear death even more than the Islanders. Then he had wondered if Lamars might be spirit people who, after death, lose the memory of their earth lives. As a young man he had thought that the Lamars might be like his own people, among whom only the priests and chiefs have knowledge. Jakara had boasted of a great land filled with knowledge which the Lamars themselves owned. C'Zarcke now believed him. He knew the vast world of the stars, and he did not believe that the horizon of the sea dropped into space. He knew that as far to the south as the most adventurous canoes had voyaged there lay a great land. True, the people seen were black in colour, but they were very different from the Islanders. Might not a land of Lamars lie farther away still? If so, then what learning their wise men must have! But what ineffable knowledge they must possess if they were really the spirits of people come back to earth!

With his brooding face almost likeable in its pathetic yearning, C'Zarcke stood up within the darkened Zogo-house, and, sliding open an aperture, gazed steadily up towards Jakara's Lookout.

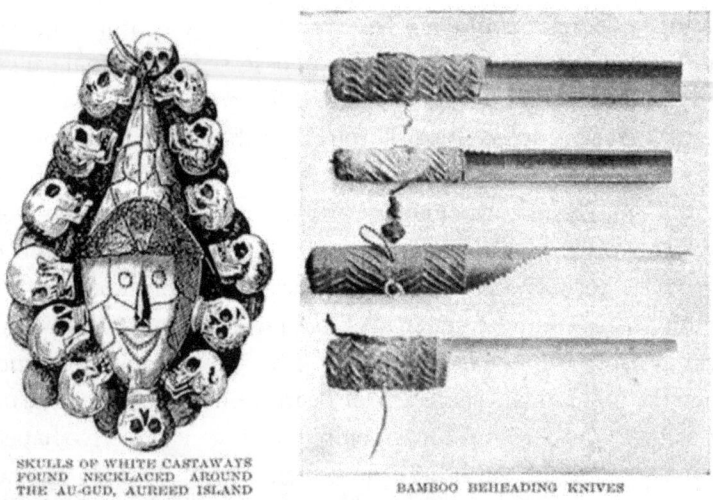

SKULLS OF WHITE CASTAWAYS FOUND NECKLACED AROUND THE AU-GUD, AUREED ISLAND

BAMBOO BEHEADING KNIVES

CHAPTER V

The Coming Of Kebisu

The sun gleamed brightly on Maiad Bay with its beach like a crescent moon clouded with palms. An expectant throng waited, all shining eyes and laughter and singing. Everywhere strong men and lithe women and rollicking children and excitement. Even the trees on the hill-sides whispered it! For Kebisu was coming; Kebisu the Brave, who led in war and the larger tribal raids; Kebisu who had looted Lamar ships; Kebisu the Undefeated.

Reverberations boomed over the sea to a tattooing of the drums of Mer. For Kebisu's sail was sighted, and a mighty shout arose. Again boomed the welcome of the drums, vigorous yet queer of note, like thunder muffled by the beat. The canoes sailed prettily upon the blue of the sea, picturesque in their barbaric strength. As their tall bows foamed through the surf, the people plunged towards them and rushed the big vessels high up on the sands, while the women pelted the laughing warriors with hibiscus and russet blossoms. The song of the clans echoed the throbbing of the drums.

Then the chief Mamoose of the Island nations stepped ashore, and Mer thundered to roars of "Kebisu! Kebisu! Kebisu!" Far above the din, within the crater-top in welcoming crescendo came the sound of the drums of Mer, while the Miriam-le and the emissaries of Eroob and of Ugar massed around the war Mamoose and waved the cruel shark-tooth swords and spun their killing clubs to the frenzied sway of bodies. It needed but a spark to set these inflammable savages at one another's throats in a bacchanalian riot of clannish feuds. The women, crushed, yet not to be denied, fought their way into the crowd, shrieking adoration of Kebisu's proud warriors while their gestures and voice inflamed the blood of their own. Then called the harsh voice of the Mamoose of Mer. "C'Zarcke! C'Zarcke awaits."

Instant silence: a sigh arose as if from some vast animal. Grudgingly they stood back, light badinage broke out, and from heaving chests escaped laughter as animals became human again.

Kebisu stood out big even among the striking men there, his stature emphasized by enormous shoulder muscles; his limbs long and powerful, his bearing sheer untamed arrogance, his face unexpectedly pleasing because of a boyish happiness which occasionally lightened the grim jaw and broad, savage cheeks. The full brow was noticeable between the ringlets that fell upon his shoulders, arranged to hide the fact that the left ear was missing, bitten off in a fight. When he was angered, Kebisu's face flushed red, particularly around that part where the ear had been; and at that ominous sign his savage warriors grew subdued and mild. Worthily accounted the brainiest chief of the Island nations, this man was possessed of unbridled ferocity, and yet he had been known to cry because he could not relieve a child in pain. Apart from the supermen of culture who had come with the Bomai-Malu, and of C'Zarcke in the present age, this man was the greatest organizing genius that the Torres Strait Islands had ever known. Both for war and for trade he had made his own tiny island of Tutu the key position for all commerce and war that came from far down the Australian coast, right across the length and breadth of the Strait, to New Guinea's shores. Nothing could come, nothing could pass, nothing could go across the seas, without paying heavy tribute to Kebisu of Tutu on his tiny sandbank by the historic Warrior Reefs. His men were better fighters than those of Mer. He had an alliance with the Eastern Group because of their numbers and their importance for trade. Had it not been for the supernatural power which C'Zarcke wielded over all the Strait, Kebisu would long ago have taken Mer by force. He stood now with eyes gleaming in pride at his reception.

Then Bogo, the Mamoose of Mer, strode heavily forward. They greeted by lifting outstretched arms and placing the hands on each other's shoulders, smiling with a side touch of the face to each cheek; but only the highly initiated few noted the secret signs of the Bomai-Malu that passed between them. Then Beizam, proudly erect and smiling shyly, stepped forward. His hawklike eyes shone as the people shouted his name, and he trembled with happiness when the great Kebisu smilingly touched his head-mai. The youth thrilled when the crowd shouted in renewed approbation; an ecstatic premonition of greatness to come coursed madly through his brain and heart. Then out strode Kesu, Mamoose of Eroob, as "broad as he was long," with arms knobbed like the roots of trees and paws that swung at a level with his knees. His face was that of a killer who could accept death with a laugh. Kebisu greeted him with the geniality of long friendship, then turned to Orama, Mamoose of Naghir. This man was tall, a fitting representative of the towering, needle-like peak which marked his own cold grey island. He walked with stealthy litheness. His form was splendid, his face should have been that of a god. So it was-a devil-god! Cruelty personified, his handsome features expressed a vindictiveness that had never shown mercy to any living thing. His piercing eyes adored Kebisu, but only as the Killer. Next came

Maros, Mamoose of Ugar, idol of his people, unadulterated bad man. Of all the unscrupulous scoundrels known to the Islanders, Maros was the worst. He was fairly tall, and his body was nuggety and muscled like that of a horse. He stepped forward with a grin that stretched from ear to ear. An ugly man, his grim face was rendered striking by the menace in the rolling black eyes which could, however, twinkle into laughter in a second. Maros lived! He did not know what fear was, found joy in daily life, and loved a fight even more than he loved women.

Then out stepped Jakara, with a devil-may-care defiance, with head erect and smiling face, a strongly-formed man of living bronze. His steel-grey eyes and long brown hair contrasted strangely with the black eyes and hair of the mixed tribes. Kebisu joined with unfeigned approval in the shouts, "Jakara the Wise!" "Jakara the Lamar of Cunning!" "When will Jakara flash Lightning again?" And in varying degrees of high estate among this throng were those of the Bomai-Malu. By secret signs these also Kebisu greeted, but they alone knew when and how.

Then the Island Mamooses and village chiefs and councillors formed a body-guard and escorted Kebisu along the pleasant village street towards the Sacred Grove where the Zogo-le and attendant Tami-le priests were waiting.

The people thronged around the Tutu men and laughingly quarrelled over their entertainment, as with songs and joking they led them across the village street to where the feast was hot in the *kop-maori* ovens. And Jakara was at liberty to notice Eyes of the Sea.

Eyes of the Sea, in the centre of an admiring group, was all vivacious movement and gay repartee under the excitement; her sweet little laugh echoed in Jakara's heart as he pushed in among the crowd. She was small compared with the girls around, her skin was berry-brown, her body slim and rounded, with the silken strength of the dancer. She had come arrayed in the softest though shortest of skirts, with a necklet of mother-of-pearl round her comely throat. Her restless limbs were braceleted with mottled tortoise-shell: rich brown hair played upon little round breasts. Her face was a cameo of happiness made startlingly beautiful with eyes of intense blue – laughing eyes under long black lashes, mischievous and roguish. Obviously a happy girl.

She smiled impulsively at Jakara, saying demurely, "Greeting to Jakara of Mer," and he smiled back with a wealth of good wishes in eyes that had grown very kind. Shyly, but serenely, she gazed at this Lamar of whom she had heard so much. The on-lookers watched delightedly. Jakara laughed boyishly amid the sudden silence, and took her hand and turned, leading the way into the village.

A boisterous shout arose as the people scrambled to tear down palm-branches to wave over them. The girl's blood quickened, for among this people such a proceeding was a sign: when a man boldly took the hand of a girl, he was bidding for the possession of her. No one guessed at the hurt in the heart of the Pretty Lamar.

But Eyes of the Sea broke away with a prevaricating laugh that hid her quickened thoughts. She instinctively realized that something would come of this. The world, as she knew it, had been her playground. All her wild life she had been the independent favourite of a people who determinedly suppress their women when possible, and now she felt, though without understanding, that the playground held other players, perhaps a master.

Jakara leaned against a palm. Life was suddenly interesting. His world had changed, too; a brightness had come into it, something pleasant to think about, something to look forward to – it felt nearly like happiness.

The vivid blue of the girl's eyes had surprised and enchanted, as her brown skin had shocked him. He remembered his dreams of a white-skinned girl, forgetting that the sun and sea had browned her ever since childhood. And the gold fringing of her hair! Constant sea-diving turned the ends of the native girls' hair a bright brown, but this girl's hair was fringed with gold. Above mere prettiness, she represented something very dear – the heart and mind of a white girl. So he held a wealth of reverie until sundown, to stare uncomprehending into the harsh eyes of a Maid-le messenger. Quickly he woke. That whispered name busied his mind as he strode through the palms, then up the hill-side track that vanished within the Wongai grove. It was oppressively silent and gloomy in there, for Wongai-trees are rugged and almost squat, and their lowlying, grey limbs carpeted the ground with shadows. Finally, across the open of the tree-walled amphitheatre he hurried, guessing with certainty what was required of him, yet not thinking of it, for he was planning to keep Eyes of the Sea now that she was here. Almost subconsciously, he noticed Beizam standing alone among the Wongai-trees and gazing longingly towards the Zogo-house. "The black pup would love to bark inside among the Council," thought Jakara. "Mer will crown a Caesar when Beizam gains the crescent-mai – though not if I can help it."

The Zogo-house doors opened to Jakara, and then shut noiselessly. He strode forward and saluted the Au-gud. He could never make cringing obeisance to this thing, but he gave it military salute in recognition of the undoubted powers behind it. And the ways of Jakara the Strange were accepted.

He gazed boldly around. An alien though he was within this chamber of terrorism and of material and spiritual power, he felt the glow of a new feeling, a challenging defiance. He did not realize that it was because he now fondly imagined he had someone else to fight for beside himself.

C'Zarcke regarded him from black eyes as wise as the crocodiles' teeth plaited in his beard were grotesque. On a coloured mat of sacred patterns he was sitting before the great Au-gud. To his right and left sat the two others of the Island nations, and the Bomai-Malu Zogo-le. Joined with them, and completing the circle, were the lesser Zogo-le of the allied Island groups. Attendant Maid-le priests stood statuesque between the mummies. Old Passi, the chief medicine-man, was there – a slight figure, but the brain within had an expert knowledge of herbs, and the kindly eyes were piercing with hypnotic light. Kebisu, with Bogo and Kesu, sat fronting C'Zarcke. High above all, out over the Council, there floated a pale blue light.

Quietly Jakara, with the grace of long practice, sat in his place on the mat beside Kebisu. A brooding silence was within the Zogo-house. It framed C'Zarcke's deep voice

"Jakara, we wish to exterminate the people of the Two Brothers. Their Maid-le are clever men, with doctrines at various points not harmonizing with ours of the Bomai-Malu; also they are a warlike people and ambitious. They have interfered, and cleverly plan to interfere still further with our trade-canoes coming north from Spirit Island and the canoes coming from far south up the coast of the Great South Land. Also, in speedy fighting-canoes, they are beginning to intercept our heavily laden canoes that carry trade and payment to the south. Now, during a recent voyage Bogo sailed round the Two Brothers, so that you could see it closely. You remember! From the sea he pointed out to you the nature of their land, their principal fighting hills, and the approximate position of their villages. Your eyes have always had a keenness for an unexpected landing-place: we know that your brain sees differently from ours and can therefore plan forms of attack wholly unforeseen by Island peoples. We trust in you for a plan to cripple our enemies, if not to wipe them out with one blow. And – the Au-gud wants heads, many heads, for the monsoonal ceremonies so nearly due."

A chill crept upon Jakara.

"Kebisu will now give you all information," continued the deep persuasive voice; "then we will command the silence in which your plan will be born."

Kebisu gripped Jakara's shoulder. With expressive eyes and nods of emphasis, and an occasional broad smile, he spoke eagerly and rapidly, his voice booming in the quiet of the Zogo-house.

"You have seen the place, Jakara, and know how its teeth can be drawn. We can quickly muster a thousand men; everything except the fall of the blow is planned and ready-canoes, men, water, all waiting to be collected as we sail. Winds are propitious: everyone is lusting for a fight. Show me, Jakara, exactly where I must strike to shatter these people into the sea."

Jakara leaned back, and the brooding face of the Au-gud stared down into his. As brutal as the certainty of destiny, that face yet wore an almost wistful smile, as if wearied of the puny arrogance of man. It held an expression of life, that huge mottled face, a frightening expression of quiet, living thought. The very mummies round the walls seemed to be listening in the silence. Wonderful how he could think: on these occasions! His brain cleared and worked smoothly into coherent thought, free of all effort. He felt that around him were waves of brain-force coming out to him, which, with but the indrawing of the breath, he blended perfectly with the essence of his own thought. He seized the opportunity, for intermixed with the planning of the raid came an inspiration which he hoped would please C'Zarcke and gain a little of his friendship. The minutes passed as if in that atmosphere time were non-existent.

Jakara sighed. As if tired, he stroked the back of his head. A Maid-le stepped from the shadows and placed before him a white square of bark and a charcoal pencil. C'Zarcke looked on silently; Kebisu and the Mamooses leaned eagerly forward. Jakara spoke in a droning voice, mapping the bark and explaining his plan clearly and in detail. The night wore on, until Kebisu laughed. The spell was broken, for when Kebisu laughed the hills heard it, and, if he was in a house, the walls boomed. His great hands thumped Jakara's shoulders, his fine black eyes were rolling in unholy glee. The Mamooses joined in congratulation, while Maros pulled Jakara's hair in bovine play. Jakara, flushed with the praise and the creation of a plan which was excellent in every detail, smiled up at C'Zarcke, and immediately remembered. Every man present, except C'Zarcke and Jakara, arose and quietly left the Zogo-house. Jakara uneasily realized that C'Zarcke had read his mind, and that a secret sign of the Bomai-Malu had dismissed the others.

"You have something to ask of me, something to give," insinuated C'Zarcke softly.

Jakara stared, and then leaned forward impressively: "I should waste words in talk with you, C'Zarcke, who can read my very thoughts. I will just say that I crave something of you, and in return I will give you my greatest treasure. I will bring it now, and then you can judge. Afterwards,

I pray you to grant me my wish."

He hurried from the Zogo-house, away through the chilly Wongai grove, then up a hill-side path toward his Lookout. As he climbed, the revelry from the villages fringing the island shores came singing up to him – most of the villages of Mer were right on the sea-shore. Many pandanus torches twinkled deep down among the coco-palms. As he climbed higher still, the voices became indistinct and were lost as the path wound through the dark jungle where flashed and vanished and flashed again blue and yellow diamonds within the gloom. Out on the forest patches the night was open and beautiful: the moon, and clusters of God's lovely stars: the air sweet and cool and whispering over the grassy slopes: the sea dark and peaceful.

Jakara walked more slowly, for he was about to part with the companion of years. It had shown him the ships of his countrymen; he had drawn a comradeship through the distance until they dimmed away. He remembered the agonized hours of hope while a ship drew slowly near, only to glide by. Several had actually anchored, but the hand of the all seeing C'Zarcke had reached between him and rescue. This sea-battered telescope had been his chief friend. Countless hours had he spent here with his mind abstracted from the island below. Of these passing ships, two had sailed so close that he had actually distinguished their white crew – white men, white men, white men! Jakara sighed; for nothing of value is gained without sacrifice.

C'Zarcke was waiting in the shadows outside the Zogo-house. And Jakara spoke: "C'Zarcke, you know the stars in their courses, you study the heavens, continually seeking guidance of the weather as affecting the fishing-season and the crops. This, my present, will help you. It will show you wonders invisible to our naked eyes-wonders on the sea and upon the land. Much more, this is the eye of a god which will show you worlds in the highest skies."

He trained the telescope on a cloud whose edges were brightening with molten light.

"There, C'Zarcke, watch the moon as it peeps from behind that cloud. Hold the telescope so. No, this way! Why, I believe you are trembling! Ah, that is right! Now move these 'tubes,' as we call them, in or out, like this, until your eye sees perfectly."

The moon peeped, then rose from the clouds all burnished silver. Majestically it glided up across the sky. Still C'Zarcke gazed on, and Jakara grew impatient. Besides, his fear had given place to a satisfying certainty. He spoke. He spoke again! C'Zarcke took not the slightest notice. Jakara spoke loudly, then with a curious thrill touched one of the big muscles. C'Zarcke might have been a mummy, except that his arm felt warm and firm. Jakara touched the telescope. Instantly he was thrown to the ground, with C'Zarcke's weight crushing him and the dreadful face glaring into his. Jakara was a powerful man, but the chief priest of the Bomai-Malu simply twisted Jakara's windpipe; he snarled like a bear as Jakara struggled to gouge his eyes.

Suddenly C'Zarcke's face changed into something pathetically human, he whimpered like a child, and, running into the Zogo-house, laid Jakara upon the mats. He touched the Au-gud, and a long blue flame shot above the fainting man. Jakara struggled to consciousness with his head pillowed upon C'Zarcke's arm. Big eyes gazed into his with almost a mother's anxiety for her child.

"Forgive, Jakara," he whispered, urgently. "I thought you were going to take the wonderful thing away. But it is mine – and are all its powers intact?" There was a pitiful questioning in his eyes.

Jakara nodded weakly. C'Zarcke sighed, and then smiled warmly. "I was a fool, Jakara, but I knew not what I did. Tell me your wish; it is already granted."

A great fear slipped from Jakara. He looked up and managed to whisper: "I – want – Eyes of the Sea." C'Zarcke gazed astounded, then his big head went back and he laughed until the Zogo-house vibrated and the Wongai-trees echoed back the voice and threw it down the little hill-sides. On the beaches below the dancing people halted, amazed. It was the only time in its history that Mer had heard C'Zarcke laugh! He shook Jakara's shoulders as a playing child shakes a doll; then, sobered: "She is yours," he said with a smile. "Take her! If you want her to wife, I will marry you now."

Jakara sat up, coughing but smiling. He grasped C'Zarcke's hands. "Thanks with all my heart, C'Zarcke! But I must woo her first. We are both Lamars, you know, and it is our custom. Afterwards –"

"Well," protested C'Zarcke, "surely you want more than that! Pick out any girl, any number of girls! They are yours for the asking. Or if you have seen any maid among our enemies, name her, if it costs the lives of a hundred men."

Jakara shook his head vigorously. "There is only one that I want, C'Zarcke; just Eyes of the Sea. I have a notion that she will keep me busy, too."

C'Zarcke was disappointed. Gravely he spoke: "You have given me a wondrous thing, Jakara. You do not understand how I have dreamed of such a thing. I had thought that such knowledge was only the property of the spirit world. And I was partly right, for you are a Lamar, though I know you are no spirit. Your wish is granted. Take Eyes of the Sea whenever you wish, and no man dare say you nay. Can you not ask for something more worthy of this great gift?"

Jakara's brain worked quickly. He hesitated, then whispered breathlessly: "Give me my freedom, C'Zarcke. When I have won the girl, give me a loaded canoe and let me sail to the first passing Lamar ship." C'Zarcke's lips opened to say "Yes." He thought soberly for a moment, and then said with growing emphasis: "It is granted, Jakara, on one condition, and you can easily grant me that, for you have the knowledge. Tell me, Jakara," he leaned forward and whispered with a terrible earnestness, "tell me of the Maker of the world! Does He live beyond the stars? Who is He? What are we for? Why does He let us live? What is He going to make of us? To what does the spirit-life lead us? And shall we ever know all? What power made us? Why?"

Jakara stared in incredulous astonishment. C'Zarcke watched him with blazing eyes. Striving for time, Jakara's wits whispered that he must be very careful. "C'Zarcke,' he said slowly, "you have asked me questions that the wisest men of the Lamars have striven for thousands of years to answer. I am not a learned man, and I can only repeat what our wise men tell us. To explain would take many nights of talk. Let me go now, and I will think over all these things."

C'Zarcke stood erect, disappointed. "But, Jakara," he pleaded, "you know who made the world. Tell me!"

"God," said Jakara, as if unaware of himself.

Instantly C'Zarcke's eyes blazed. "God! Who is God? What is He? Where is he?" And Jakara gazed into a face quivering in its lust for knowledge.

"C'Zarcke, you ask me questions that are as vast as the limit of time. I am only a worm. We are all insects, and God made every one of us. How, then, can I tell you of God! When you make a bow, can that bow sing to other bows of you who made it? Heavens alive! Let me go, and I will try to explain in the nights to come."

C'Zarcke rose and half turned his face. His lip quivered sulkily, and Jakara thought that this curious giant was about to cry like a disappointed child. But he turned and asked quietly, "What are 'heavens?'"

Jakara waved helplessly towards the Zogo-house roof. "You saw the heavens to-night, C'Zarcke; you peeped into them through the present I gave you."

C'Zarcke's face brightened instantly. He lifted Jakara to his feet and patted his shoulders, smiling as a happy boy might smile. He took him to the door and stretched out his hand towards the Wongai glade. "C'Zarcke is now Jakara's friend for all time," he said warmly. "Whatever you wish for, whatever you desire, take it, or do it without fear of any man. Tell your wish to the Mamoose, and see me at all times, if you should want something that the Mamoose cannot give. Go now, and in your own time explain to me the knowledge of the Lamars. And I will seek within the 'heavens!'"

Jakara went, a very subdued Jakara, painfully aware that in this queer world there are matters of greater importance than Love.

SMOKING HIS ZOOB

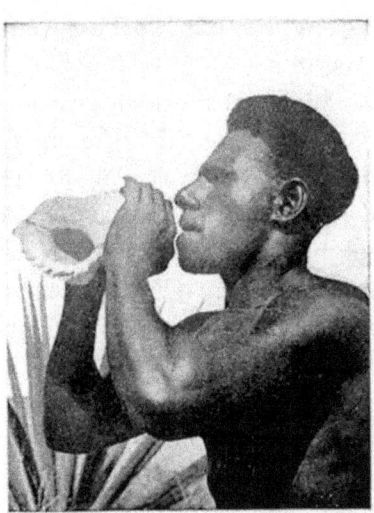

BLOWING THE BOO SHELL

CHAPTER VI

War Dr ums Of Mer

Mer slept – with Silence for her blanket and Death for her bedmate. Suddenly Death ripped the blanket aside and sprang erect to the rolling drums of Mer. Those shark-jaw drums! Unhappy, sobbing drums that swelled to pulsing waves of sound which drowned the quiet of valleys and villages and boomed across the bays far out to sea, drums that throbbed the knell of death from the heart of great Gelam.

Jakara sprang from his sleeping-mat and listened in breathless alarm: with alert body and tingling ears he drank in the warning of the drums. Every glade in the island echoed their changeful sound, grown now to a rolling throb, dreadful in its intense effect upon the passions of men. The echoing sea, and the air, and every tree and rock and leaf were sobbing into the ears of men a physical hysteria.

Jakara laughed, for the thrill of a maddened energy was racing through his blood. He snatched out Lightning, and the steel trilled to the drums. Drums of war! A thousand men sprang to club and bow and arrow, to spear and shark-tooth sword. A rumble of feet came from the houses as men hastened into the night; women lay a second longer, then, like tigresses, snatched their babes and leaped out beside their men; tousled-haired maids, all frightened-eyed, sat up, crouching, from sleeping-mats; children clung to their parents' legs, and stared out into the night.

Then came an eerie whisper – of relief – in many villages for the *boo* shells brayed of an embarkation for war, not of a night attack upon Mer. So, joining the song of the drum and the *boo*, roared up a note of exultation: with those steely rays of dawn Mer was an awakened ant-bed.

Stridently called the *boo* shells, bold, insistent, compelling. The misty valleys echoed while the damp cliffs blared their challenge across the now lightening sea. From every village poured terribly excited men: scolding, advising, questioning, laughing, and crying, wives rushed after them to twine across their hurrying backs dilly-bags of sling-stones. Maids with thumping hearts tripped along, scanning the lads who pushed roughly by. Naked children came running and screaming war-songs, and dogs with bristling back and tails erect snarled at scampering strangers. Along every village path the bushes swayed and hissed at being brushed aside as things of no account. From jungle tracks across the shadowed beaches welled out lines of scurrying people, all disappearing into jungle again, all hurrying to the increasing sound of the *boo* shell, all bustling in the one direction, while the island and its sea-washed sides and hilly slopes between soon became deserted. All the paths gradually converged under the palms of Maiad.

The sun crimsoned Gelam, and a black cloud streaked the crimson with flame. As village clan after clan poured upon Maiad beach, their shouts were drowned in the roar of welcome from the gathering throng. A roar of the Beizam-le, of the Zagareb-le, of the crocodile men, and the dog men, and the pigeon men – a roar that rose with the clashing weapons and shrill of fighting rattles and with the booming *boos*, to merge with the methodical sobbing drums of Mer. And high above the Zogo-house rose a steady prism of light, a weird blue light that shone only at war or at the death of a Zogo or at some great Island calamity or victory. It was from the *booya*, a round stone which was a miracle to Jakara, in that it emitted this piercing light from some property held within itself. Set in a large bamboo socket heavily decorated in designs of the Bomai-Malu with teeth, shells, hair, and colours, only three of these light-belching stones are known to have been in existence, one the property of Mer, one of Eroob, and one of Ugar. A secret, as yet not rediscovered by white men, was lost with these stones when the Zogo-le of the Eastern Islands nation, foreseeing the inevitable conquest by the whites, buried their secrets.

Unexpectedly, Jakara felt quick warm fingers on his arm. He liked the Pretty Lamar as she deftly fastened a palm-leaf armlet above his elbow. Though she smiled so gaily, he felt her fingers trembling. "A good luck armlet for Jakara the Unkillable," she whispered. "The leaf has slept against my heart. It will guard Jakara from any weapon, though it may not save his heart for me." With a gay wave of farewell she stepped back among the people.

Distinct from the excited crowd, each village chief, in perfect discipline, took his orders from Bogo. And now arose a peculiar note, a wailing of anguished men who were detailed to stand by Mer. With the quick orderliness of perfected plans, each village quota marched to the sands, where ten huge war-canoes were drawn up in alignment. Within them, packed to a nicety, and loaded to suit the rising wind, were foodstuffs and massed bundles of arrows and bamboos of water. The canoes comfortably averaged forty men each. Several of the grizzly weapons which these men carried are worth mentioning.

The *kamoose* was an arrow with a barbed but detachable head which stayed in the body when struck. The arrow-head fitted into a hollow socket in the haft, and the haft fell away with the shock of contact. The *doad* showed remarkable mechanical ingenuity. It was a short bolt rather than an arrow-head. It also fitted into a bamboo haft, with a screwing motion. The point was broad and fashioned with a view to penetrative power. Running down from the point for a length of five inches were two flanges of broad tempered bamboo. These had each three sides, razor-keen. Underneath them, pressed against the hard-wood of the arrow-head proper, were compressed springs of bamboo. Immediately the arrow-head pierced the body, the springs were loosened, and the flanges flew out with a twisting motion, thus making a whirling disk ten inches in diameter, which cut up the opponent's body inside. The weapon was also designed with a view to terrible shock. No man ever arose when once the *doad* entered the body. It was fitted into a bamboo haft, and fired like a bolt from a very strong bow. Crossing the centre of the bow was a bamboo tube: the haft was thrust through this, then the *doad* was fitted on. At the butt-end of the haft were two knobs, which would not allow the haft to pass completely through the tube. The bow was drawn to its full limit and the string loosened. The haft shot out, but the knobs caught against the bamboo with frightful force, adding to the *doad* a spinning motion as it thrummed heavily with terrific speed on its way. Some men carried slings of plaited fibre, and expert marksmen could bring down a bird on the wing.

The men did not all carry the same weapons. Every man carried his *gaba-gaba*, and each wore, hanging from his neck, the *upi*, the bamboo head-knife, and the *singai* loop. Each man was an expert with one weapon and different villagers were adepts at different arms. Thus there were the sword men, the club men, the arrow men, the *doad* men, the *sukari* men, and so on. The *gaba-gaba* and bow and arrow were the favourite weapons. The bone dagger was a deadly thing at close quarters. It was carved from the shin-bone of a man or a cassowary.

With warriors lining the canoe sides and with song from every throat, the vessels were rushed into the water, and, as they splashed, each man sprang to his place. Up flew the sails, and the wind bellied them into life. The women of Mer, how they sang! How their black eyes flashed while they screamed to the maddening rhythm of the war-song! As the bows of the canoes dipped to the bay, the very hills echoed back the song from the men, the sun bronzed their muscles and proudly ornamented chests. Cheerily they waved the *dadu*, with each canoe proudly flying its own *dadu*, a coconut-leaf flag at the end of a pole in the stern.

The crowd rushed the departing canoes, and in hundreds the forgotten children plunged into the water, swimming and shrilling their triumph song. The girls and women swam through the foaming wakes until the free sea-breeze hurried the canoes over the reef. The women swam far out, tailing off like sheep until distance made mellow the song from the canoes. And on the beach face downward lay the men who were not allowed to go and fight. Then the crowd, with drenched hair, ran panting up the grassy headlands, shrilling their wild, grim song with straining voices until the canoes grew dim on the misty sea. And over all, permeating the hysteria, even within the throb of the drums, brooded the spirit of C'Zarcke.

In Kebisu's canoe were also Jakara and Eyes of the Sea. A shrewd move this of Kebisu's, going ajaunting with but a few warriors and, above all, women! Thus by telepathic communication the Maid-le of enemy islands would conclude that Kebisu had been paying but a ceremonial visit to Mer.

They would not visualize him standing now, handling the Eagle's Claws, his eyes fierce as that pirate of the air! These claws were a pair, and were symbolically used by the chiefs of clans when fighting on sea or shore. Thus, in a few nights to come, as the canoes crept closer to the doomed island, Kebisu would grip those claws tightly and thrusting them in the direction of the Two Brothers, haul the claws slowly back towards him, muttering the while. This signified his "grip" on the island, and the final rush of the canoes would symbolize the rending of the talons. Similarly, if a sea-fight occurred, the Eagle's Claws would be thrust out to "grip" the enemy canoes. Symbolical, of course, but with a distinct meaning which added materially to the fighting-power of these people.

Jakara looked at Eyes of the Sea, and she smiled cheerily, then blushed, vaguely annoyed at not understanding why she wrapped her disarrayed skirt around her. Had there been only tribesmen present, she would never have thought of her skirt, for all had great things to think of far above the limbs of a girl. Jakara the Lamar was different, his ways were new and uncertain. He always seemed to be expecting something different of her, something she did not quite understand. She was annoyed with herself, too, that she wanted to be as this man expected her to be. Still, he was handsome and a noted chief! So were other men also, but this Lamar attracted her most strangely. Many a girl pined to be his humblest slave. Lively curiosity puzzled her as to why he refused to wear the head-mai, insignia of warriorhood. She sat almost buried between fat bunches of bananas, and Jakara stepped over an outrigger spar and squeezed down beside her. His manner was possessive, and the quick men of Tutu laughed with their eyes, and nudged insinuations. And Jakara laughed with the girl and said pleasant things, and talked as if he owned her, and she joked back, thrilled by the hard grey eyes that spoke so meaningly while his lips talked lightly. Girls of Tutu from adjoining canoes called to Kebisu's warriors, who answered amid laughter at the lovers among the bananas.

Jakara noted a scowl behind Beizam's laugh as he called boyishly from his canoe: "Blue eyes of Tutu, how quick you were to tie upon Jakara's arm the band of love!"

Jakara had to satisfy the instant curiosity of the girl. "So Jakara already loves," she said merrily in reproof, and refused to accept his denial.

Little waves rolled to spank the sterns of the canoes, but could not quite reach, while the derisive wind hissed spray once and again into the jaws of crocodile and shark. The warriors grimly remarked that soon their figureheads would drink of something else. The sun sparkled on the water, and life seemed very happy. Then Eroob stood out grandly, with the grassy slopes of Lalour climbing down into the sea. Presently came faintly the *boo* shells: the warriors answered with one voice and broke again into the war-song, while all eyes searched Eroob – except those of Jakara, pained that the girl had turned from him to gaze in intense excitement at the emerald valleys and golden beaches.

She turned such an excited face! "Oh, Jakara, you hear them? The *boo* shells of Eroob! Hark! the sea throws back their voices, and they growl like the spirit of thunder. Hear the drums of Eroob! Oh, how they throb out the deep song that carries with it the wail of a child! The drums of Eroob, calling. the men to war! Oh, how I wish I were a man! Jakara, how proud you are! You are a leader of men!"

She leaned towards him, and he thrilled to the adoration in her face and voice. But he was deeply pained. This was no fondness for him, this was simply native hero-worship. Her eyes sought the circlet at his neck, so that he could *feel* the accusation.

"Jakara," she whispered, "where is your head-mai?"

Startled, he stared at her. "I have not got one."

"Why not?"

Jakara drew a long breath; the kindness left his eyes. "Because I am a white man," he snarled, "you little white savage!"

She sat back among the bananas, then turned again towards Eroob, bewilderment in her eyes.

The *boo* shells brayed loudly, and the drums throbbed from the heart of Lalour. Its green slopes became blackened as with ants that came crawling up from every jungle path until the lookout knolls were covered and the lazy waves hummed to the roar: "Kebisu! Kebisu! Kebisu!" And *boo* shells from sea and land joined chorus, a blasting of loud musical sound, each shell a note to itself, long-drawn-out, insistent, the voices in the song of the rolling drums of Eroob. The ants with one accord ran down the slopes and disappeared down the jungly ravines to burst forth on the village paths and spread out thickly upon the little beaches. They ran along the beaches and disappeared among Saidee's palms, and reappeared farther along the beach, while behind them hurried still more files, and others, all singing the stirring song of the war-god, all the clans hurrying for Medigee Bay. A great throng, with the screaming chorus of the women, hastened on while Kebisu's canoes raced parallel towards the point. Like pigeon-hawks under a sure leader, the canoes swept into the bay, and, as they skimmed the great Sai, their inverted V-shaped formation in pairs came gracefully about, with Kebisu's foaming canoe leading up through the lines until the flotilla was facing out to sea in inverted V-shape again. With bows to the wind the flotilla floated like waiting swans.

On the pretty beach at Medigee a mad crowd surged around eight canoes, but never delaying the detailed men who, breasting the vessels, rushed them to the water and swung up the big sails. As they took the breeze, Kebisu's sails filled, and the flotilla, in two inverted V's, stood out to sea to a repetition of the leave-taking at Mer. Kebisu, his brawny chest swelling with pride of life and power, turned to Jakara, the exultation in his smile making vividly alive the shrewd, savage face.

"Give me a fleet such as these, and not only a flotilla, and we would conquer the world, Jakara," he laughed, in his big rolling voice.

Jakara smiled. "All the earth would tremble if they knew of the power of the Strait, Kebisu; and if my world knew of the wisdom of the Zogo-le, they would wonder much."

"And the plans of Jakara the Cunning," answered the big Mamoose; "do they include the maid?" And with a laugh at the bashful girl, he turned again to thrill at the picture of his canoes.

"You can sing again, Eyes of the Sea," said Jakara gruffly; "Kebisu notices us no more."

"You do not like me to sing," flashed the girl. "Why so, Jakara the Strange?"

Jakara's stern face relaxed. He leaned towards her, and said gently: "Because, Eyes of the Sea, you are white! A girl of the white people should not sing at the sight of savages bound for murder and things more terrible."

Her voice was troubled, her face defiant: "But, Jakara, these are our warriors going to fight a people who have slaughtered numbers of us and would kill us all, were it not for our fighting men: they would carry our heads back on the *koon*. Besides, I am one of them, and I am very proud. They are my people!"

"Listen, Eyes of the Sea," Jakara said earnestly; "can't you realize that you belong to another race? These very people slaughtered your own father and mother and would have done so to you, had you not been claimed as a Lamar. We are English, you and I, white people! Don't you understand that we must keep our pride of race and cling to the ideals of our own people?"

Jakara ceased at the puzzled frown on the angry little face. "They should call you 'Jakara the Mad.' These are my people! I will have no other."

Just then Beizam, from the fighting-platform of his canoe, called to her, and, beckoning with his shark tooth sword out to sea, laughed aloud as he started the war-song again. The girl jumped up among the bananas, a figure of graceful youth and wild loveliness, stretched out her arms towards the foaming canoes of the Mamoose of Eroob, and joined in the wildly musical song.

Jakara frowned at the *koon* she had mentioned. This ominous pole stood aft in every canoe, its masthead gay with leaves and cassowary feathers, a single great plume at the very tip. Down below at an angle, lashed to the pole, were two shorter poles. On these would be hung the heads of slain enemies.

The sun sank like a ball of fire and crimsoned the rolling waves. From the Erubian canoes a voice inquired why the sail of Kebisu had stained to red? To the swish-swish-sh-sh-sh of the sea and the trill of the wind, the canoes sped on while night splashed the sky with brilliants. Then a half-moon peeped from a fleecy cloud and silvered a road upon the sea. The voices from canoe to canoe tinkled with laughter and song. Just before the moon disappeared a blue flame shot up from black Ugar and was answered from Kebisu's canoe by the blaring, far-reaching call of a *boo*. The canoe men shouted the chorus, the strange wild music speeding into the night. The blur of Ugar was speckled with torch-flame, and a hundred fire-flies burst into light upon the beach, while from every village rose the counter-challenge of the *boo*. Kebisu's canoe men burst into the war-song, which was returned from Ugar by voices fresh with excitement.

Into the bay sped the canoes and came about with eerie precision in the night light, rocking quietly while five fighting-canoes of Ugar took swift form as they sped out from the beach. Then on again to wilder song, with clarion voices of the *boo*. And right out in the bay fire-flies suddenly dimmed as the torches of swimmers were drowned by the sea.

Through dark night sped the canoes, and stars speckled the warriors' faces with dancing points of. light. By the stars Kebisu sailed, for the stars in their courses had for centuries been familiar to the navigating Islanders of the Strait. At dawn appeared a low small island, only a sandbank capped by mangroves and surrounded by the greatest coral reef (apart from the mother Barrier) in the world.

The island of Tutu was named by Bligh, "Warrior Island," because while in 1792 the great navigator in H.M.S. *Providence,* accompanied by the brig *Assistant,* had all the boats out taking soundings in Basilisk Pass, the Tutu men attacked with an enveloping fleet. The boats met them with musketry, but were forced to fly to the man-o'-war. Captain Portlock signalled for assistance, and the *Providence* came up. The cannon of both vessels had to rake the canoes with grapeshot before they broke their way through. The warriors got so close to boarding the brig that they killed one sailor and wounded several. Kebisu's boastful warriors claimed that their fathers had won the victory because "the Lamar ships never came back." Furthermore they asserted that they were as good warriors as their fathers had been. To-day, in their dances, the descendants of these men pertly commemorate the event in which they claim that their forefathers hammered His Majesty's ships of war. Bligh described the Tutu men as "dexterous sailors and formidable warriors."

And now the people of Tutu crowded the coral-specked beach in mad hero-worship at the return of their chief. But the *boos* were silent, and bursts of song were sternly suppressed, although all was hysterical excitement. A huge feast was spread, and the warriors ate, and continued to eat, and the women tried to force them to eat more. The Maid-le of Tutu walked among the groups with Kebisu and the Mamooses, and impressed upon the chiefs that they should urge their men to sleep and, above all, suppress dancing and singing.

A HOUSE OF MER

CHAPTER VII

The Massacre On The Two Brothers

Night came, but few slept. How could they? The warriors of Tutu prowled among them, their tribal pride entirely unconcealed as they swaggered in plumed head-dresses and cassowary *kadik*, twitching their cruel stone clubs. Barely suppressed excitement rioted among every clan or Island tribe. And the Tutu women, urged by the wild-cat Eyes of the Sea, with gesture and eyes and lisps of song added continually to the tension. Presently, with unspoken accord, group after group sprang up, column after column formed, weapons clattered, a hum arose sky-ward, the earth murmured and then burst into a roar of stamping feet and maddened war-song from two thousand throats. How the women screamed, their voices shrilling above those of the men and vibrating with terrible passion! In vain the chiefs sought to smother the fire in all those hysterical eyes.

Kebisu and the Mamooses rushed from the Council House, headed by a fiend who was the Maid-le. Only fear of a punishment after death stemmed that mad, abandoned dance; the Maid-le shrieked the penalty in the awful threat of the Bomai-Malu; men stood aghast, their song strangled, while women glared with hatred but terror at the Maid-le, who raved against all with words terrible in his fury. And the panting of a thousand chests was a homage to the power of his words.

Beizam, clenching his hands in the mangrove shadows, snarled to himself, for since boyhood he had secretly hated the fact that the Tutu warriors were classed as the greatest in the Strait. All the Strait, right to New Guinea, knew that, if it were not for the spiritual power of C'Zarcke, the men of Tutu would be the overlords of Mer.

Rustling through the moonlight in tune to eerie whispering, warriors manned the canoes; the Tutu men filled another five, while the women threw their arms around them and sobbed. Girls bade farewell to lovers who, with a warrior's pride, looked ashamed. Jakara, who stood looking on, feeling desperately lonely, thrilled to a little hand upon his arm. He smiled into blue eyes lovely in their moon-bathed mistiness. Surprised into warm happiness, he pressed her to him and kissed lips sweet and trembling. Eyes of the Sea loved that kiss and clung to him. The world seemed to fade away, leaving only happiness. His eyes smiled as he whispered: "Eyes of the Sea, little sweetheart."

A cold voice said: "Kebisu awaits," and Eyes of the Sea hated the Maid-le of Tutu.

Jakara kissed her with all the pent-up longing of years. The girl, happy despite the pain at her heart through fear for his home-coming, followed his canoe into the water and kissed him as he leaned from the fighting-platform. The canoes sailed in four inverted V's, but at this embarkation there were no drums, no noisy farewells, just the sobs of women sighing into the cool night air.

In the deep silence sat the Zogo-le in their groups of three upon each Zogo island; and upon all the allied islands stretching right across the Strait sat the Maid-le priests. C'Zarcke, inside the Zogo-house of Mer, sat as if hypnotized into the unseen life. His eyes, gleaming blue-black, told that his mind had drawn upon the mind-power of the Zogo-le and the entranced priests, and was rapidly concentrating that power in order to will to sleep one lone watcher on the Two Brothers.

This flotilla from the grand fleet of Kebisu was an impressive sight of savage power – twenty-eight huge canoes skimming across the starlit sea like mammoth bats of a pterodactyl world. The vessels had been built by the war-canoe builders of New Guinea, men whose ancestors had been constructing this type of vessel for over a thousand years. Kebisu's canoe was seventy feet in length and capable of carrying a hundred men. Made of one giant Mah-moro tree, and shaped like a gigantic torpedo, it was buoyant and yet exceedingly tough. With incalculable patience and labour the inside had been burnt out and then chipped as smoothly as if planed by tools of civilization. Every chip of surplus weight had been scooped away. The lessons of centuries had been put into the scooping out of these logs, for therein rested the secret of their immunity from swamping when caught in a storm. The narrow opening along the entire length of the log was only two-and-a-half feet wide, and the warriors had to stand sideways when climbing down into the body of the canoe; but, inside, it was hollowed out roomily. The extreme narrowness of this "hatchway" practically defied the greatest wave to fill the vessel. The bows were deeply grooved within and supported by cross pieces. At midships, and at an equal distance between bow and stern, the sides were widened and yet supported by massive forks of tea-tree; each fork, though one stick, was really three branches and so gave to the sides of the vessel great resistance against the crash of the waves, while at the same time the forks were light and resilient. The stern tapered upwards, to be cut off sharp. The depth of the vessel was five feet. Another two feet of height was added by a gunwale of planks fastened through bored holes by lashings of lawyer-cane as firm as twisted wire, and were made rock-firm amidships by the long mangrove poles of the outrigger booms. These long side planks once more defied the elements against swamping. A man standing on the bottom of the canoe was invisible from the outside. These side-planks were loopholed at intervals for arrows. Inside were rows of lawyer-cane loops which held sheaves of arrows. The archers stood at an angle in order to obtain the room necessary for drawing back the big bows within that narrow space. Their system of fire was mostly that of two rows of men, each man firing at an alternate angle to the next. Thus each side of the canoe could direct a cross-fire. The archers stood to their required height upon cross-pieces deep within the canoe, which also helped to strengthen the vessel. The bows, stern, and particularly the fighting-platform, were also fought from. The impenetrable cover afforded by the hull of the vessel was generally taken advantage of only when the enemy were in overpowering numbers, or else were disciplined and so more dangerous fighters than the ordinary. At about one-third of the distance from bow and stern were the outriggers. These greatly added to the vessel's buoyancy, helped it in speed, and made it practically non-capsizable in the roughest weather. There was an outrigger on each side, reaching about twenty feet out from the vessel, and, as Kebisu's canoe was of extraordinary length, each outrigger float was over twenty feet long, shaped like a huge cigar, and of Duar wood, very light – the same wood from which are made the torpedo canoes that skim along the surface. Uprights about four feet in height were drilled into the middle and ends of these floats. Standing out from the canoe were booms of black mangrove wood, lashed to the outrigger uprights. Twisted ropes of brush-vine stayed these booms to the masts. So taut were they, and the outriggers set at such an angle, that they seldom touched the water when the canoe was on a quiet sea, but in the trough of the waves these floats spanked the water and were bounced high and forward, thus helping to shoot the vessel along and offering a great leverage, one outrigger against the other, to keep the canoe upright when big waves came rolling side on. The outrigger was platformed with lashed-down planks forming a broad deck right across the canoe and far out on each side. Around the sides of the platform were long box frame-works of bamboo, inside which were placed food-stuffs or cargoes. Lashed as a secondary floor to the platform were crates of bamboo, which in a trice could be fitted round the platform, enclosing it with a breast-high bulwark loopholed for, but impervious to, arrow fire. The vessel was steered by a man manipulating a long board somewhat similar to a ship's rudder.

The larger vessels had two masts of an elastic seasoned wood, fitted firmly into the canoes by stays of tea-tree, but in such a way that the mast-butts had the necessary "play" against all strain. Ropes and cordage were of specially prepared hibiscus-bark fibre. Instead of pulley-blocks, loops of lawyer-cane were used. A vessel less than forty feet in length had but one mast, and generally one outrigger.

The Zogo-le have records of four-masted vessels, but these appear to have been used more as slower trade-vessels, while the vessels described here are Kebisu's main fighting-fleet.

The others of Kebisu's flotilla varied in size and strength. Bogo's canoe measured sixty feet, the others fifty and forty. The Islanders were exceedingly proud of their vessels. Each was aptly named; thus Kebisu's was the *Skull Chief*, Bogo's the *Tiger Shark*, Maros's the *Headhunter*, and so on. The canoes bore the clan sign of the chief in command, so that high over the bow of Bogo's canoe was the viciously open jaw of a tiger shark; over Kebisu's canoe the gaping jaws of a crocodile, the forequarters of the loathsomely lifelike bulk clawing the bows; on several canoes was the big snakelike head of the Turtle clan. Some again flaunted the figures of women, wild goddesses whose faces were set to incite men to attempt anything. Water was carried in long bamboos used as cylinders.

Kebisu's canoe carried the *kupi* – a stem of coconut-palm with a number of leaves adhering. This was the calendar of dates. At each setting sun a leaf would be torn off, and Kebisu would know exactly the passing of the days – for all voyages were set to a definite time-table, right to the return to Mer. At Mer a Maid-le attended to a checking *kupi*. Thus was Kebisu's planned whereabouts known day by day (barring unforeseen circumstances) at Mer. Unforeseen happenings, especially if tragic, were detected only by the mysterious divinatory power of the Zogo-le. The Zogo-le always chose the sailing times carefully; they knew exactly the prevailing winds and the distances; and the weather of the near future was compiled from the stars.

The canoes sped on. The moon slid to rest as if unwilling to see; fleecy clouds veiled the stars that peeped like misty tears. The sea's slow waves moaned a restless song. In their ocean bed slept the Two Brothers, sleepers of a million years. And within their shadows the villages slept, and the air breathed sounds of sleep, even to the whining of the dogs.

But the chief Maid-le was fighting against sleep, fighting hour against hour the dread premonition that disaster drew near. It was in the small hours that, haggard eyed, as if driven by a will more powerful than his own, he threw himself upon his sleeping-mat and fell fast asleep.

A shriek – and the night shrieked. Upon a dozen villages broke a wave of men with crash and shout. Quick screams, wail of children, howl of dogs, bursting walls in ravaged houses, tattoo of drums, grunts of fighting men, and the awful cries of pierced women!

Skyward roared their terrible triumph as the allies of Mer thrust and stabbed and hacked and swung the clubs, the rattles on their speeding limbs shrilling in vibrant chorus. Startled seabirds flapped into the night. Throughout a dozen villages men thudded upon the sleeping-mats in the sleep that awakes at Boigu, Isle of the Blest. Others were hacked to their knees and died against the tearing walls: odd sleepers did not even awake to receive the club. The heads of women, wonderful in their wild-eyed amazement, showed plain in the melee a moment before they fell. Crunching noises silenced the wail of children. The one awful chorus was, "Kill! Kill! Kill!" Overhead hissed blazing snakes that lit the thatched roofs into bonfires which illumined the quiet bays. The fighting soon writhed in madly beautiful groups under the leaping flames: the men of the Two Brothers were going down very, very fast.

Now thrummed the *doad*, and the sobbing gasp of the stricken was but a sigh in the uproar amid the twang of bows, whistle of arrows, whizz of sling-stones. A terrified cur with bared fangs and tail between its legs leapt at Beizam as he clubbed its master, while Sakor of Eroob, pinned by a spear through his belly, croaked strangely while his talons tore the grass. A mother brained her child, then shrieked into the fight, clenching her husband's broken spear: she avenged his spirit too, before she was stunned and thrown into the flames. Pathetic things happened, as when a toddler tried to shield her puppy from the club: and a sea-gull, confounded by the uproar and dazzled by the flames, sped out to hiss in the sea – a throbbing ball of fire. To this omen the raiders roared lustily that the star of the Two Brothers had fallen! They pressed the harder on the fast diminishing villagers, and the groups dissolved when the disciplined fighters died. Then maniacs sped among the flames, and Jakara was one of these, just an animal seething with the awful physical energy of "Kill! Kill! Kill!" Taking their ringing blows upon the up-flung shield, he thrust with Lightning to throat or belly or heart, and thrust again in leaping fury upon antagonist after antagonist-and always at belly or throat, as the unbalanced body of fighters gave opening, for thrusts through the heart demand strength, and such quick, continuous work tires a man's arm. Beizam also was fighting with a savage fury, but cleverly; burning to make a name for himself in this, his first great battle, he yet fought with the cool self-control of the old campaigner. And several times, as fortune favoured him, he fought his way behind Jakara, and, while fighting his own battles, studied, when opportunity allowed, the way in which Jakara fought his.

In the uncertainty of the first mad rush the attackers had no time for the Dance of Death, but when came the flight of the remnant, the roars of the pursuers changed to animal howls as the *upi* knives whipped out and runaways at bay fought from the standing to the kneeling, and from the kneeling to the lying attitude, until their heads rose again to laugh on high.

Then Jakara remembered! He left the fleeing men and sought only the weak people. Under smouldering walls, crouched among bushes, he sought them, and it meant only one sharp thrust to the throat. Instant death – incomparably more sweet than the Dance of Death. Women and children, all he could find – these did Jakara the Strange seek. He left the comely girls, for they must work out their own destiny. But to all the helpless ones he gave the swift kindness of death.

And with the flush of dawn all was over, except that scattered animals were being chased by other animals over the hills. Jakara, his arm hanging limp and leaden, sobbed in mental sickness.

The pick of the young girls only were saved. Everyone besides – man, woman, and child – went to the killing-clubs. Here was the greatest slaughter by the allied men of Mer, the entire annihilation, in one attack, of an Island population. To this day the big island remains uninhabited and deserted, the Two Brothers brooding over the harvest of skulls gleaned on the night of Kebisu's raid.

WAR HEAD-DRESS OF KEBISU (NOW IN BRITISH MUSEUM)
WOODEN CLUB, MER

CHAPTER VIII

The Return

Drums of Mer! Welcoming drums! *Boo* shells calling across the sea. Kebisu's fleet had swelled to giant proportions with the canoes of several Island populations and the congratulatory emissaries from allied groups, causing the enemy islands from northern Australia to New Guinea to wonder uneasily at this further gathering of the tribes, for the telepathy of their Maid-le had spread the news.

The home people of Mer ran from the hills to the beaches and back again in seething excitement as the fighting-fleet of Kebisu sailed first in flotillas of inverted V's, and behind them, in bellying crescents, the canoes of the populations. Three hundred canoes were there, and as Kebisu's Tutu flotilla swung into the tiny bay, a grand collision seemed imminent: but when, nearing the beach, Kebisu's leading V ran straight on, the V directly behind swung to the right, the following V to the left, and the two remaining swung out and flanked the first three. Kebisu skimmed in magnificent fashion straight up the golden sands almost to the palms, followed by the complete fleet in ever-spreading couples. So skilfully performed was the manoeuvre, so buoyantly built were the canoes, that the fleet glided to rest without even jolting the crews. The indiscriminate vessels which followed landed boisterously.

Around the warriors surged a sea of people, while C'Zarcke, statuesque and silent, stood apart with the Zogo-le groups until the froth of excitement should subside. Eventually, in answer to a Bomai sign, Kebisu strode towards him. Instant silence enveloped all. A gull, flying overhead, croaked harshly. The two great men met with smiles and placing of hands on shoulders – Kebisu strikingly tall, and carrying himself with the fierce hauteur of a savage chief, C'Zarcke broad of form, with rugged head, and reasoning power from which even Kebisu shrank: the fighting-idol and the dreaded idol of the people.

A shout roared up which startled the sea-gulls and made the leaves shiver upon the palms: "C'Zarcke the Wonderful!" "Kebisu! Kebisu the Great!"

Excitement burst into hysteria as the crowd surged upon the warriors and brought many to the sands by weight of embracing arms. Others rushed the canoes, and with roaring triumph-song, struggled to snatch out the baskets filled with heads. Also a wild and pitiful cry arose, the lamentation of women for sons and brothers and sweethearts; and there followed a terrible rite, as newly-made widows rushed the carriers' legs and with maniacal strength brought the contents of the baskets rolling upon the sands, when each snatched up a head and, with screaming song to Bomai, gouged out the eyes with her fingers. Thus she took material revenge for the spirit of her husband. A weird chant arose from thousands, the spirit-song to Bomai: they wailed in eerily-rising, softly-falling cadences of chilly musical beauty to Malu and Kulka and Segar, beseeching those spirit-gods to receive unto them the souls of their dead and ever send down spirit-power to the material body of C'Zarcke for the uplifting of their nation.

Miriam, her sweet face frantic in its grief, stared down at her lover's head, with the sand speckled upon its lips. Shrieking, she ran across the beach like a mad thing, raced through the village and along the banana-paths, and sped out of the jungle where the sea-air crooned about her face, "Come! Come! Come!" And straight to Geedee's Lookout she flew, and leapt far out and down to the sad welcome of the sea.

From the beach rose the triumphal home-song, rhythmic and sustained, swelling into fevered volume with praises to the gods, the Zogo-le, the warrior leaders of battles hard won. For now the Zogo-le and Kebisu with the Bomai-Malu priests, and just behind them the Mamooses and Jakara the Strange, followed by the warriors in clans led by their several village chiefs, and around all the mad, mad people, marched and surged through the palms up and up towards the Zogo-house to lay out the heads before the Au-gud.

A great crowd jostled that day up the grim hills of Mer, forcing new paths through the jungle ravines and flowing among the banana-patches like a crowd of mammoth ants spreading down the green dales and over the hills.

They passed the Shrine of Barbaker with good-humoured greetings to the little stone god, who gazed whimsically back almost with a twinkle in his eye. It was a pretty shrine, set among the trees. The god squatted on a black volcanic stone, and this in turn rested upon a block of granite, which in ages past must have been brought from the Great South Land, the Western Islands, or New Guinea.

As rank upon rank thundered into the Sacred Grove, they lapsed into silence, but the dry leaves under their thousands of feet whispered their marching-song. They formed into statuesque phalanxes in crescent form facing the Zogo-house, the men of Tutu in honour fronting the Au-gud, flanked by the men of Mer and Eroob and Ugar. And the people filled the grove, packing far back among the trees, while children, not daring to climb the sacred branches, whimpered to their parents for a shoulder-perch to view the great Zogo.

C'Zarcke and the Zogo-le officiated upon finely woven mats, patterned in sacred designs of the Bomai-Malu, artistically dyed with colours extracted from fish and plants and minerals.

Upon its coral dais dreamed the gigantic Au-gud, carved from plates of shell selected from a thousand turtle. Men of a vanished race had carved that figure, men of a great migration who came from the south bringing with them a culture which taught these people all that they knew and much that they had forgotten, and who created works of utility in stone which have defied time and weather to this day. The legends of these islands give it that the great migration, led by the supermen, Bomai, Malu, Kulka, and Segar, came from Ekinpad in the Great South Land near the granite mountain range enclosing the Pascoe River in North Queensland.

Embraced by the Au-gud was the Booya, and behind it leered a carved crocodile, a shark, and a snake. These represented the principal clans, and crocodile, shark, or snake men were the best educated and most resourceful classes. A half-shark or half-turtle man was classed lower in the social scale. This system represented a classification similar to that of the European nobility, except that here every man had to prove himself before he gained respect. Some classes worked with their heads, others were tradesmen in carving and in the making of weapons and instruments of utility; others again were agriculturists, others fishermen, while yet others were "hewers of wood and drawers of water."

Those figures of the crocodile, snake, and shark could move and run and squirm by virtue of some inner force – a fact which had caused Jakara much fruitless thought. For even if the Zogo-le understood an unknown kind of mechanism, still these figures were centuries old and had moved upon these hills possibly centuries before the first European mechanic was born, possibly even before Atlantis sank beneath the sea.

On mats fronting the Zogo were placed in rows the cane baskets filled with heads. It took two men to lift each basket, for heads are weighty. On the following day these heads of kinsmen and enemies alike would be handed to special women who would clean them and prepare the skulls.

But Jakara had seen all this before. When etiquette permitted, he impatiently moved away. He was now, since the affair of the telescope, in much less dread of C'Zarcke. He knew now that the priest valued him apart from his cunning in planning raids, and for as long as C'Zarcke wanted him he knew that he would carry his own head.

It was the Pretty Lamar who smilingly showed him where she was, but he eagerly pushed by the native girl without noticing the savagely pained look that she flashed after him.

As usual, Eyes of the Sea was getting all she could out of the moment. Perched on the shoulders of two brawny warriors, she delightedly kicked their chests as Jakara pushed towards her. "Oh, Jakara the Planner," she laughed, "two rogues hold me a prisoner; they fancy my head."

With a concerted movement they flung her into Jakara's arms. She gasped, and so did he, and he held her close for the sweetness of her body and the allure in her laughing eyes. The throng roared gleefully, and mischievous girls shrilled, "Jakara takes Eyes of the Sea." With flushed face the girl pushed from Jakara's arms and demanded her seat again. But the warriors turned their backs and emphatically declared that she had spurned them and flown of her own accord. Thereupon she turned and rated Jakara for her lost position, until he swung her upon his shoulder and turned towards the Zogo-house.

"There's your view, Blue Eyes, but give me just a smile."

Her eyes answered the meaning in his. His dreams might all come true, he thought swiftly, if he could only escape with this girl. The world was big, life was sweet, and fortune could change; God was good. Eyes of the Sea laughed to the sallies of friends, and chattered to hide the fact that she was furiously conscious of the man upon whose shoulder she sat. And when he whispered: "Blue Eyes, you are very pretty; some day I know I shall love you," she blushed and shyly touched his hair.

Jakara longed to take this girl away to the quietest beach he could find, somewhere in God's clean sun-light. He knew that opportunity would not occur later on, on account of the constant rehearsals for the grand dances, those outlets for the feverish enthusiasm in which the women could at last take active part. And Eyes of the Sea was noted as a dancer throughout all the islands!

Jakara turned abruptly, and the crowd made way with laughing sallies concerning the marriage day. The girl quickly saw that he was not moving to a more advantageous position.

"Where are you taking me, Jakara?" she wonderingly asked.

"To a place where you will look very pretty, within the shadow of the rocks," he said, and smiled up at her; "down by the crooning old sea."

"But I don't want the sea," she replied impatiently. "I shall see it again when we return to the village. Take me near the Mamooses, where Beizam stands. How proud he looks! He is smiling, too – I hate him! *You* ought to be there! Come back, Jakara! Look, C'Zarcke is about to anoint the Zogo-stone! We shall miss *everything!*"

But Jakara strode on. "I'll anoint you with kisses," he promised, "which will be better than anointing a lifeless Zogo-stone."

"I tell you I do not want to go. I will not go! Come back at once!" She savagely tugged his hair. Jakara was surprised. He gazed up with a frown.

It was the first time for years that he had been spoken to so. Among these people he was a man of authority. Hundreds even among the warriors bowed to him in passing. He walked quickly on, and Eyes of the Sea kicked until her feet were thumping hammer and tongs. When Jakara savagely stopped their thumping, she tugged his hair, to a murmur of delight from the people. Jakara strode straight for the Wongai-trees, madly savage when he glimpsed the mocking eyes of the Pretty Lamar. Through the Wongais he strode, and out into the soft light of a village path. The applause of the crowd grew fainter while Jakara strode on, cynically pleased that the girl had to let go of his hair quickly in order to protect herself from the prickly branches that met overhead. Presently she sobbed, and instantly his anger evaporated. He took her from his shoulder and kissed her. She liked it, and, closing her eyes, nestled close and sobbed again. Presently she sighed lingeringly and opened to the love-fevered Jakara entrancing eyes of blue. He kissed the eyes and the lips. Tenderly she touched his cheek: he kissed her hand. She whispered, "Please let me go, Jakara; I will be so very good." He set her down quite gently, kneeling to smooth away a vine which tangled her feet, and stared in amazement at the empty path! Eyes of the Sea had turned and vanished, leaving Jakara the most angry man in all Torres Strait.

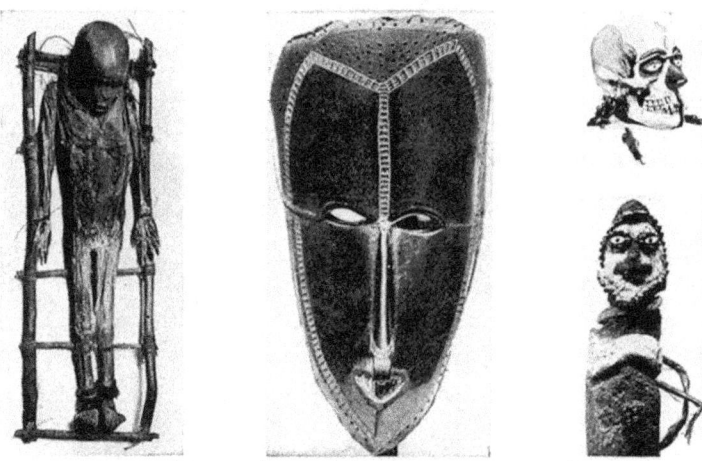

MUMMY OF A CHILD—FUNERAL MASK—DECORATED SKULL AS USED FOR DIVINATION—RAIN CHARM

CHAPTER IX

Jakara Makes Love

Jakara lazed upon his Lookout, dreamily absorbing the beauty of the day. His eyes roamed past the gorge of Werbadu-pat, till a movement at the small cape Tur-Pit caught his eye. It was a Maid-le and his satellites tending the shrine of the Wag-Zogo. Jakara grunted deprecatingly. Himself convinced of God, he came near to scorning these people for setting up stone images to intercede between them and what they believed to be benevolent spirits who brought the rains and the seasons and gave life and fatness to the crops and fishes and all things that are. He detested their reverent and frightened belief in the great Au-gud, even though he knew they realized that it was but a medium between them and the "Great Thing That Is." When they spoke – as they seldom did – of the Au-gud and the Zogo-le, it was but in whispers, and, as for Bomai and Malu, these were sacred words and only to be used as such.

Jakara grunted, and lifted lazy eyes towards the west, where swift clouds of Torres Strait pigeons were flying towards the Great South Land islands. With the seasons these pretty, plump birds migrate from New Guinea to nest on the northern Australian islands.

Then, near the snub nose of Gelam-Pit, but just above the big cliff, a moving figure caught his eye. No, two figures! Geedee of the mischievous eyes, and her eager shadow, Sasak! They vanished in the beckoning grass. "Geedee's Lookout" was facetiously named, but her angry parents had better "look out!" So far they did not dream that, though the girl went almost daily to her Lookout, it was not to sulk alone. Anyway, mused Jakara, why shouldn't she wed Sasak? He was a likeable lad, and worshipped her very feet. He had a decent garden too, and his father would ultimately leave him a share in the hereditary fish trap. Even though Sasak did not belong to the shark clan, he was as good a man as they! And though Geedee's people had sworn by Malu that the lad should never marry the girl, well, how could they stop it? Of course, they would probably arrow him afterwards for breaking a rigid tribal law. Jakara smiled sadly. Love really did seem complicated. He thought of poor broken-hearted Miriam, half wondering if the little girl and her lover were really happy in Boigu, Isle of the Blest. Geedee's Lookout, Geedee's Leap as it is now called, holds a grim reputation in native history. Many tragedies those black rocks below have witnessed.

Hazily to the south-west lay a sail, idly moving. A schooner, and its wings were black. But Jakara knew that immediately she changed to the starboard tack the cloud that shaded her from the sun would be outranged, and the sails would gleam white. He longed for his telescope to glimpse the white men aboard. They would particularly avoid Mer. The Eastern Group was dreaded by mariners; even the maritime sailing directions warned against it. Jakara wondered how this great pearling-rush must ultimately affect the Islands. This lonely Coral Sea, hitherto only sailed by pioneers and adventurers, was fast becoming dotted with schooners and brigantines, ketches, luggers, and cutters, all hungry for pearl-shell. There was a rush for fortune within the Coral Sea far more exciting, more thrilling, more dangerous than any gold-rush on land. And the adventurers, despite the warlike native, would persist in landing more and more frequently on the islands. Their bullets and steel must eventually defeat arrow and club. Jakara was thrilled. He knew nothing of the doings of the outside world, but he did realize that the distant black sail, cruising now in trepidation, was the writing upon the sea that spelt the beginning of the end of the Dance of Death. Jakara must ultimately be rescued. Other Lamars had been rescued; from this very island, too.

But Eyes of the Sea! Oh, dash it all, a savage in a white skin. Yet he must tread warily, and not be so critical. She had lived on Mer some months now, and had responded more to his love-making than to his attempts to educate her. She was a baby as regards knowledge of white people, and the more she learned of them the less she liked them. But he was learning patience, taking a delight in this moulding of a soul, confident that finally he would win. He must gradually turn her into a white girl. Sometimes he felt tempted to take her by Island right, but if he simply took her, she would never rise above the outlook of an Island girl.

Jakara grunted, and rose on his elbow. Yes, she was worth the trouble. What was life worth living for, anyway, if it was not for the love of a woman whom a man could respect? God knows, he might have to live out his life on this island. If so, then with a white woman for wife he could at least live to the white standard and not sink his birthright into savagery.

He stood up eagerly, for away down on a shingly beach she had just stepped from a jungle path. He gazed awhile, admiring her confident walk, smiling at the grass skirt, which he knew was cut and draped with such careful regard to her figure; he mused a while as to this little white savage who could look after herself so well in a world of savagery. She seemed to be to the manner born. Leisurely he walked down the slope. His Lookout commanded a view of numbers of village paths where they emerged into the open from jungle or forest or gardens. He did not hurry.

Why should he? He knew that she would wait. Besides, he was a Chief of Mer, and she was merely a Lamar. He even dawdled a while when passing through the great garden of Maiad, chatting to the guards lounging under shady trees, and flinging a word in answer to the women's sallies as they toiled among the rows of vegetables and fruit and tobacco. Squads of fighting-men were daily detailed to escort the women to and from the gardens, for life on all the Islands alike was often startled by enemy attacks, and, quite apart from the danger of more formidable raids, a toiling woman was liable any day to lose her head to the bravado crew of a single, swift canoe.

Presently, from the bushes, he surprised the frowning little face.

"Blue Eyes looks pleasant to-day," he said, with a smile, "and she has picked the prettiest of crotons to twine in her hair. I was so afraid of disappointment that I dared not hurry to the meeting-place."

"You will be disappointed," she answered, smiling, "I am on my way to Ulag."

"Never mind Ulag," said Jakara, as he invitingly held aside the bushes; "come along to the Glen of Dreams."

"You *are* a dreamer, Jakara," she said, as they walked along a grass-lined gully. "Do not wake some day and find that you have lost your head!"

"I lost that when first I saw you," he laughed, "and my heart, too."

"Jakara makes love again in the words of the Lamars. Jakara looks very pleasant when he plays at love. And he smiles pleasantly, too. But I remember times when his mouth looks like a shark's."

Jakara's eyes widened: "Go easy, Blue Eyes! Say things that are as nice as you look. Where did you get the pretty tortoise-shell comb?"

"Beizam gave it to me."

"Oh, did he!"

She smiled mischievously: "Maros said it suited my hair."

"Have nothing whatever to do with that big dugong!" said Jakara grimly. "And the less you have to say to the Shark, the better."

"But why?" she asked innocently.

"You know very well," answered Jakara. "But let us sit down here. Why, Eyes of the Sea, you have grown a freckle on your nose!"

"That is to match the tortoise-shell," she replied demurely.

He kissed her, and laughed as she laughed. "I believe you flirt as much as the sunbird," he grumbled. Idly she pulled at the grasses. "Anyway, the Pretty Lamar wove you an armlet w hen you sailed to the big raid!"

Coaxingly he drew her head to his shoulder. "You are a dear little girl," he said softly, "and you do not dream how wonderful you could really be. It is a shame that you do not understand all about the big white world where you and I belong."

Earnestly he yet again tried to explain about the white life from which fate had debarred her. He tried to express the ideals of the white race, of their ever struggling to perfect those ideals, of their disgust at any lowering of the standard. With sympathy and tender understanding, he tried to impress upon her mind that she was a daughter of the great white civilization, and that she was heir to the ideals which had been left by the Christ.

From time to time Eyes of the Sea changed her position so that she could see his face, and her expression grew often puzzled, sometimes indignant and petulant. Once a look of tenderness touched her eyes and mouth. He took her small face between his hands, but the expression had passed, and the eyes were clear and laughing.

He was puzzled, and a little hurt, but had sense enough to understand that to break through this girl's lifetime of savage environment and awaken to understanding the white life deep within, could only be accomplished by time, deep sympathy, and unswerving patience. He wondered if he could ever accomplish such a task, but the touch of her hair against his cheek, the thoughtful look in her eyes as she tried hard to grasp the meaning of what he said, made his heart beat more quickly in a fierce determination to succeed.

But when, in answer to a question, he described the white girls' clothes, Eyes of the Sea sat up indignantly. "I will *never* be like the Lamar women. I will *never* wear such skirts! White people cannot be pretty, or they would never cover themselves up so. Why are they ashamed!"

Jakara laughed. He gave the subject up for the time being, and spoke more in the way that she could understand.

"You are prettier than the sunbird, Blue Eyes," he whispered, "and just as saucy. No Lamar in all the world is as nice a girl as you. Oh, dash it all, sweetheart, that's the *boo* shell of the Maid-le calling for me. C'Zarcke is anxious that every day I should teach him a little more about the world of the Lamars. He is a much more patient pupil than you. Meet me to-night under the palms of I'Laid, and we will continue the lesson; and I have something to tell you. But before I go, Eye of the Sea, I want a promise."

She lifted a flushed face from which smiled pleased but suddenly wary eyes.

"We have spoken of it before. I want your promise that you will not walk so often and so early to Ulag village to see Geedee. Now listen, dear," he continued earnestly, "you know that only a week ago some Naghir raiders collected three heads from Masig Island just after sunrise. You know that lurking warriors often make a private raid on any island. Eyes of the Sea, your head to me is far more valuable than it would be to the greediest raider, and all because I love just you. Promise that in this you will do as I say."

Jakara was very earnest and handsome, too. She nodded, and whispered, "I promise."

But that night Eyes of the Sea lay coiled upon her sleeping-mat in deep thought. She loved this Lamar, she felt happy when thinking of him, and her half-formed dreams of the future were sweet. But over that future there hung a dread – the dread of the Lamars! He had not forgotten his strange land – he loved it as much as he loved her, it seemed. He wished to take her to it, and this, to Eyes of the Sea, meant terror indeed. He could take her, too, if C'Zarcke remained his friend. The girl shivered, remembering the stories told, from her childhood up, of that infernal, spirit-harassed world of the Lamars.

Whence did they really come, these pale-faced spirit-people? From the stars? From the sky? The girl's tribal beliefs had it that those Lamars who were found on land came from the bottom of the earth, those found on the sea came from the bottom of the sea. What strange rites, then, must be carried on down there! Jakara had assured her that the Lamars really lived on a beautiful land, much like Mer, but far larger. But –

And how did they treat their women? Did they really have children? They surely could not – they were spirit people! And yet Jakara seemed very human, and kinder than any man she had met before.

These and many other questions troubled the girl as she fought against the savage environment, the heritage of centuries of superstition which was all that she had known since babyhood. She cried softly, in her unsolvable perplexity, to think her love, her dream of all to be, should have come in the form of a dreaded Lamar!

It was dark in the densely-thatched house. She heard the breathing of her sleeping companions though she could not see them. She could see, however, the iridescent gleam in the pearl-shell eyes of the one-time master of the house standing mummified in the centre of the floor, guarding the living from evil spirits through the dead hours of every night. She was quite used to such as he, but not to the unknown terrors of Jakara's world.

Presently she lay very still, trembling apprehensively for dimly from the thickets outside the village hummed the sinister whirl of the *lo-lo*. She knew it was the voice of a "Something," a something to frighten women.

She guessed that the men understood all about it, but they would never tell, and no woman who found out had ever told, for she died quickly.

Plaintively the *lo-lo* sighed away. The girl breathed with relief, and began thinking all over again of Jakara's world. She knew the fears of her own world, but she looked forward with abject terror to journeying into the unknown Lamar world, even with Jakara.

TORRES STRAIT ISLANDER

CHAPTER X

When The Blood Lust Calls

Eyes of the Sea stepped along, humming a native melody. All the world was happy. Birds twittered the fact, and the flowers nodded: the breeze whispered pleasant things about her small brown feet. The sun cast aside his fleecy blankets, and was love-making in the sky, beaming bright kisses on earth's shadowed ravines. Eyes of the Sea liked the sun. He played upon the flowers, the birds, and the bronze of her breasts, and was so burningly eager to light up all the dark places for her to see. Everything was so friendly: the trailing sweetheart vine that brushed her face with scented breath, the sheen of the hill-side grasses, the serenity of the coco-palms as she emerged from jungle and sea-girt track. Distantly she got a glimpse of the Tomog Zogo-grounds, and could not forbear a peep. There were long lines of great fusus, helmet, and clam-shells concentrically arranged, and queer-shaped heaps of volcanic rock. The little that Eyes of the Sea understood about the whole business was that she had no right to be spying. Also that each shell, each stone, each group, and the shape of all, had a definite symbolical meaning. In the centre was a stack of enormous clam-shells, glistening in the early dawn like snow-white petals of an enormous flower. Upon this shrine was a symbolic stone, and upon the stone the representative of the Tomog Zogo, a wise little man, quaintly carved.

Squatting solemnly round the stone were a few eager but serious men, while a Maid-le stood asking questions of Tomog. For here was the shrine of the Tomog oracle, to be consulted reverently only at break of day.

But Eyes of the Sea was a woman and must not pry into the learned affairs of men. Guiltily, and a little afraid, she passed on her way.

She climbed higher, quite noiseless upon the creeper-shaded path. Over hillocks and down valley glens and up slopes again, to skirt the big black cliffs by Gelam-Pit. It was the very morning after she had promised Jakara that she would not visit Ulag until all the villagers were astir, until the women were in the gardens and the men in the fishing-canoes out on the reef, or spearing the daily catch in the great *sai*.

But it was so silly, and, really, she had started out before she had remembered the promise, and to turn back would have been unlucky! Besides, though this impetuous Lamar was an interesting lover, she must not give in to him too easily. She almost stopped – wondering at that strange thought.

She wished something *would* happen. She felt a longing for excitement. She did not want too violent a thrill – she shuddered and involuntarily glanced back. But her head felt firmly set. With a soft laugh she walked on, her eyes bright as they peered down the ravines and towards the shadowed jungles and rock-hidden shores.

How angry Jakara would be! She smiled, with memory-filled eyes: she loved even the name. Nevertheless she was determined on having the pleasure of a little naughtiness; she felt deliciously triumphant too, now that she understood that she was the only girl Lamar: she was realizing that, with his determined, unusual ideas, he could love no native girl while she was there. She did not quite understand why he did not take her, as by tribal law was his chieftain's right at any moment, but until he made up his mind she decided to mould him to her desires. This nameless castaway was burningly ambitious, unaware that it was the urge of the white blood that made her so. She had determined not to leave the Islands for that unknown ghostly world of the Lamars. Her quickening dreams were to reconcile Jakara, to see him chief Mamoose of all the Island nations, to force every group under one leadership. If only something would happen to C'Zarcke! She switched off thoughts of C'Zarcke very quickly. He would be managed later perhaps, for Jakara was brave, a leader of men with the shrewd brain of the Lamars. That was what she counted on, that unknown quantity, the brain of the Lamars! Perhaps distant Kebisu too could be coerced. If not – well, his geographical position would keep him well away on his own tiny island. His terrible warriors were far fewer in number than those of Mer. But – Kebisu commanded the sea. He could block all trade coming to and going from Mer. The girl frowned, then sighed deeply. Surely Jakara's cunning could weld all the fighting tribes under one great figurehead, himself! Perhaps it could all be done without risky fighting, by cunning, a cunning working unseen into the minds of men until every Mamoose naturally recognized Jakara as the Chief Mamoose, Jakara the Wonderful. With flashing eyes the girl made up her mind that she would be the unrealized factor that would make of Jakara a king. Jakara desired her above all else in the world. Well, he would have to sacrifice before he could receive. He could have her in any way he wished, but in return he must make her the leading woman of the Strait!

She knew that the hardest obstacle to overcome was the one thing imperatively necessary to success. Jakara must be made to overcome his aversion to making some slain foe dance the Dance of Death! Otherwise the Islanders, no matter how much they respected him, would never acknowledge him even as a minor Mamoose. As a chief, yes – in recognition of the cunning of his brains and his terrible fighting reputation, but never as a Mamoose. Somehow she must persuade him- very cleverly and quietly sow little insinuations that would bear fruit in his mind days after; perhaps she could begin during the times when he was making such delightfully queer Lamar love.

She smiled wistfully. Jakara was wonderful, she knew; she loved him when he smiled, and yet even for her he would not do the one little thing which would confirm him a warrior in the eyes of every Islander. Thinking deeply, her eyes to the path, quite unmindful of her surroundings, she stood shocked as a scream rang up from down the hill- side.

She peered down upon the feathery tops nodding over grass-roofed houses. Along the beach there halted abruptly some early Ulag men *en route* to the fishing-traps. She heard the crash of blows, saw seven painted men burst from a house and two race in screaming triumph for the beach, each waving a dripping head. The remaining five, berserk at being baulked, rushed another house. Too late! They were met by shark-tooth sword and club: every house poured forth warriors raging with hate. The raiders, their chance of success having depended on a quick surprise and escape, had, unluckily for them, picked a large house sheltering only two heads. The five men in shrieking execration rushed to rejoin their friends who were dancing by the launched canoe. Too late again, for with exultation Eyes of the Sea saw the fishermen racing back along the beach, heard the warning shouts of the canoe men, and saw their comrades redouble their efforts as the men of Ulag strained every sinew to intercept. The canoe men waited until the last moment, and then pushed off and trained their sail to the wind. The canoe was a fast raider, and it foamed out into the bay, its occupants jeeringly waving the heads towards the fishermen now tumbling into their own canoes. The stranded raiders turned and, racing round the village, plunged straight up into the bush. They would travel for their lives straight across the island and make a dash for any handy village canoe. Just a fighting chance, with the hornets' nest now aroused, for the signal *boo* of Ulag was braying in loud jerky blasts, and there throbbed the raid drums! Every valley, village, and headland fairly hummed to the warning note.

The girl crouched. The instinct of a wild thing told her that to move was to be seen. She was not afraid, only excitedly scared. Big-eyed, she peeped for a sight of the warriors chasing the hunted men. She knew that now from every village encircling the island were pouring men who would run out until flank after flank joined each village quota and formed an avenging crescent closing in on Ulag. The raid drums would throb orders of movement and the *boo* of Ulag would call to them instructions where to concentrate. Suddenly Eyes of the Sea shrieked and fled. Behind her sounded a curdling howl of abandoned, exultant triumph. In one glimpse she noted that the raider swung the *gaba-gaba* and not the little stone throwing-club. But she screamed again as another head-dress burst from the bushes ahead and ivory teeth were bared in triumph. With quivering nerves and body racing to save her head, she leapt aside through the vines, and kept shrieking in crescendo to guide the Ulag warriors in the chase. She jumped high among the bushes, saw a grassy knoll, and ran straight towards it, for then she would be in sight of all, and the villagers would hurry towards her while she sped towards them. The hunter behind her exulted; for how this girl's keyed-up nerves would move when he clicked her head for the Dance of Death!

She burst out on to the open grass, and screamed for joy when she saw ahead of her yet another raider hotly pursued by three warriors. He glanced behind, and his eyes gleamed white. She sped behind them, praying that his end would be swift, for well she knew that the Ulag men would not turn aside to save a mere girl while the head of a man was already within reach. In whining eagerness they swung their *gaba-gabas*, but the hunted thing leered back, just clear of the stunning stroke. His face spelled doom when a fourth Ulag warrior came running with his right palm lovingly clasping the dreaded throwing-club. The hunted one strained towards the shelter of a jungle, but the warrior's club-arm swung back with such a lithe movement as the missile hummed through the air. It struck like a hammer on wood. Paralysed from the hips down, the man fell clutching the grass, with three warriors upon him. Even then with leering face he troubled them as much as he could, vexatiously jerking his temples as the wolves above him savaged each other for his head. They stunned him hastily, and, as the girl screamed past, the head crunched off, and the fleetest snatched it to his mouth and ran, the others chasing him. She circled towards them, and saw that their work was well done, for the corpse moved convulsively in the grass. The girl moaned in imagining her own body dancing in a manner so ludicrously ugly. Dodging, she saw the hair upon her pursuer's chest, and glimpsed the dog-tooth necklet of the second man behind. She sobbed and raced straight back for the sea and the villages by the sea! Pain stabbed her heart, and she gasped for breath and speed, speed, speed! She heard the animal panting behind as she burst clear of the shrubbery and raced out on to a headland. Then she realized that she was too closely pursued to turn: cliffs fell away on either side, both raiders panted behind. She could only race along the headland with Geedee's Lookout at the end of it, and she could not stop – she must race straight on and over—

She screamed in frantic despair when, far out over Geedee's Lookout, she saw the blue of the sea. Then feathered heads of Mer's warriors bobbed up over the headland sides, and the raiders, howling in recognition of the trap, put forth the very last of their strength to secure the fruition of the chase before their own day was done.

The girl saw the green shimmer of the corals far below, she heard the hiss of an indrawn breath, and instantly ducked her head. The *gaba-gaba* missed. She caught one gleam of Lightning, and howls of triumph mingled with the buzzing in her ears as Jakara tripped her, and was himself hurled to the cliff-edge, with two bloodshot eyes laughing into his while claws gripped his throat and rapier hilt.

Jakara fought with his face contorted at the thought that this thing had sought to take the life of his love. The raider gloried in a fight to the death in physical ecstasy with the desire to take another with him. He wrestled with a frenzied strength that meant a fight of moments only. Jakara sensed the cliff awaiting him, and so jerked his shoulder under the other's jaw and strained forward with all his strength of mind and body, striving just to hold his adversary until those moments of maniacal strength were spent, while over the man's greasy shoulder he saw the second raider clubbed and writhing across the body of Eyes of the Sea. The villagers wrestled over his head, and the corpse staggered up drunkenly. Warriors came rushing along the headland howling in feverish excitement, their heaving breaths audible to Jakara while he fought and they watched the fight. He could expect no help: the result was a foregone conclusion to them. If he had been hurled over the cliff, they would simply have gaped, not believing their eyes. He heaved to break his man's ribs – and felt that his own back was cracking. The legs twisted round his own were tearing their very toe-nails in the strain to push him over. He swerved suddenly and hurled his arms straight out. The raider flew over the cliff, and his scream was echoed by the warriors as they scrambled down – the head was dead, but the skull was of value and belonged to the first comer.

Mad with excitement, and yet trembling with a cold anger, Jakara glared down upon Eyes of the Sea. She was exhausted and piteously frightened. Jakara forgot his anger. He knelt down, and, lifting her tenderly, kissed her trembling lips.

PORTIONS OF THE KWOD
The training ground for youths.

CHAPTER XI

Velvet Claws

Jakara loafed at his house door, though the morning invited him to walk. He was a chief, and, as such, was entitled to idle during the times when his presence was not required in the Councils. His share of the produce of the island was daily brought to his door, so that he wanted for nothing. On this day he gazed towards Dauar islet, by Waiar, where lay the schooner *Woodlark*. Ominous vessel! Jakara wondered uneasily at the intentions of the fighting-crew aboard. Maliciously he loved that grim vessel;. through his telescope he had in time past seen every man aboard, white, brown, brindled, and black. On some nights he had lain awake expectantly, awaiting the startled blast of the *boo*, the shouts and screams, and the rolling echoes as the valleys thundered to the fire of the Lamars.

The *Woodlark* was ever hungry for women; she was a devil-ship for women. They were all that the crew ever came ashore for. In these raids either Islanders or men of the vessel's South Sea crew got killed, and that meant a few more head-hunters the less. Looking back over the years, and especially of late, since the *Woodlark* had come to be more troublesome to Mer, Jakara remembered again all the cunning of C'Zarcke – how, when at the occasional close approach of a Lamar ship Jakara had rushed outside, it was into the arms of guards. Once, long ago, he was confident that he was unobserved. He had made a dash for it, but an arrow through his buttocks had made him very sorry for weeks afterwards. On two occasions he had been called to the island centre for ceremonial duties, to find on return that a Lamar ship had actually anchored a while that day. He glumly recalled the heart-burnings of those times, and then remembered that he had thought hardly at all of rescue during these last few months. Eyes of the Sea, of course, and C'Zarcke's still unanswered questions!

He turned again to the schooner. He was amazed at the whole-hearted devilry of those men. Cruising over an uncharted sea with its thousand reefs, nosing among islands inhabited by thousands of war-loving men, they yet chose one of the grimmest strongholds of savagery as a rendezvous. What a sign of the times their presence was! The schooner was heavily manned, the crew were armed to the teeth, and thoroughly understood Island warfare. The crew was made up of a mixture of South Sea Islanders, Malays, Rotumah men, Eromangan savages, and coloured ruffians from the Solomons. They loved a fight, and were willing to indulge in one to a finish. Every man knew what his fate would be if he were taken alive. Liable as they were at any moment to be attacked by overwhelming numbers, it was their ceaseless guard and thunderous guns that had time and again saved the vessel. Recently they had actually raided a Mer village, several times Eroob, while on hilly Maubiag can be seen to-day a huge cave in whose black recesses the women hid whenever the sail of the *Woodlark* hove in sight.

But now Jakara wished the *Woodlark* would shun Mer; he hoped they had plenty of women. On Geedee's Lookout he saw the little figures of sentries gazing down towards the troublesome vessel.

Yawning lazily, he sauntered down the path towards Las, feeling in happy mood. He noticed in passing that the guards scattered among the shore gardens were trebled, and he smiled sympathetically at the glances of the women towards that grim vessel lying in company with those two islets of ill repute. As he passed among the houses, people greeted him jovially, and youngsters demanded a game. Jakara gossiped a while and passed on, to presently find himself on the path leading to the pretty village of Las. Las was a large village, the "modern" village of the island. Its houses were better made, with the sleeping-floors higher and more comfortable; its cooking-utensils and weapons were more finished and artistically shaped. The Las women wove the strongest and closest sails for the great war-canoes, they fashioned the neatest and best cooking-pots, while their prettily made, shaped, and dyed skirts were the envy, not only of all the other Mer village girls, but of the entire Eastern Group. Their wig-making was sheer art. For, strange though it may seem, these savages with their splendid hair were adepts in the making of wigs, and would sometimes shave the head just for the pleasure of wearing them. Moreover, wigs of various designs were used in a number of the ceremonial dances. It was also trained experts among the Las people who carved the turtle models for the great "Sacred" masks, and supplied the dyed tassels of reeds, shells, berries, and gorgeous puffs of feathers, and the intricate skirts of plumage, used in the Bomai-Malu dances which were looked upon with such reverence. Especially intelligent in all things were these people of Las.

Jakara generally avoided Las, for it was difficult to pass through. This morning he was mobbed in the village centre by a shrieking crowd. Little Mesi and plump Carra each grasped a leg and entwined their own round it: chubby hands clutched his belt, and others clung to his grass skirt. Nimbler children climbed his back. Jakara shook himself. They laughed gleefully at Lightning rattling in its scabbard. Quite resignedly, amid the laughter of the grown-up folk, Jakara dragged himself across the beach into the nearest *sai*. In the deep water of the monstrous fish-trap he held under as many of the children as he could, and then plunged, staying under water for a long time, only to come up for breath and then dive again. But the boys and girls could swim like fishes, and he therefore splashed laboriously across to the walled *sai* with laughing youngsters clinging to his body. At the *sai* end he dumped them on the beach, for this was the boundary of Las and it was forbidden that the play should be carried on into the next village, whose people were rather staid and austere; also they would never allow children to disturb the water of their own great *sai*.

Coming from a banana-patch, he met the Pretty Lamar, quite accidentally on his part. She smiled a quick welcome. "Jakara comes to visit the Pretty Lamar," she mocked.

"And Jakara is rewarded."

She laughed to the mischievous question. "How prospers the love-making, Jakara?"

"Promising, Pretty Lamar," he said. "According to village gossip, you also have promised."

"You are a fool, Jakara the Wise; whom have I promised?"

"Beizam," chided Jakara.

"Damn Beizam," she said emphatically. "You see, I have learnt the Lamar language, Jakara."

"Yes," he drawled reminiscently, "that's what Eyes of the Sea learned first, too."

"Two damns Eyes of the Sea! She has gone gossiping to Ulag, so there's little chance of her returning this way. It would be awful, Jakara, if the Lamar ship made another raid on Ulag and took Eyes of the Sea."

She watched Jakara's face to see the effect of her remark.

"Let me spread out a banana-leaf for you, Jakara. Mind! do not sit on that thorn-vine or your skin will be spoiled, and your temper, too."

Jakara sat down cautiously.

"All right, Pretty Lamar. Now talk to me, but mind the birds do not hear! Especially the sunbird!"

"The sunbird has told me wonderful things about Jakara," said the girl, her eyes very bright.

"Good little sunbird! That must have been the one that built inside my house and whistled of your beauty all day long."

"If Jakara's heart spoke with his tongue I would kiss his feet," said the girl softly.

"Your lips are meant for other lips, Pretty Lamar," said the man uneasily. "But do not be serious, the day is too beautiful."

"Then do not talk about the weather, Jakara! I see you so seldom, but the weather every day. For once let us talk about our own little world. What would happen if Eyes of the Sea were to see us now?"

"There'd be a hell of a row," answered Jakara decisively.

"What is 'hell,' Jakara?"

"It is where the bad people go when they die."

"What do they go there for?"

"Oh, to frizzle."

"What is 'frizzle,' Jakara?"

"Oh, to burn."

"Then why do they go?"

"Good heavens! I don't know!"

"Are you going there, Jakara?"

"Heavens! I hope not."

"What is 'heavens,' Jakara?"

"Heavens? Oh, heavens is – is – it's away up beyond the stars."

"How do you get there, Jakara?"

"Fly."

"How?"

"Lord bless my soul, Pretty Lamar, ask me something easy."

"You would not grant it!"

"Yes, I would, instantly."

"Then marry me, and we will be wonderfully happy, and when we die we will go to Boigu, Isle of the Blest – together! It will be much better than hell, Jakara."

She leaned towards him, her every word a caress, her lips trembling, her big eyes misty.

Jakara stared, while joy fled.

"Jakara," she whispered entreatingly, "I would do *anything* for you; far more than Eyes of the Sea could even dream of! You are the only man in the world to me. I cry at night when I think of you! If you go to hell, I will go to hell; if to heaven, my spirit will follow you through the stars! Take me, Jakara; it is for only a few short years! I will make them beautiful years for you. You will bless the mother that gave me birth. Afterwards – we must go together where all the Island peoples go, to Boigu, Isle of the Blest; and we will be happy there for ever and ever."

Jakara pressed the hand that trembled on his shoulder. "Pretty Lamar," he whispered, "some day I will surely return to the land of the Lamars."

"Take me with you! I am not frightened. Keep me near you, and I will go anywhere, anywhere—"

"I wish you were Eyes of the Sea and she you," said the man almost savagely. "Why weren't you white!"

"Why, Jakara, I am far whiter than you!"

"Yes, by some freak of nature. With a gown on, you would look like a lady of Spain. But, Pretty Lamar, our children would not be white!"

"Why, not? If you want them white, then our love would make them so."

"I am afraid it would take something a bit stronger than that," said Jakara, smiling sadly.

"I do not understand," answered the girl wonderingly. "Why, we are the two whitest people in all Mer."

"Oh, Pretty Lamar, I cannot explain, but your children, certainly some of them, would revert to a darker colour even than your father."

"But, Jakara—" the girl drew him close to her and whispered: "Is that all you fear? How funny you are, man of my heart! What matters the colour of the children! You would find me so wonderful you would not even think of the children!"

It was at this moment that Eyes of the Sea rustled a banana-leaf. Jakara stared stupidly; the Pretty Lamar, her arms tightening around him, in proud defiance.

Eyes of the Sea, drawn to the very tallest of her little height, looked down upon them with the silent dignity of an outraged queen.

Jakara jumped up, but Eyes of the Sea treated him to such a blaze of blue eyes, such a scornful tilt of the nose, that he stood abashed. She strode down the path in a speaking silence, accentuated by the "frou-frou" of her short grass skirt. Jakara could not help smiling as he watched her go.

"The fat is in the fire," he remarked, "I shall go 'frizzling to hell' now, for certain."

"She did look 'hell,'" sighed the Pretty Lamar. "I wish she would go there."

"You are picking up our language fast," Jakara laughed, "But Eyes of the Sea has proved that she is jealous."

THE ARCHER

CHAPTER XII

The Menace of Lamars

Bustling activity livened all the islands – outfitting of canoes, twisting of fibre ropes, plaiting of mat sails, filling of long bamboos with water, tightening of outrigger platforms, strengthening of every vessel against the tempers of an uncertain sea. For the south-east season was nearly over, and soon would howl the wild north-west. Just before it broke, the Islanders would sail on their great trading cruise, commencing from the north-east of the South Land and proceeding far up the New Guinea coast.

So all was preparation. Every day canoes sailed in from outlying islands, bringing their quota of trade to help swell the bulk of the great fleet. Soon now would arrive the flotilla from Spirit (Forbes) Island, away down the coast of the Great South Land, and their canoes would be loaded with rich things bartered from the savages-ochres and colouring paints made from roots and flowers and minerals; cassowary skins, animal, lizard, and snake pelts, bundled feathers of brilliant birds, hardwood for spears and arrows, resins and gums and beeswax, kaolin, and many other things.

The Komet-le of Mer were especially busy, for among the Eastern Group it was this clan that were the experts at trade and barter.

Now a section was fitting out under Bogo, to sail for the produce of the Central Group, a hundred miles westward. This Group traded among their own larger group, and, like the people of Spirit Island, they traded particularly with the South Land savages. To the Islanders, the Australian aboriginal was a "savage." The Central Group sought his skull, but with the northern tribes of Cape York Peninsula, and down the western coast of the Gulf country, far distant from the Spirit Islanders, they had long since opened up trading relations, for the great mainland possessed treasures which the Islands could not grow or produce, and materials which were especially valuable to distant Doudai (New Guinea).

So the aboriginal coastal tribes throughout the year bartered and collected from the inland tribes large quantities of goods for the seasonal Island trade. In this fashion, for centuries, articles from the very centre of Australia have found their way inland into gloomy New Guinea. Across the vast Australian continent there may be traced spider-web tracks which are the primitive trade-routes of stone-age man.

Jakara was to sail with Bogo's section. C'Zarcke had explained that, because of the fast-growing number of Lamars sailing the seas; the Murralug people were actually afraid to risk themselves and their canoes in bringing their accumulated trade to Mer. C'Zarcke spoke savagely: "And, Jakara, the Lamars, your countrymen, are working to strangle our national life. They have established a settlement which they call Somerset, close by the northern point of the Great South Land. They drill warriors in a Lamar Kwod, and have actually," C'Zarcke's eyes blazed, "trained savages in the use of the thunder-weapons to use against us! Their big ships call there often. Some are fighting-ships whose thunder-weapons hurl destruction. The settlement has almost paralysed our trade with the savages. Several tribes friendly to us they have annihilated, and disorganized the others so much that trade does not flow evenly up the land and across to Murralug (Prince of Wales Island, Central Group). Their chief especially harasses the Murralug peoples. I wish I could get my hands on the throat of that Lamar chief, just for one minute!"

Jakara endeavoured to hide his exultation as he took his leave of the furious C'Zarcke. Never before had the Zogo spoken to him like this. And how utterly he had failed to realize the fast-closing hand of his countrymen over these islands. Little wonder! Everything of that nature was kept from him. And he could not see for himself. The stream of *bêche-de-mer* and pearling-vessels came up the east Australian coast to Cape York, and then spread out fishing, mainly among the Central Group and down towards the great Warrior Reefs towards Tutu. Since the settlement at Somerset, numbers of them were beginning to concentrate on Island bases supplied by fast schooners, with the ultimate object of dispensing with the long and risky southern voyage to Sydney and Melbourne at the close of the season. Cape York Peninsula was over a hundred miles distant from Mer which only glimpsed the sails of the most venturesome boats cruising far east of the then known pearling-beds. And Somerset! Jakara light-heartedly pranced in the jungle path. A settlement! A white man's settlement with soldiers! Heavens! A civilization! The end of the Dance of Death! The end of the Island nations! Prosperity and progress and the white man, and freedom for himself! And white people again!

Jakara turned and raced along the upward track leading to his Lookout. He longed to gaze on one of those dear sails that meant so much, with the hundred others in the invisible distance. He wanted to cry to the cold black stones that his years of fear were ended.

C'Zarcke had not told Jakara that it was expedient just then to get him out of the way, since a massed meeting of the Zogo-le and the chief lodges of the Bomai-Malu were to discuss at Mer a means of striking a decisive blow at this menace of the Lamars. For some time two big schooners, the *Melanie* and the *Bluebell,* had been cruising in Eroob waters, and C'Zarcke's chiefs were desirous of attacking them. Strangely, however, the flotilla had not started when these two distant vessels unexpectedly spread their wings and sailed away.

With smiling face Jakara reported to Bogo. And Eyes of the Sea! How propitiously events were shaping! This little cruise would just fit in by giving her time to get over her pique. Jakara believed that absence sweetens the heart. Among the throng, when sailing day dawned, he tested her feelings by asking for a kiss, and gazed in mock alarm at her icy disdain. He waved farewell from the canoe, leaving the girl in annoyed surprise.

The deep blue waters of Albany Pass, which could look like a mile-wide street of turquoise, were now a maelstrom under the lash of the terrific tide. Long and hillocky and brown-cliffed, with dainty white beaches, was Albany Island. Across, on the opposite side of the Pass, was the mainland, with Somerset, capped in beauty upon the baby cliffs, the coast-line hemming in the Pass with frowning little headlands all dense green with scrub. But Somerset, famed right away to England as the new and most northern settlement, an embryo Singapore, stood out plain from the tangled wild. A sign of the times, almost a threat, Australian civilization stretching out its farthest tentacle in conquest of savage lands!

On the flat summit overlooking the Pass stood Somerset House, with the tall flagpole in front of it flaunting the Union Jack for all to see. Historical Somerset House, the house of noted men in a noted age. And romantic has been its hospitality; its cedar walls have echoed to the clash of swords while a French count vindicated his honour in a duel. Noted explorers, prospectors, men-o'-warsmen, soldiers, naturalists, missionaries, have slept beneath that roof. D'Albertis in feverish enthusiasm planned his desperate voyages there. Chalmers rested there from his great labours; even there he discussed his problematical fate which, alas, was realized later in the cooking-ovens of New Guinea. Others also have walked its broad verandas, though tasting less of its hospitality – Nikolas the Greek, man of twenty lives; Captain Strang, whose guns, even in port, were crammed with chain-shot. Many others, all of note in their own way, have called there when the Strait was growing her eye-teeth, splendid men, good men, medium men, bad men, very bad men, and men as bad as men can be; and arrogant but troubled native chiefs have been housed there, to feast out of the hand and sense the hidden bridle.

Guns frowned from the steps of Somerset House, and guns frowned away down below on the beach close by the friendly trees whose branches have shaded more than one writhing wretch flogged on the triangle. By itself apart was the business-like barracks of the marines, aloof from the native police barracks. Houses were dotted here and there among the red ironstone rocks. Among the trees, where the scrub had been felled, were bare brown ribbons, which were the "streets" laid out for the new settlement. For this was going to be a second· Singapore, and its allotments had been gambled for in Brisbane, Sydney, Melbourne, and London.

In the miniature bay below the House few craft were at anchor. A lugger or two and a native dugout, that was all. For the men of the Gudang tribe were encouraged around the settlement; they were a splendid buffer against the fierce Yardigans of the interior and the warlike Koregas of the Strait.

Unluckily H.M.S. *Blanche* had just sailed away, for a shipwrecked crew had floated in, and the man-o'-war had sped on succour bent. No vessel going to the Chinas was anchored in the Pass. It was deserted. But in that wild tangle of scrubs and green hills and whirling water the human activity of the tiny settlement appeared very great indeed. On the parade square smartly uniformed native troopers were drilling under the supervision of their white officers.

Jardine, autocrat and Government Resident, by virtue of Authority from the Queensland Government and Great Britain, walked the big veranda, telescope under his arm.

His stern eyes were clouded with thought, for he was worrying as to the probable replies to his last long overdue batch of mail from the Colonial Secretary. In this isolated post a man was exceptionally lucky if he received letters every four months. Jardine desperately wanted a favourable answer to his requisition for more horses for the troopers, a new issue of rifles, pistols, and a much more liberal supply of ammunition for the defence of the settlement. And he urgently wanted a more efficient police cutter and reinforcements for the water police, also more equipment, clothing, plant-seed, and food-supplies. And those scurvy rough diamonds among the marines had been playing up again, procuring coconut-rum from somewhere, heaven knew where! He would flog the hide off the swine who was supplying them, if he could only catch him!

On top of all his mainland worries, there was constant trouble throughout the islands of the Strait, fightings and threats of fightings among the whites, the blacks, and the browns. The pearl-shell rush was spreading so alarmingly with vessels from the big southern cities that a definite outbreak was to be expected at any moment. Earnestly Jardine hoped that his plea to the distant authorities for a warship to be permanently stationed in Cape York waters would be speedily granted. He would then have a great check upon not only the mainland natives but also every fighting-island in the Strait, and, joy of joys, over those damned blackbirding buccaneers among the whites!

Grim and ruthless though he was, in his great isolation and responsibility Jardine was the right pioneer in the right place. He searched Albany Island opposite, spying as to whether the graves of Wall and Niblett of the ill-fated Kennedy expedition were still left intact by the natives. Then he swept his glass over the only patch of open sea that was visible, away over the lower hills in a south-easterly direction. Beside the cliffs below raced Albany Pass, hemmed in by the big island and, on the settlement side, by foliage-smothered hills. And there, just rounding a rocky point, raced the government cutter *Lizzie Jardine*.

Jardine gazed down upon her, for the bellying sails, the alert manner in which she was handled, the men gazing up from her decks, all told that she brought news of serious import. She tacked into the bay, and, .as her sails came tumbling down, the anchor rattled overboard before her head was brought up to the wind. As the boom thumped the deck, the dinghy was slung overside and raced for the shore. Jardine waited while the captain quickly climbed the zigzag path up the cliff-like hill to the house.

From the veranda steps the captain saluted, then ran up and reported:

"Sir, while returning from Booby Island, where we were ordered to place in the cave the government stores for the relief of shipwrecked crews, we passed Prince of Wales Island. By Friday Island we spied a schooner, the *Sperweer*, Captain Gascoigne, with wife and boy of fourteen years, and crew seventeen strong, looted by the Murralug people and the Koregas. Blood is plentiful on the decks, and in the captain's cabin. He had evidently been speared through the skylight. We found no living soul on board. Under a bunk was the chopped-off arm of a man."

Several minutes later Somerset echoed to the bugles' alarm. Instantly the settlement was seething: marines buckled on their equipment as they ran to form up statuesquely on the parade square, and the black police troopers, eyes bulging to the echoing alarm, formed up fronting the marines, their claw-like fingers gripping their Sniders. The regular men, and the flotsam and jetsam of the settlement, stared, startled, towards the barrack square, or rushed into houses for arms, convinced that the long-expected massed attack by the native tribes had come at last.

To sharp commands and rhythm of arms, a file of marines, followed by native police, were winding down the zigzag track. An odd *bêche-de-*

mer man, a pearler or two, hurriedly joined them on the beach. Dinghies raced back and forth to the *Lizzie Jardine*. Her sails flew up, the anchor-chain rattled in, she glided and then raced towards the setting sun.

It was dawn when Jardine cautiously landed on a beach of Murralug. A dinghy lay there, and in it a coil of new rope and a log-book with blood-stained pages. Jardine looked around and found the clean-picked bones of several men, a barbed arrow-head still embedded in a thigh – and the pelvis-bone of a child. He looked in the log-book and saw that the captain's wife had been aboard. Where was she now? Jardine gazed towards the sand-sprinkled bone of the child, and needed no other answer.

There was nothing that could be done – as yet. For his tiny force to venture into the fastnesses of this, the largest island in Torres Strait, was madness. Always thickly populated, Jardine knew that it now swarmed with savages from the surrounding islands, hot with their successful blood-lust. The experience of an old campaigner warned him that they were even now eagerly waiting for him to venture into the hills.

The small force withdrew, and the sails of the *Lizzie Jardine* appeared despondent as she slowly headed back for Somerset. Nothing could be done – as yet.

Next day every available craft hurried from Somerset – the *Lizzie Jardine* towards Eroob, where cruised somewhere the schooners *Bluebell* and *Melanie* with their fighting South Sea crews, the other vessels to comb the seas for vessels seeking *bêche-de-mer* or pearl, or for any vessels manned by good men or bad. Particularly were vessels wanted manned by South Sea men, for their delight was in a fight with the Torres Islanders.

Almost alone, Jardine paced the veranda of Somerset House. With head bowed, he was determining that for all time the Murralug group of Islanders must be taught that the white man had come to stay. These people, not content with massacring shipwrecked crews and the crews of any vessel they could catch napping, had even sent their envoys with challenges to the Lamar settlement at Somerset. Moreover, this was not the first white woman who had fallen into their merciless hands, and the fast-developing industry, resulting from the exploitation of the *bêche-de-mer* and shell-beds of the Strait, could no longer be permitted to be dominated by terror of these groups of Island savages.

CHAPTER XIII

The Leaden Fist Of The Lamars

The Mer flotilla made all haste, helped by a stiff breeze. Depression sailed with them. Jakara had never before felt aware of such a collective reign of the "dumps." He was delighted because of this "shadow of the Lamars." These people were afraid of they knew not what; they tasted the fear that civilization would know if a race of Martians were to threaten our life. "The beginning of the end!" laughed Jakara to the wind. Up rolled heavy green waves upon which the canoes rose and fell like flying gulls. They passed islands of friendly and unfriendly people, islands varied in shape and size from gleaming sandbanks to the rugged range of Moa, islands well-wooded, others bare and waterless, islands of coral, islands thrust up by volcanic action, and islands of solid mother earth. They passed Massig, lying in savage beauty then as it does to-day, with its mile-wide collar of foam as the wind thundered a swirling tide across the reef – just a long strip of silver sand rising barely five feet above sea-level. Weeping casuarinas cling to its crooning shores; down its centre sway the tops of coco-palms, and below them rest the brown houses. Jakara wondered at the vitality and the cunning necessary for those islet people to cling to life, for in the event of a raid there were absolutely no hiding-places and no means of escape: a man could run across the island in a few minutes. If it were not for their coral ramparts, the waves would long since have ravaged these jewels of the sea. The inhabitants insured themselves against human foes by making trade treaties with their larger neighbours and supplying a quota of men for Island war. Thus they bought protection from the grim peaks looming upon the horizon.

They anchored at Coconut Island, for here Bogo had conciliatory business. Coconut Island is a tiny replica of Massig, but with only one village. Trooping down to the beach came men, women, and children, glad indeed that their welcome was to a friend.

Up sail next morning to a boisterous breeze, with tall Mount Adolphus away to the south-west and behind it the hazy outline of Cape York Peninsula, a dread land of mystery to the Islanders now, for from somewhere far within it were coming the Lamars. Ahead, faintly seen, lay the massed islands of the Central Group, not richly fertile, very green of grass and trees after the wet seasons, but during the dry months much resembling the harsh conditions of the Great South Land.

Bogo steered to take his canoes between Thursday and Hammond islands, where King had sailed. The narrow waterway in between was deep-blue under the shade from the rugged little hills, all scrub-covered, of Hammond Island, and the open forest hills of Thursday Island. Jakara never dreamt that he was gazing at an island of which the fiery Chester was soon to take possession, thus starting the building of what soon would be a busy Australian town.

Then they saw the shores of Friday Island, where lay tragedy – the ribs of a vessel burned to the water's edge. All saw those blackened spars, all asked the silent question. The islands seemed deserted, and instinctively all eyes turned towards Murralug. A black pall had enveloped its gloomy hills with the setting of the sun.

Bogo laboured under a state of indecision. The cruise had started pessimistically, and the telepathic sense of the native mind warned the leader of a disastrous voyage.

Jakara would have been madly excited, and Bogo would have started straight back, if they had known that the Queensland Government cutter, *Lizzie Jardine,* had also seen those blackened ribs, and that even now, as Bogo's canoes crept up the long northern coast, the schooner *Bluebell,* packed with native police and South Sea men and white men volunteering from every vessel within call, was creeping up the southern coast. The canoes and the avenging vessel were both making for Port Lihou, so named by Captain Lihou. Hoping against hope even now, the whites aboard debated the forlorn chances of a rescue. But most shook their heads. With all lights out, the vessel crept through a silence accentuated by the oily clicking of Snider-bolts.

The night wore darkly on, alive with that listening stillness of the tropics. Bogo's canoes crept along like giant bats which dread the light. With every mile Bogo wished more and more that he was on the homeward tack. Uneasiness gripped the men. They whispered. Ordinarily they would have been noisily excited at another victory over the Lamars, but on this night they all sensed the paw of extinction reaching out over the Strait.

Jakara was a prey to bitter memories. He thought of his mother, clubbed on such a night as this – a night of hazy stars, like tearful eyes seen through a veil. The black clouds draping the heavens had vanished, leaving the sky darker and farther away. A moaning sigh came from the sea, its waves moved surlily, like the breast of a labouring woman who finds no joy in sacrifice. The mass of the island loomed higher and darker, until the canoes seemed to be creeping through pitch. Jakara looked up at the hill-crests standing in fantastic silhouette against the sky. In the chill hours before the dawn they crept round the point of Port Lihou. And round the opposite point there crept the invisible schooner *Bluebell*, the spirit of vengeance wrapped about her.

Bogo hugged the wooded shores of the bay. He ordered the lowering of sails, the noiseless ply of paddles. He wished to turn back, but could not without some definite reason. All was indefinite, except the depression which had followed them into the bay.

Crimson fires stabbed the hills behind the beach. The waters echoed the voices of the island's warriors in wild song. A sigh of relief whispered from the canoes, but no one spoke. Bogo ordered the vessels inshore, and they noiselessly grounded by the mangrove-shadowed beach. To whispered orders one half of the men filed behind him, the remainder stood by the canoes. Quietly they walked along the beach. Bogo stood for a moment, listening. In throaty chorus welled the barbaric song. There was no other sound except a sighing among the trees, and, muffled across the bay, the cough of a crocodile. Bogo left the Leach and vanished into the bush.

Within a grove of pretty trees they caught the gleam of coals heaped in a line upon the sands, the ashes of cooking-fires. This was by the trading village of Murralug, where the people should have been waiting. Excitedly the party grouped itself around the fires. Jakara was sick with horror – bones newly picked lay scattered there, gleaming like pearls from the leavings of swine. Crowning a heap of flattened sand, in a little pyramid, were the skulls, a child's on top. Forlorn in the starlight, those skulls, grinning at the dying fires!

Jakara was lonely too, and very unhappy. He did not wish to kill the owners of those exulting voices from the hills. He felt mentally sick – tired of everything.

Piled-up bundles and packages and native crates were strewn upon the sands, for the Murralug men had been ready for the trade. Bundles of wommeras, of long hafts of hardwood; huge coils of mainland barks and fibres for string and rope-making and for the lashing of outriggers; carefully wrapped packages of cassowary feathers, black cockatoo feathers, grey feathers of the crane; banana-leaf packages from which peeped the vivid feathers of parrots; cable-like coils of elastic lawyer-cane; many bundles of pandanus bark; bark boxes in great numbers enclosing ochres of many colours; fibre-lashed bales of goanna and snake skins; "fire-sticks," scarlet-knobbed, in bundles; dingo and crocodile teeth and scarlet berries for necklaces; flint, quartz, and granite stones for sharpening and cutting; piles of crocodile hides; bark-enclosed swathes of zamia flour; gourds of lily-seeds, and bark bags crammed with dried water-onions – even a few carefully wrapped parcels of that precious narcotic, pituri – these and countless other bundles made up the much-diminished trade of the year.

The Murralug men should have been ready to load. A howl of triumph came from out the fire-lit night, and Bogo glanced up scowling; He ordered his men to hurry the trade to the canoes. Each man grasped a bundle and slipped like a shadow towards the beach. Jakara crouched beside a tree, his face hidden upon his arms.

The east was dawn-streaked when Bogo spoke: "Jakara, we must go! C'Zarcke is calling me. The spirits of evil are abroad. I feel the chill of death with the dawn, and I know not which way it is coming. Quick, we will return, and let these howling fools find later that we have come and gone."

Jakara glanced up listlessly, and suddenly awoke to the present. He suffered agonies of remorse. He saw trodden upon the sand a ribbon of lace, and instantly knew that the woman's skull was not yet added to the pyramid.

Bogo ran after him, and Jakara struck back savagely. "Why did you not tell me – you *knew!* Fool, I will not run away! Stand by the canoes, and I will soon be back."

Bogo shrugged irresolutely. Jakara hurried on to where he could glimpse a battalion of painted figures in a surging circle among the flames. He unslung his bow and fitted an arrow. Dawn streamed icily upon the hills. Trees hid his shadow as he strained forward to see.

The heart of the scene was clouded, for the crowded dancers whirled around it, and a thousand watchers massed close around all. Those who danced were of glistening ebony, for their bodies were anointed with human oil, and the breeze-blowing flames were reflected upon them. The women feeding the blazing fires with oily bark of the tea-tree kindled a raging fury within Jakara's heart.

He strove to see what was within the circle, but the painted bodies masked it with rhythmic movement. So intent were the tribes upon this sport that a regiment of soldiers could have marched unseen against them. Jakara climbed a tree and crawled out on a leafy branch. Over the heads of the dancers he peered down into the circle, then drew his bow, for lying on the hard ground was a white woman. Even as Jakara aimed for her heart, the darkness burst in ribbons of flame, a rifle volley roared and rolled and roared again among the close-packed hills. The play ceased in utter silence, dancers and lookers-on petrified, appearing the more moveless as some fell and lay quite still, while others writhed. What awoke them was the twang of a bow and the Mamoose of Murralug writhing with an arrow through his lungs.

The crowd broke as another volley thundered through the valley. Again Jakara's bow twanged and he screamed with the lust for vengeance as again flame spat after the runaways. He saw white men run from the shadows and kneel beside the lone white figure. But they stared into eyes glazing in death. Recklessly Jakara jumped from the branch and ran towards the gathering group. He never forgot the faces of those men as they looked up. He fell flat on the ground and Snider-bullets screeched over him: he bounded sideways into the bush, crying that his own countrymen took him for a savage! He heard the crash of brambles, the whine of bullets that splintered branches, but took no pride in the knowledge that he could easily lose these men.

Down towards the cooking-fires he spied three painted men racing as if from the devil. He called, and they stopped, their chests heaving, and with a great fright in their eyes that turned to unbounded relief when they recognized Jakara. They stood there while he thrust them through with Lightning, paralysed astonishment on their faces, the three of them.

He rushed down the beach and along the shore to where an agonized Bogo awaited him: the canoes were already under way. They sprang aboard, the sails filled in the strengthening light of day. Across the bay floated a shout, a spit of flame: a bullet smacked the water. Jakara laughed – a hard, unnatural laugh. There would be only half a dozen men left to guard the avenging schooner; they could not possibly sink Bogo's canoes. They did not hit a man. The light was uncertain, and the distance widened every second under thrashing paddles allied with sails. Bogo sighed when the last canoe rounded the point.

As they skimmed back along the coast, the echoes swelled until the valleys roared. Filled with intense excitement, Jakara shook impotent fists at the greying cliffs of Murralug. He knew the geography of the place, and he guessed what had happened: the conglomeration of tribes had rushed, after the first volley, down the nearest way of escape, which was an enclosing valley whose walls swiftly closed in to abrupt cliffs. The avengers had herded the tribes in an inescapable cul-de-sac. And as the growing echoes confirmed his belief, Jakara laughed hysterically.

That was the first great lesson the Lamars taught the Island nations, when Jardine caught the Central peoples in the Valley of the Hills upon Murralug.

Stone fish traps - built by an unknown race.
Mer.

CHAPTER XIV

Within The Crater Of Mer

When the canoes returned to Mer, Jakara hurried to Eyes of the Sea, but found her to be still aggrieved, so he left her alone, feeling thankful that she was alive. When C'Zarcke sent for him one evening, he answered immediately, glad of a break in the monotony of existence. "Come," ordered C'Zarcke, "the time has arrived when you must tell me of the Lamar God."

The command depressed Jakara. He thought hard while he followed the big priest over the hills of Mer and down into gloomy Deaudu-pat with its huge crescent-shaped valley, ghostly in its stunted vegetation, its still, tufted grasses, its solitary palms, almost all leaning, its grey enshrouding hills in such utter contrast to the outer fertile lands. The winding track led them through tabooed Zogo-grounds and presently turned in towards Gelam. Presently they reached the base of the shadowy, circular rim of the ancient mountain crater, on country which only the Zogo-le and the Maid-le dared to tread. Jakara had often spied this forbidden land through his telescope, but the gullies and peaked hills and patches of jungle looked eerily different in starlight. He was worried as to how he should explain to C'Zarcke.

The shadow of the mountain cloaked its base, merging the rocks and hillocks, trees and shrubbery, with the towering bulk above. C'Zarcke bandaged Jakara's eyes with a cloth of banana-leaf. "You are the first living Lamar to take this path," he explained. "This is going to be one of the most interesting nights of my life. Come!"

In hesitation Jakara felt himself brushing among bushes, until C'Zarcke's guiding hand checked him and he heard the harsh grating of stone upon stone.

Stepping forward, they walked with a noiselessness that did not even betray the whisper which bare feet make on a path. Jakara felt that he was treading upon a rock floor carpeted with softest sand. No breath of the night fanned his cheek, no trill of insect could be heard, and he knew that the stars were blotted out.

Jakara smelt the smoky oil as C'Zarcke lit a pandanus torch; he blinked when his wrappings were undone. He stood in a tunnel, a twisting passage-way riven by volcanic torture. The walls were almost smooth, of black volcanic rock; the invisible roof was a chasm rising up to denser blackness. C'Zarcke walked on. Jakara lost all sense of direction in the bewildering length of passage. He fought against a feeling that he was an alien in a silent world where lived beings that saw things, heard things, knew things! So overpowering grew this impression, that he felt like striking C'Zarcke just to make a sound. The priest glided on as if he were a shadow of that living silence.

Presently they turned right into a rumbling sea of noise. C'Zarcke waited; his rugged face under the torch seemed to be cast in copper. They stood in a mammoth tunnel, and Jakara gazed back puzzled at the silence. But he could not understand. The big tunnel had suddenly ended and eight huge pillars stood before them. C'Zarcke walked past these and into a smaller tunnel which sharply boomeranged around, then halted on the edge of an inky pool, while Jakara was overawed by a beauty of darkness. The light of the flame reached to the centre of the pool, and the ripples made by a waterfall quivered like reddened quicksilver for one wall of the amphitheatre was partly visible and down this there sprayed a veil of water from the upper darkness. The walls themselves were deeply fissured, and from rugged buttresses loomed down gargoyles and hunched monstrosities of black stone. Jagged beards of wispy rock trailed from fissures in the clefts. Shadowed forms shrinking into the blackness showed dimly behind them. Fronting the way along which they apparently must go came a restless volume of sound which Jakara recognized as that of the imprisoned sea. It moaned underneath in laughing sobs that receded in panting sighs. They were deep within the dead crater of Mer.

"Awful things live down there, Jakara," said C'Zarcke in a gentle voice, "things that would frighten even you. Monstrous things, and mites so small that you cannot see them. They are the worst! What you hear is the sea coming in from far under the coral reef. That tunnel leads down into it. All the things that live among the coral swim and float and crawl up that tunnel. The waterway could tell wondrous and fearsome tales, Jakara, but – and it leads directly to Beig."

"We Lamars do not believe in Beig," said Jakara, "although some among us believe, like you, that the spirits of the dead go to a waiting-place where they are taught the mysteries of their environment before being capable of ascending to higher spheres."

"You are right in that," answered C'Zarcke meaningly, "and I have brought you here to-night to see whether you are blind to other things of truth."

Jakara's hair stood on end when a bell tolled: the sound floated down in rings which spread and softly flooded the amphitheatre, to drone sadly down the under-sea passage-way and sigh into silence. Abruptly tolled the bell again, pealing from the invisible above, its melody flowing down the walls and enveloping space in liquid sound. Minutes passed amid trilling whispers that faded into silence again.

"A ship's bell," said C'Zarcke. "It tolls on this night every twelve moons: it has tolled for centuries, as it tolled while the strange ship was sinking. But do not think that there are any people, live human people, here. We are the only two. No earth-born hands ring that bell."

He slipped into the water, and, with the light upon his fine face, looked up impressively. "Watch me, Jakara, and do exactly as I do."

He walked into the pool, one hand holding high the torch. He swam directly towards the waterfall, and, on reaching it, thrust his hand straight through. Then he turned questioningly towards Jakara, who nodded, for he guessed that C'Zarcke's fingers were gripping a ledge of rock. C'Zarcke waved the torch until it flared noisily, then with a quick upward leap he vanished through the waterfall.

Jakara gazed on a beautiful sight, for the waterfall appeared like a veil pierced by torchlight, every sparkling drop a rainbow, with the rugged form of C'Zarcke waiting in silvered outline behind it, while blackness framed the picture.

Jakara crept into the water, feeling queerly alone. He swam as if through ink, his eyes never leaving that rainbowed silhouette, and, as he swam, he experienced a shrinking feeling that something was threatening to pounce upon him from the blackness above.

Thankfully he leapt through the water-veil, then gazed back into the gossamer drops, startled that he could see nothing of the pool and the darkness behind.

"We are in the heart of Gelam," said C'Zarcke, and, turning, walked on. Again they threaded a passage-way that had no visible roof, and the only sound was a cold, steel-like tinkling of the water falling behind. They walked until the sound dimmed to that of a fluted organ, with honeyed voices floating back from the uttermost roof to sigh away through honeycombed crags.

He tiptoed into a broadening passage, and paused, shivering. Someone had whispered to him! He glared into the darkness, and C'Zarcke turned. "It is the Passage-way of Whispers," he said quietly. "Come!"

Jakara hurried after him, and then felt impelled to look behind. Nothing spoke. He wheeled and jumped back upon C'Zarcke, for someone *had* breathed over his shoulder. C'Zarcke watched him covertly. "I see that, after all, you are not familiar with the real Lamars," he mused.

"But come, I assure you that you and I are the only two earth-people within the heart of Gelam."

C'Zarcke walked to a wall and lit a torch. As it flared, so Jakara's eyes widened, for, crouching directly beneath the torch, was the hideous caricature of a man, naked and withered, with glaring eyes of nautilus shell.

Jakara shivered in relief, but he drew close to C'Zarcke, who had moved to light a second torch. Under this also glared a mummy, and under twenty-three more. Twenty-five others claimed the light when C'Zarcke moved across to the opposite distant wall; and, vanishing away into the darkness, Jakara sensed others waiting. All manner of men they were physically, so queerly coloured for human bodies, from sickly yellow to grey, and some brown with a greyish tint, others hard ebony black: all were hideous. The hair of most was in wild tangles, though some had carefully combed curls, and an odd one was curiously bald. Jakara experienced an eerie feeling of repulsion that a human being, a being like himself, could become such a thing, even though it were a thousand years old. As each torch lit up, it showed littered things upon the floor.

"Only those chiefs of the Zogo-le who were also of the Bomai-Malu, and, before them, they of the Ad Giz, rest here," said C'Zarcke reverently. "The history of four thousand years lives here, but speaks only to them who understand. It would take years to explain the realities that are here, so we will only seek that which we have come to learn."

Jakara eagerly followed him along systematic lanes that divided many stacks of things. And again, and yet again, Jakara exclaimed in astonishment, for books of his school-days rose before him as he saw ghostly relics which he could have sworn were the heads of Egyptian or Phoenician galleys. C'Zarcke urged him towards an arresting heap upon which a torch concentrated its light. Jakara halted with a startled cry, for there loomed overhead the white figure of a Madonna, gazing calmly down from the shattered bow-sprit of a Spanish ship. His eyes bulged at the sight of kegs and chains, and queer old silver cutlery, and flagons, and iron-bound cases: at swords of strange design, and culverins: he stared at the polished blades of battle-axes, and, as he struck his clenched fists to make sure that this was wide-awake reality, he was unaware that C'Zarcke searched his face with blazing eyes.

Jakara impulsively wrenched up the rusted lid of a chest and cried aloud at the dull glitter within. He turned over rich coins, yellow and heavy, and laughed up into C'Zarcke's face.

"Treasure trove! Yo ho! for the land of gold!" – words which C'Zarcke could not follow. "You might well look excited, C'Zarcke, you old Midas!

Where did it come from?"

"What is it?" questioned C'Zarcke eagerly.

"Why, money, pieces of eight! Doubloons! Dollars! Spanish Gold! Gold!"

"Lamar money?"

"Yes, yes!"

"Does it answer to our shell money?"

"No – why, yes! We can buy anything with this!"

"Can it do anything?"

"Why, what do you mean?"

"Can it do anything? Can it work? Can it explain the stars, or teach knowledge of any kind?"

"Why, no; it is just money."

C'Zarcke turned away a bitterly disappointed face. "Look," he said gruffly, and flared his torch round to a niche in the wall. Jakara stepped back in sudden fright from the threat of a Spaniard in polished armour.

Such an awful face, with shimmering eyes and teeth of pearl-shell! His haughty white moustachios and pointed beard were carefully combed. Jakara gasped in astonishment. Those who had mummified the man had preserved with wonderful likeness to life his appearance of arrogant hauteur. Jakara instantly knew that he had made the acquaintance of an aristocrat.

"Who is he?" asked C'Zarcke tensely.

"A Spanish don," whispered Jakara in reply. "Am I dreaming?"

"Was he a Lamar too?"

"Yes, a Spanish one. Just as a man of Tutu is a man, but not the same as a man of Mer."

Again disappointment clouded C'Zarcke's face. He ground his heel into the floor, his big flat foot tapping in bitter exasperation.

"Tell me about him," said Jakara.

"It would waste time," answered the priest harshly. "Someday I may show you his history by spirit power. He and his followers are responsible for Las. When their ship went down, they landed in force. Our ancestors' weapons were impotent against the clothes that these men wore. Our men of those days accepted them as Lamars, thinking it impossible to kill them. They took the young girls by force, and made the village of Las. In the course of years our men found out how to kill them. One great day they all died. So did half of the men of Mer. He was their leader. I have often spoken to him in spirit, wishing he would tell me of the stars, but he speaks a language foreign to me and delights in his still living hate to explain, so that I cannot understand."

C'Zarcke sighed in remembrance.

When Jakara opened a casket he cried aloud in astonishment.

"What are they?" demanded C'Zarcke.

"Rubies, diamonds, necklaces, pearls! Don't you even recognize the pearls?" And Jakara incredulously held up a string of gems.

C'Zarcke spat upon them. "Fools!" he sneered. "When I saw the stones of blood and light, I thought they might teach me something, but when I saw the stones of the sea I recognized that the Lamars were fools! Are you also a fool? Have I brought you here to teach me knowledge, and are you but a child that crows over things of the mud?"

Jakara stared up at the savage face which threatened him. He dropped the pearls.

"Look!" commanded the priest, and lit a torch in the wall. Jakara gazed at the sweetest face ever modelled by the hands of men.

C'Zarcke held his breath as he looked on Jakara's face. Then he dropped his torch and seized the white man's shoulders.

"It is He," he whispered hoarsely. "Quick! It is He?"

"Who?" asked Jakara absently, while he looked upon the wonderful figure.

"The Lamar God!"

"No," whispered Jakara, dreamily, "it is Jesus Christ, His Son."

Intense amazement succeeded the radiant hope on C'Zarcke's face. "His *Son!*" he exclaimed; "the Son of the Lamar God."

Jakara then dimly realized what this explanation meant to C'Zarcke. He was amazed at the hunger for knowledge that possessed this strange man. He turned again to the crucifix.

A large silver crucifix it was. Once it had been sacred to some ship's company. One glance told that the craftsman had not fashioned it for money; it was a labour of love. Love through all ages gazed from that silver face. Patience and utter understanding shone gently through the expression of pain. The sweetness of humanity cleansed of all dross was upon that thorn-pricked brow. Jakara gazed enraptured, worshipping the message of this work of art born of love.

"Tell me about Him," whispered C'Zarcke urgently, "and about His Father, God."

"I can tell you about *Him*," answered Jakara, "but no man living could explain God. Listen, C'Zarcke! Recently an insect alighted on my hand. It was so tiny that my eye could barely see it, and yet it had perfect form. It had wings dressed in colour. That unconsidered thing could fly of its own power – a thing which men cannot do. But, C'Zarcke, the head of that insect I could not see, though within that invisible head were sight, hearing, and brain. It could reason, and had a knowledge of things which I cannot dream of. And it experienced love and hate, and thought itself a fine creature, and me it considered no more than we consider the mountain we stand upon. Now, C'Zarcke, God made that wonderful insect. Who is God? For he also made me! All this island of Mer is a big thing. God made it, every particle of dust that is in its stones, every leaf, every insect, every man, every fish and bird. He also made life. What is life C'Zarcke? I see that you do not know; nor do I. Then how can we understand God, Who *made* life! God made death too. God breathes the beauty into the flowers. He whispered to the hibiscus to be scarlet, and urged the lily to be white. He makes every sunbird to shine in beauty, feather for feather, and breathes the one wild call in the throat of every gull. He made all these islands, all New Guinea, all the Great South Land. He made all the world; He made the sea. But, C'Zarcke, He made that tiny insect! How, then, can I explain what God is? He made the stars, the sky, the heavens. He made every hair upon your head. Now, C'Zarcke, why is the sea ruled by the tide? Why does it not pile up in one overwhelming mountain of water that would reach to the skies and come rolling and smashing upon the earth? Why do the mountains stop in their place? When you throw a stone, why does it fall to the ground? It is because of the law which regulates everything to its appointed place and work. God made that law! A law that holds the waters back from drowning the earth, a law that makes a house to stand erect, a law that makes the greatest mountain on earth firm in its allotted place. That law keeps the whole world harnessed. Otherwise everything would fall apart into space, the mountains and the seas, the islands, and everything. Even that little insect, C'Zarcke, would fall straight away into nothing. God is that law. Now can you tell me who God is, C'Zarcke?

"He stretched out the skies, and made every star, fastening it within its limit. Why do not those stars fall? Why does not the sky close together and blot out the stars as the darkness blotted out your torch in the chamber back there? Because, C'Zarcke, God made a law that such ruinous things could not be. Who is that law? What it is? Who is He? You do not know: the Lamars do not know. We only know that He is God who made everything – who *is* Everything.

"I will explain our traditions, C'Zarcke, passed on by human prophets who spoke the word of God. Had you lived in their day, C'Zarcke, you would have been such a prophet. Then I will tell you a much closer human knowledge of His Son."

Jakara went through the Bible as closely as the memory of childhood allowed, and C'Zarcke listened with tense eagerness to every word, his eyes burning with desire. Jakara realized that he held C'Zarcke for all time when he described the witch of Endor and the raising-up of Samuel. A startled comprehension expressed itself in C'Zarcke's face, and Jakara realized that the priest understood thoroughly the methods of the witch, though Jakara himself knew only the story.

These people were steeped in a practical spiritualism. Their priests studied death more than life, convinced that this existence is merely a passing phase whose object will be understood only in the life to come. For centuries their wisest men had delved into the secrets of the spirit after death, and, like other coloured. peoples, they had glimpsed something behind the veil. They studied the future, whereas we study the present.

C'Zarcke, with a throbbing joy in his heart, felt at last that he was on the way towards piecing together the mystery of life. This Lamar, who was a fool, had the secret coming from his tongue, but he was blind and could not see.

The fighting and trials of the Israelites C'Zarcke enjoyed and understood, but he could not understand that love should govern life. There were other things that he misunderstood, but he stored up every word for a future dissecting. Finally Jakara, grown very confident, told of the Christ. He was on a much surer footing now, and confident because he realized that C'Zarcke understood better than he. C'Zarcke understood the miracles perfectly, and actually by what forces they could have been brought about. Jakara little knew that, as he spoke, C'Zarcke visualized and understood the reason and cause of those happenings of nearly two thousand years ago. When Jakara came to the death of Christ, C'Zarcke seized him with trembling hands.

Horrified amazement corrugated his face; then his expression changed to an awful fear.

"Surely *No!* Jakara!" he shouted. "Even the Lamars could never be such fools! They could never do that! Never!"

"C'Zarcke, I am telling the truth," said Jakara frowning, "and you are hurting me."

C'Zarcke's grip unwillingly relaxed: he was gasping. "Answered like a fool," he muttered, "fools who killed the Christ."

Jakara scowled, hearing the contempt in the tone of the priest.

"Speak on with the story," commanded C'Zarcke furiously.

Jakara thought it better to continue. At the mention of the Resurrection Jakara became frightened of C'Zarcke, the man's interest was so appalling. And when Jakara spoke of Christ's appearance at the dinner of the disciples, C'Zarcke sprang up with face literally shining, and hurried straight out between the torches into the darkness.

Jakara sat wondering; then he moved about and immediately forgot everything in the delirious joy at sight of the treasure. Long afterwards something startled him, and he gasped, for a voice had whispered. C'Zarcke, visible in the gloom, was gazing up at the crucifix. Presently he sighed, and turned towards Jakara. His face was inexpressibly sad.

"Why, Jakara," he said evenly, "the favoured Lamars had the knowledge of all things within their hands; they had life itself; they had this very love you speak of; and they extinguished the light and left us to grope through the centuries in darkness."

Jakara said nothing. He felt uncannily certain that now C'Zarcke understood far more than *he* himself would ever know. "We will go now," said C'Zarcke at last; "I have much to think of for moons of time. Afterwards I will question you on what I cannot understand."

Jakara hesitated by the caskets.

"Fool!" snapped C'Zarcke, "you make me very angry! You think only of dead things, when the very secret of everlasting life is all around you! The Lamars are blind fools who would deny the very light of the sun. The insect you spoke of is more fit to live than the entire Lamar nation in their ignorant conceit. Have anything you want except the Wonder Man ... Come!"

Jakara snatched jewels from the casket, and then ran after the disgusted C'Zarcke. Not for all the gold of the Indies would he have remained alone in that Chamber of Whispers.

Jakara was staggered when they emerged into the open, for it was afternoon! He turned to C'Zarcke. "Now, C'Zarcke," he said eagerly, "I have only to remind you of your promise, and it is granted."

C'Zarcke returned from the clouds. "Ask in your own words," he said with a smile.

"You promised me a canoe," said Jakara quickly, "and Eyes of the Sea, and liberty."

"Go," answered C'Zarcke, "when you will. The questions I would have asked I can best unravel for myself."

Jakara snatched the big hand in undisguised joy, C'Zarcke watching him as a scientist might watch a beetle. Jakara raced along the track towards Maiad. He fairly jumped through the door of Obi's house, and swept Eyes of the Sea off her feet.

"Pack up," he laughed; "cram full the bags and the hat-boxes and the other things. We're off to the land of paradise where the orange blossoms grow." The girl clung to him in amazement. Obi stared; Obi's wife stared, and so did all their friends upon the sitting-mats. Jakara laughed at their amazement, and swung the girl through the doorway, hoisted her to his shoulder, and hurried into the nearest banana-patch. Laughing faces peeped from doorways and children shrilled after them. Jakara hugged the girl tightly in the shelter of the broad green leaves. "We can sail right away, little girl," he said, softly. "Sail, sail, sail! C'Zarcke has given me permission to take a canoe of our own. We can fly to the first ship that sails along, and we will make a kingdom of our own, and eat Lamar bread-and-butter and salads and pies."

The girl drew an understanding breath, staring at the man until her wits flashed together.

"I will not go," she said slowly.

"Why?" he asked in surprise.

"Because I should be leaving my country and friends for a land and people strange to me. I like you, but I do not like your friends. I am happy here; I should be miserable there. I will not go."

"But, Eyes of the Sea," insisted Jakara hastily, "you cannot live here for ever! Does not your own blood call to you at all? Are you always going to be a white savage amongst niggers?"

The girl did not understand the word "nigger," but she sensed the insult. "You can go yourself," she said freezingly. "I am content to stay with the 'niggers,' and—" for she had understood the look on Jakara's face, "if you force me to go, I will never be any more than a 'nigger.' I will never be to you what you are trying to teach me to be. I shall remain a 'nigger' always."

Jakara smiled wryly. "A fine sweetheart you are! You would not raise a man up to the skies!"

The girl clasped her hands and whispered: "But I could, Jakara. You are cruel to think so unkindly of me. I should love to raise you to be the greatest chief of all the Island peoples."

Jakara laughed scornfully. "Jakara, king of the niggers! What a kingly ambition!"

The girl clenched passionate hands as if to strike him; then with blazing eyes she ran back to the village. Miserably he hid the stones away. Eyes of the Sea was a dear little thing; her soul was sleeping, that was all. But he despaired of being able to awaken it. Life was very complicated-women more so.

"What the hell am I to do?" he asked himself, and savagely kicked a banana-plant. Shrugging, he walked along to old Kewa's house, for he must be present at the initiation of the boy.

Kewa was preparing for his first fight. He was only fourteen, he had just passed through the Kwod. He stood now, erect and serious. Around him were grouped warriors, with their eyes fixed on his. While relations chanted low toned in solemn ceremony.

His mother held a small bamboo gripped tight to her breast. The bamboo contained a mixture of water and grated portions of a warrior's organs, killed by his father in a previous battle. To a quick, low order Kewa stepped to his mother, facing her. He drank, and the liquid seemed to come from her breast. Low and serious was the chant as he drank this liquid Augud-ui-osa (Give you God). Then the father seized the boy, rubbing his hand down over his mouth and chest.

For the boy could not fight otherwise. That liquid made him fierce and strong, imbued him with a warrior's cunning and blood-thirst. Then the father gave him a small piece of alligator liver to eat, which gave the boy courage and a "strong heart."

Then Kewa's maternal uncle seized him and rubbed under his arms and over his heart a mixture of chewed paiwa-tree, which he spat out of his mouth.

The ceremony over, the warrior's crowded around Kewa, and congratulated him.

A definite change had really come over the lad. Fire shone from his eyes, his chest seemed to have expanded, he stood erect with a litheness that seemed ready to spring. Young Kewa was "ready." He was burning to kill a man.

CHAPTER XV

Women

The Woodlark again lay over by Dauar, with Waiar islet but a bowshot away. The three were a grim company. It was impossible merely to glance at the Woodlark and look away, for the spirit of her sinister history gripped the mind. It was a dark spirit, like her crew, who now worked in scattered dinghies out from the reef but keeping close around the schooner like chicks around the wary mother bird, all carefully placed within rifle-shot of one another. Any rash raiding canoes would thus be caught between two fires which would rapidly develop into a circle of fire if the dinghies should be forced to race for the schooner.

The crews were diving for *bêche-de-mer*, and their brown and black skins flashed in the sunlight as man after man popped up from the depths. And, as each broke the surface, somehow his face turned towards Mer, and his eyes gleamed. Not with the pleasure of the catch, as he threw the beloved delicacy of the Chinese mandarin into the dinghy, but with the red-hot pleasure of anticipation.

For the boys of the Woodlark wanted women. They always wanted women – young ones; and pretty ones were prizes. They got women, too, when they could take them!

The captain and mate on the Woodlark's deck searched the island through glasses. They knew it as a hornets' nest, but they had tapped it before and meant to tap it again. But again to bewilder these savages necessitated a change of plans.

"Mer grows the best girls," growled the mate; "they are pretty, too, and bite like the devil. A man is never certain whether he is to get their lips or their teeth. The taming of them is grand."

"Their men, though," said the captain thoughtfully, "are damned handy with their blasted killing-clubs. I don't want to lose any of the crew – not while we are getting plenty of fish. We're coining money now."

The bucko mate searched with his glasses trained long and carefully on the village of Ulag. He pointed out the easy landing-place, the cover afforded by the palms, the feasibility of encircling the houses by separate parties of men scaling the headlands which flanked the village. The captain nodded, adding suggestions also.

"Some day the missionaries will spoil this place."

"For us," grunted the mate.

"H'm," said the captain. "Well, the crew must have women; they toil contentedly when woman-happy; they never growl at the long hours or the tucker, they think only of the night."

The crew were men whose daily round was determined by the passions of primitive life – virile hot-blooded passions, but ruthlessly cruel when the inclinations of others went against their own. They worked, and loved, and fought, and sacrificed themselves and one another and others, quite pleasantly and mercilessly – all in the day's work, all in the cycle of life. They toiled in the sunlight, they loved and fought and slept with the moon, and in between they died when they had to, mostly by violence, with a laugh or a sigh or a scream, just as Death took them. And they took others with them – if they could.

A few white men were among them; some had so far forgotten they were white that they even used native names. There was also a squat devil with a slant to his eyes and yellow in heart and body, but mostly they were fighting savages from the South Seas. Tanna men and warriors from Api, savages from Eromanga, from Fate, and from nameless islands in between. There was a flaxen-haired giant whom the sun had scorched black, like his heart. He was the worst of the lot. A girl in Norway had waited years for him – was still waiting.

A few mornings later, the crew bellowed in lusty chorus to the clang of the creaking capstan, and in the steel-grey dawn the Woodlark sailed away. To joke and song the crew worked and as they hauled on the stiff tough ropes, the sting of their hands was felt by the rumbling sails. They laughed with their eyes turned towards Mer, and they left their minds behind them in her villages by the sea. When the island became dim in the distance, some grouped themselves in the bows, bare-chested to the spray, others squatted upon the deck, toying with well-oiled rifles, pouring lead into bullet-moulds, and lingeringly thumbing the blades of cutlasses. For her size, the *Woodlark* carried almost the armoury of a man-o'-war, and her numerous crew thirsted with lust to use their weapons. While they filled their cartridge-belts, they boasted truthfully of conquests they had made, for they made their own little wars, but the conquests which they loved always had frizzy hair and frightened black eyes.

The watchers upon Gelam suspiciously saw her melt into the mists towards Eroob, but they breathed with no relief until, hours later, C'Zarcke sent a telepathic message to the Maid-le of Mer that the ship of prey was heading towards Maubiag. For C'Zarcke was with the Zogo-le and the majority of the warriors of Mer, who were assembled in strength at Eroob, for the reason that two large Lamar ships were again hovering around the shores of Ugar, and the Zogo-le of the Island nation had decided to try definite conclusions with the Lamars at the first opportunity, hoping to prove to their uneasy people that this menace was vulnerable. But the mind of C'Zarcke was troubled, and his heart sore, for he alone understood that the Wonder God of the Lamars would stand by them. C'Zarcke had the knowledge, and he despaired. Clearly he saw, with each new sail upon the Strait, the approaching end of their national existence.

From sombre Maubiag the Watchers of the People spied the bird of ill omen coming with the gloaming of evening. And so the boo shells blared a snarling warning and quickly another sound answered it, though only the cool evening air heard – the patter of bare feet as along many paths hurried the women of Maubiag. They scurried into a huge cave, the young girls from afar clutching panting hearts, and the women and the children and the old people hobbling after. The bushes swished behind them, swaying up over the cleft-like mouth, and nothing was visible but foliage and frowning rock.

Soon the dark night came; the air whispered as with many voices, and the reefs roared under foam. Everything was unseen, but electrically alive, in the air and on the land. The sea was surging with phosphoric splashes against the bows of a ship that sped through the night like a thing alive. Certainly a thing of life was that ship, every timber whining in sinister eagerness, every block with its own slight squeak, the stays hissing like the breath of a straining man, sails bellying, impatient bows dashing away the rough caresses of the sea. Every man was tense with the expectation of a fight, working up more and more madly with the growing woman-lust.

Ugar slept, and so did Eroob, and Moa, and Naghir, and all the islands, and Mer! And dawn was born sombrely in clouds of black, streaked with fire from the father sun, and there was the *Woodlark*, laying to just off the reef opposite Ulag, while stealthy men were surrounding the village, eager men with eyes straining to outstrip the light of dawn ere it could warn the sleepers. On the shelly beach waited dinghies, and men expectant to handle the catch. Then came the rush, a swishing of banana-leaves, tearing of vines, dry crackle of hurrying feet upon coconut-leaves, the bursting in of a door, a hoarse shout, a scream, two quick rifle-shots – and hell had broken loose.

Birds twittered at the dawn, tweaking feathers with sleepy beaks. The sun kissed the palm-tops, and mists like bridal veils moved from the valleys of Mer; But the human beings awoke to the thunder of Lamar guns.

Hesitantly, then in frightened chorus, brayed the boo shells for most of the warriors were away and, above all, C'Zarcke was away, and the dreaded Lamars had come! Beizam would be angry, for he had been very active of late in trying to stir up his tribesmen definitely to attack the Lamars, but now that the chance had come the Islanders themselves would be forced to fight – and nearly all the warriors were away.

Smoke rolled up from Ulag and formed a pall for Samsu and a youngster trodden underfoot. Men and women and children were crashing through the bush, for every path was blocked. Those who ran to the beach doubled back amid the laughter of the raiders, and with bullets hastening their pace.

Screams came from the beach where men were dragging girls down to the dinghies. The catch had been good in quality, but small in quantity. Five young girls. "They're lively little devils!" panted the bosun as the captives kicked, screamed, and scratched, and, when prodded in the ribs, sprang at the men and tried to bite them.

Up on a hillside where he lay gasping in safety, Obara heard a screaming entreaty that tore his heart. With a moaning cry he bounded back down through the bushes to help his girl wife. He had only his bamboo knife, and they hacked him to pieces across the dinghy bows. The raiders, quite mad, rushed the paths to the next village, for the ecstasy of the most merciless hunt of all mankind was boiling through their veins – the woman-hunt!

They tore along the higher paths which cut between the villages and the interior: here they met parties of uncertain villagers hurrying away into the heart of Mer. The *boo* shells of six villages were calling for aid, musketry thundered over all, organization was gone for all sought escape in the moment. As parties met, twigs were snapped clean off by musket balls, there was a scatter for the jungles and the vales, while hunted women and hunting men raced over the south-east shore of Mer. Gabru, a South Sea man, and the best diver on the *Woodlark*, writhed to earth with an arrow through his belly. When confusion was complete, cunning men hunted separately, for the prey goes not so often to the swift as to the cunning. Nagabulu, with knife-scar making his cheek hideous, crept like a huge black cat through the quiet jungle patch behind Las, where he lay quite still in the green gloom. Presently his heart raced and his eyes gleamed as he spied the legs of the Pretty Lamar hurry-ing along the path. She was scared, but believed she was safe, and so spared time to glance back towards her village of Las. Then Nagabulu sprang! They crashed among the vines that whipped around her, almost choking her heart with shock, while with a gurgling laugh he glared into her twisted face. His surety cost him all, for she snatched his paw from her throat, and Nagabulu found he had tackled an animal as wild as himself. He gloried in the struggle and snarled his delight as he rammed his knee into her stomach to block her wind. Her eyes blazed with unbridled madness as she bit his thumb to the bone. Nagabulu screamed and cracked the top of his woolly head into this wildcat's face. Her body opened out, her arms clenched round his shoulders, her legs unexpectedly swung round his back and pulled him tight. He lifted his head to laugh into her eyes the ecstasy of his triumph-and her teeth fastened upon his windpipe and bit deep, deep, deep through hair and skin and flesh and deeper still, and Nagabulu rolled and sprang up and dashed them both against trees; then they fell and rolled over and over. He could not gouge his thumbs into her eyes, nor break the ribbed body jammed leech-like against his: his life was sobbing out as his jugular vein burst and the vampire simply swallowed as her terrible teeth met nor did she for a moment let go until she had drained the last gasp of the life of Nagabulu.

At Serwaged the South Sea men hurried westward, and two Tanna men killed Laagot because she was too old. At Keweid feeble Komaberi waved a sem-leaf and cried "Peace! Peace!" for he could not run and hide. They shot him for sport, and at the village of Mei they trapped a man and forced him to fire his own village. Laughing, they cut his throat and threw him into the flames.

Away behind I'Laid crouched Eyes of the Sea among the flowering creepers. She listened in terrified excitement while she smelt, not the honeyed air, but rather the pungency of smoke. The thunder was apparently dying away while from the distant side of the island swelled a fierce joy-song that flooded her heart with delight – the roar of warrior voices:

"Jakara! Jakara!" and "Kill! Kill! Kill!"

Confident of the result Eyes of the Sea came out from among the vines and stepped quickly but cautiously towards the sound of the diminishing thunder. Women have gazed back at a burning city – and Eyes of the Sea was primitive.

A dozen crazed raiders, just because the girls of Gelam were so maddeningly fleet of foot, hacked old Baksu's shoulder when he fell gasping, and ran him through when he stumbled to rise. An easy shot brought down Gobar, a lad of ten; then they hacked Tek's sister, Kali, and quickly killed old Bidam, Baksu's sister. They raced down the valley between Gelam and Zaumo and shot Kawer, Irabai's wife, and their little girl, Gasi, because she was so very young, too young. It was sad that the little feet of Moira should have betrayed her as she hid high up among the coconut-fronds. The hunters peered from the ground up the slender trunk and stealthily asked whether they were the toes of a boy or of a girl. An impatient Malay raised his rifle but the devil with the slant eyes slugged him under the chin, and then swung an axe into the tree. Every blow trembled up through Moira's heart, and the leaves shivered in sympathy as the palm leaned over and then fell pitifully and quickly; and Moira screamed. She bounced high among the crashing fronds to the raiders' roar of delight for she was a young girl, pretty in her terror, and quite undamaged.

Racing along the slope of Gelam, some of them outwitted young Sauiri and, when the demented lad turned upon his pursuers, they shot him and shot again as his body rolled down Gelam-Pit. Dense smoke rose from beach after beach along the coast of Mer: a few of the raiders grew uneasy at the throbbing of the drums, but most were blood-blind and, when a girl broke from cover, they answered her scream with a chorus of laughter and panted afresh into the chase.

Adigor, faint with running, threw her baby boy, Newar, into a bush, and fell beside it, feigning death. A Tanna man pulled her about and, savage that such a comely girl should be uselessly dead, vented his spleen by slashing the crying infant. Adigor screamed and the surprised man thrust her through. Her last scream was for her husband and Kamai slid straight down from a coconut-palm and raved towards the men: they rushed together and hacked him to pieces. Then savagely they killed old woman Gobagi – she was so useless, and could not run away.

Eyes of the Sea, who had quickened her pace when the dangers which she anticipated did not snatch at her, stopped abruptly. The bucko mate of the Woodlark stepped from the bushes and his cold, fishy eyes gleamed at the sight of the dainty round breasts of the girl. She gazed in tense surprise at this Lamar, so unlike Jakara, and yet so like him. This man was white – a taller man than Jakara, with a rough square jaw and a curl to his lip showing a yellow tooth.

She was barely out of reach, and the big fellow tried to smile ingratiatingly, but with terrifying effect. He reached out a hand, as a man would tempt a mischievous mare. Eyes of the Sea thrilled deliciously; he was only one man, she reasoned swiftly, a seaman on a strange land – she was in her own environment and felt safe. She smiled in impish defiance and slid back a step. The mate slithered his big feet from the grass and stood fair on the path. The girl stepped back again. The mate grinned and pursed his lips: "Pretty girl, pretty girl," he coaxed, in a low growl; "come to me, pretty girl!"

"Goo, goo, goo!" lisped Eyes of the Sea.

"By hell," growled the mate, thickly. "I'll goo, goo, goo you if I can lay my claws on you, you little heathen devil. You fella pretty gel, me wantem tellem you something," he wheedled in pidgin-English.

"Goo, goo, goo," lisped Eyes of the Sea.

Huskiness choked the mate's voice. He tried to lie with his eyes, but the blaze in the cold blue shouted everything to the girl. An icy feeling touched her at the sight of the uncontrolled desire in those staring eyes. As he sprang, she side-stepped and raced back along the track. The first few yards, and she thrilled with the realization that she could easily outpace this man, this Lamar! She laughed derisively over her shoulder: he thundered behind with paws outflung in trembling eagerness to grab. She looked straight ahead, then very gradually slackened her pace. To the man behind, one little brown ear was maddeningly visible but it was telling the girl that the crunch of the big feet was close behind, she could hear the wheeze of his lungs as he gulped in air. She fully sensed the terrible eagerness in his face. Then she heard the indrawing of a great breath and a quarter of a second later she sprang straight ahead. Almost too late! For the mate had staked all on that one leap. He had not snatched forward – he flung his whole great length at the girl. With outstretched arms he thumped flat on his chest as she dived from under but his claws gripped her short skirt and it ripped away, while an instant's icy fear gripped her heart. She glanced back at the crash and laughed hysterically at his twisted, gravel-rashed face. He sprang up and snatched a pistol from his belt and Eyes of the Sea bent her head and shoulders and raced and screamed, the terror of the savage at the thunder-weapons of the Lamars strong upon her. Here the path ran through short grass; there were no bushes, and the nearest jungle patch was a hundred yards ahead.

The mate was still a little "white." He jerked the pistol upward in order to prevent himself from firing at her in the fury of his feelings; then, just as she reached the jungle edge, he blazed at her flying heels. As well try to hit a breath of wind! But Eyes of the Sea screamed from among the sheltering trees and the mate grinned at the terror in her voice. He flung the pistol from him and stretched knotted arms to the sky. If only – oh, if only he could have clutched such a prize within his thick, strong arms! He kicked the grass petticoat with a sobbing curse.

Down on the grassy slopes below Jakara's Lookout a hunted girl was breaking her heart. Geedee was surrounded – no matter which way she turned, she was met by a line of panting men. How the sweat glistened on their bare chests! They joined together on three sides, then eased their straining lungs and just walked towards her, a boomerang formation of panting lips and bloodshot eyes. There was no escape – ahead was the big cliff overlooking the sea, her own Lookout that she knew so well!

This hunted thing was fiercely pretty and frantically alive as she stared in every direction. Her body glistened with sweat and blood, for her skirt had long since been torn off and the bushes were thorny. The magnet for all eyes as she faced them, this distraught wild thing, with dishevelled hair and rolling eyes, saw all, but singled out none of them.

She turned and raced straight for her own Lookout, and madness raced by her side. Speeding over the flower-strewn rocks, she shrieked Sasak's name once, but her lover was away with C'Zarcke's men. Straight over the cliff she flew and her spirit was met by that of Miriam, down by the crooning sea.

The hunters stood astonished, but their chagrin changed to alarm. Arrows snipped through the air, a *doab* thrummed and the bolt thumped an Eromanga man in the chest. His gasping scream signalled that the hunters were the hunted. Jakara, leading two hundred warriors raced to cut off the raiders from the dinghies. The avengers clubbed a few men and made them pirouette in the Dance of Death, but the majority got away by virtue of their covering rifle-fire. The men of Mer would now have rushed anywhere, but Jakara held them back from where the raiders organized themselves upon the beach, for of what avail are bows and arrows against steel and lead? Besides, Jakara had only the flotsam of the villagers, left behind by C'Zarcke.

There were some wild chases after scattered parties over headlands and up precipitous vales, but the schooner, sounding a loud return, cruised as close to the reef as she dared along the coast and her heavily armed dinghies raced to and from the shore time and time again, picking up stragglers.

The captain cursed in furious anxiety, for he realized that the crew had got out of hand and, instead of their making a quick raid and return, their easy first victory had led them to make a day of it. And now he was not sure whether he had lost more men than the crew had won girls, while his telescope showed him a huge fleet of canoes just beaching by Maiad. But the bucko mate was so mad that he troubled neither about the skipper nor about the Woodlark; he raved of a golden girl who had shown him the heels of the wind.

When Jakara, furious and disgusted with everything, returned to his house, he was met by the grim figure of C'Zarcke, gazing away down towards the smoking villages.

"So," said the big priest softly, "Jakara fights for the savages against the savages! Now you see, Jakara, that Lamars under their skin are coloured just as we are."

"There was only an odd white man here and there among them," replied Jakara angrily. "Almost all were South Sea savages!"

"Led by the Lamars!" replied C'Zarcke quietly. "Brains and savagery and mysterious weapons must triumph against brains and savagery alone. People who killed the Christ would do anything!"

And he turned despondently towards the Zogo-house, with the first droop of his life upon his shoulders. He felt hopeless – the Lamar God was with the Lamars.

WAIAR, ISLE OF EVIL

CHAPTER XVI

The Pearl Ships Of The Lamars

Mer was very busy, as were the Eroob villages thirty miles away, and Ugar Island, and Naghir and the smaller islands. Changing winds and calms heralded the approach of the north-west season. Great flocks of Torres Strait pigeons, like clouds in the sky, were travelling over from New Guinea to nest in the Strait. Distant Tutu was busy, but not with trade. They – the warriors most unbeatable of all the island groups – proudly put their energies into the refitting of canoes and the edging of weapons.

Soon now the trading fleet would sail from Mer, and every Island ally got ready its contribution. The organizing centre on Mer was the Komet-le, who allotted to the many villages their quota of canoes, men, and goods, and gave out the measurements for the assorted articles, so that each canoe should be loaded to its fullest capacity and yet remain sufficiently buoyant to outlive a storm. Each house, in every village, on every island, had its stack of neatly parcelled goods. The trade already received from the Great South Land peninsula coast was sorely diminished through the hostility of the Lamar chiefs, Jardine and Chester. But the people from Spirit Island would soon arrive, people living south of Jardine, who had free intercourse with the South Land savages of the eastern coast, and without doubt their full canoes would help greatly to make up the deficiency.

The Miriam-le whispered over the probable effect of the shortage on the New Guinea people who keenly sought the products of the South Land. Many whispered, "What is C'Zarcke saying? What is he doing?" But only silence and downcast eyes greeted the great priest when he strode by.

Apart from the skulls, their own island trade was of comparatively little variety when not intermixed with the solid goods of the South Land. The more important were shells as carved ornaments and cooking utensils; crescent-shaped chest-mais of pearl-shell, and polished necklets of nautilus shell; cone-shells and nose-sticks; arm-and leg-bands; tortoise-shell and disk-pendants. The packages of tortoise-shell were both in natural plates and in carvings of great beauty as ornaments for warriors and maids. There were sacrificial clam-shells, bailor-shells for canoes, bucket-like helmet-shells, and various kinds used for cooking.

Skulls were by far the most valuable of all the trade. A skull bought a small canoe – a great prize and a necessity to an Islander. Odd New Guinea tribes would sell a small canoe fully outrigged for even a lower jaw-bone, provided that all the teeth were intact. These skulls were traded in turn from the coastal New Guinea tribes far up into the interior. This explains why the lone skulls of white people have found their way even into the gloom of the pygmy people's forests.

Suffice it to say, trade was scrupulously honest, based on shell money and the exchange system. Women, provided that they were particularly pretty and young, had a certain saleable value, but the Islanders did not trouble much about them, having more trouble than enough at home; if they wanted any variety in their domestic life, they could always make a raid on a neighbouring island.

Visits were sometimes prolonged at each village when the haggling became acute. The Komet-le and the traders of Eroob were experienced bargainers, keenly determined to get the last possible feather of value in exchange for their goods. The exchange of skulls for canoes was carried out with religious solemnity. After that most important trade was put through, the remaining skulls were carefully packed away under the envious eyes of the New Guinea men, to be produced again at the next village that would offer good canoes for good skulls. Then came the ordinary trade.

The Island traders minutely examined every feather of the beautiful head-dresses made of the bird of paradise plumes; they examined one by one the bundles of single feathers, the long plumes for the *kadiks*, the spreading *kolber kolber* plumes worn in the belt behind; the dog-tooth necklaces; the *omai tereg*, ceremonial boars' tusks; any possible *sauds*, the petticoats of shredded sago-palm; the war *wasikor*, sacred, and dance drums, the musical instruments; the varieties of clubs, bows and arrows and bone daggers; the bundles of different species of bamboos, the piled-up sago, and the rest. Most carefully did they examine the great canoes stretched out on the beaches for sale. After a minute examination by both parties the buyers talked prices. With odd articles, such for instance as cassowary feathers and pandanus-leaf mats, the Islanders had the advantage over the New Guinea men, for they procured these and other articles from the South Land also, and disdainfully told that fact to the New Guinea men, who, uncertain as to the value of an article procurable elsewhere, sold these goods cheaply, to the secret gratification of the bargainers.

But what ensured a huge success for these trading ventures was a good wrecking year. Then the Islanders had many mysterious and wonderfully useful things to offer. Above all, plenty of pieces of iron –

knives and axes of the metal so marvellously more durable than stone. That is why explorers, patrol officers, missionaries, and prospectors have from time to time wondered when some relic from a vessel wrecked hundreds of miles away on the Barrier Reef is found housed in a jungle village in inland New Guinea.

So now the Islanders from dawn till after dark were excited and busy in preparation. And C'Zarcke and the Zogo-le and the village chiefs communed long hours as to the time, the route, the safeguards, to be employed. The leaders of the various activities of the fleet had never known C'Zarcke so ominously serious, questioning, planning, thinking deeply over every detail. For the first time in their history there seemed to be a shadow of doubt as to the success of the voyage. Some intangible disaster threatened: though no one spoke openly to the people, the leaders sensed the shadow of the Lamars.

Though the national existence of his people was in the balance, Imari of I'Laid had a matter of far more serious import on hand. He sat in solemn state in the jungle, beside him a little pile of bulbs, roots, leaves, and flowers of the love-plants. For Imari was making his love-charm. Much depended upon this: his very life, he firmly believed. His fine chest heaved as he breathed away the thought of possible failure. He chose a bulb of the *kusigor* and crushed it between two small reddish stones; then one of *mar*, which had come all the way from New Guinea; likewise a piece of *pekiau* bark, and a bulb of long-leafed *kerakera*, good plant of Mer; he added *pas*, and female of the hibiscus, crushed them lingeringly, and mixed all together. A peculiar, indefinable scent floated on the heavy air, a tantalizing scent which one would have been drawn to smell again and again, and search unavailingly whence it came. It was an odour that piqued some dreaming sense of the mind. Imari, his eyes shining, added carefully prepared coconut-oil. The scent grew acute, its exact source even less definable. A woman would have been irresistibly drawn to it.

Imari gently heated the mixture, and then swallowed a little. His eyes widened, a touch of the devil became noticeable in his face. He then bathed in a clear pool, and finally, until sundown, massaged the drained oil into his splendid young body until the skin glowed, but with no sign of oil. There was also no scent. But he was picked for the men's dance which would introduce the girls' dance that night. He knew that as soon as he should sweat, in the heat and excitement of the dance the scent would permeate the air, indistinguishable to men, but powerfully affecting the senses of the girl he loved.

Away up on his Lookout, Jakara complacently puffed his *zoob*, until Eyes of the Sea should recover from the usual quarrel. She sat with her back towards him, interested in nothing in the world but a new grass skirt. The sky smiled from hurrying clouds to a clear day; the wind came in prevaricating puffs from the north-west. Soon it would bear back to the south-east and blow steadily for a week, then there would be a calm, and then would come the first wild howl of the north-west.

Stretched across the horizon miles away, five sail were dimly speeding towards the Great South Land. Jakara had recently seen far more sail than he had ever seen before. They were speeding home to Brisbane and Sydney and Melbourne with treasure of pearl-shell after eight months of work. Could Jakara have seen across the Strait towards the Prince of Wales Group, he would have seen hundreds of vessels, barques and brigantines, schooners, ketches, luggers and cutters, all flying home – the migration of the fishing fleets. Some vessels' homes were over two thousand miles away. Back to civilization with the first of the north-west behind them, before it blew in earnest and the storms and tides discoloured the water and made diving impossible and their small vessels dangerously unsafe! Some four months hence they would all leave their home ports, repaired and painted, and with the first breath of the south-east trades come flying back, eager to cull its pearls from the Coral Sea.

But Mer is isolated, away out towards the end of the Great Barrier, and the island there at that stage of the "rush" was seldom visited. Consequently Jakara had no idea of the swift invasion of the Strait by the white man. The knowledge of the settlement on Somerset still kept his brain busy with the wildest guesses, and with a warm pride of race at the daring of his countrymen, and of joy that their coming meant the inevitable ending of the Dance of Death.

He smiled to the skies, put down the *zoob*, cupped his hands under his head, and gazed up to where a frigate-bird circled as if it owned all space. A troop of chattering gulls fished just over the sea. One dived, and rose with a fish, dodging its mates as they wheeled and screeched around it. The frigate-bird volplaned, the gulls somersaulted in bustling confusion while the bird with breakfast in its beak dodged in frantic twists among its fellows. But all effort was useless. The frigate-bird never swerved from the fisher's tail. With a despairing screech the gull dropped the fish, and the pirate had it before it hit the water. He rose in perfect mastery into the air, a picture of beauty and superb self-assurance.

Jakara leaned over on his elbow towards the girl. "It is going to be a nice skirt," he ventured agreeably. "It is shapely, and you have teased the fibre until it is soft and silken."

She said nothing, but Jakara felt that he had broken the ice. He stretched lazily back so that he could smile up into her face.

"Tell me, when will my little girl become a woman?"

"I am a woman now!" she exclaimed in surprise.

"Yes," agreed Jakara gently, "in body a pretty woman, but in mind – quite a little girl. Well, then, tell me what you are going to wear at the dance to-night?"

"Wait and you shall see."

"I am tired of waiting. I shall grow old waiting, and the bottom will drop out of the world. When are you going to marry me, dear?"

"When you become Mamoose of all the islands," she said swiftly, without raising her head. Jakara looked startled.

"Do not talk like that!" he said sharply, "You know very well that *that* can never be."

"Then you will wait a long time," she replied calmly.

Jakara glared, and sat up. He stretched out his arms and drew her possessively towards him. "One of these days you will torment me too far."

She rumpled his hair with gentle hands. "You would not, Jakara," she said softly. "You want my love only when it is given with this soul that you tell me so much about. Have just a little patience. Remember that the Lamar world to you may be like Boigu, Isle of the Blest, but to me it is dreadful past all understanding."

Wistfully she kissed him. "Why not be content with me and our island home?" she whispered. "It is the one thing I ask, and I can only ask it before we marry. Afterwards I will never ask for anything for myself, only to be near you always."

Jakara kissed her tenderly. It was hard lines – supreme happiness within his grasp, freedom, and even wealth, but all held back by this girl clinging to her environment. He wound his arms around her, pillowed her head upon his breast, and pleaded with her in a passion of feeling to make her understand. And she listened with womanly lips trembling, and she gave in, but would not let him know; the north-west season was now nearly here and the Lamar ships would come no more for four long months. He could not go away now, and who knew? Many things might happen in four months!

So it ended with the one understanding that all the world knows, and a butterfly hovering over them wondered for what purpose human beings were put into the world.

Jakara, quite happy, did not hear the *boo* shell for quite a long time, and, when he did glance seaward, the canoes of Spirit Island were plainly visible, battling against the wind.

The Maid-le were busy sorting and preparing skulls. They were carefully packed in deep cane baskets, specially made. These goods were of all shapes and sizes. They had belonged to all manner of people, and all were graded as nearly as possible according to the owner's position in life. Those of the Mamooses and chiefs and Maid-le of enemy tribes, and the sorcerers and medicine-men, were the prizes. The warriors and directors of societies came next. Then ranked in scale the skulls of different groups, and of totemic clans, according to the owner's life position.

Some skulls were cleaned and very white, without other preparation. Others were painted with bars of different colours; others were all red. Each paint was symbolic of a meaning. Some had the sockets filled with eyes of mother-of-pearl, with a black spot for the pupil, and some had plates of polished shell for missing teeth. Others looked uncomfortably complete, for the nose-socket was filled in with a well-modelled nose of wax shaped and painted to look lifelike, and the top of the head was modelled and stuck with carefully combed human hair. These skulls were awful to look upon, for their black-pupilled eyes of glaring pearl-shell gave the impression of a man skinned, and yet alive.

One basket held lower jaw-bones. These were freshened up in such way that they appeared to have been taken from a man only the day before. Under the excitement of the fight the skull part of these had been so completely splintered as to be worthless. However, many New Guinea people were content with the lower jaw-bone, and some unscrupulous ones, returning from trade, would exhibit their trophy to admiring friends, and especially village belles, and brag of how they had killed their man, adding lurid details. For the New Guinea man was accounted a warrior only when he had killed his man. When he could not, or was afraid to procure the real goods, he falsified his credentials with a purchased jaw-bone.

As the sun went down, Jakara and Eyes of the Sea walked the beach with the throng to welcome the men of Spirit Island. Jakara had to endure plenty of fun-making, for in the strange fashion of the Lamars he moved along arm in arm with the girl he loved. In reply he smiled as if he held the secret of all the ages, and hardly noticed that the oncoming canoes were at half their usual strength. His eyes asked the girl to move into the shadow of the palms. Shyly his arms caressed her neck, fastening something there. She looked very sweet, waiting there expectant of some new form of the Lamar kiss. Jakara stepped back and gazed very proudly. Her eyes lowered, widened. Excited hands flew to the brilliants upon her breast. They had graced the neck of a lady of Spain.

Eyes of the Sea gasped in bewildered delight, and clutched Jakara, whispering, "Oh, Jakara, Jakara, what *are* they?"

"A necklace called diamonds, which the fair Lamar girls wear when they dance in a great event," explained Jakara, "Apart from your own prettiness, they will draw all eyes to you in the dance."

She sighed, fingering the stones reverently and fearfully, like a child in delight at some heavenly gift. Feelings which she could not fathom seemed to radiate to her from the gems. Their flashing eyes seemed to whisper to her from the hearts of unknown women Jakara watched, his face transformed, for she was quite lovely, and her face seemed to show goodness and purity, and other things which he could only dimly define.

Suddenly she flung her arms round his neck and kissed him wildly, passionately, with a fierce strength of feeling that she had never shown before; then she turned and ran through the palms, leaving Jakara in tingling amazement. It was a long time before he was conscious that he wished he had a skull-basket full of diamonds. He would have given them all for just such another ecstasy of kisses.

TREE HOUSES, FLY RIVER, NEW GUINEA

CHAPTER XVII

The Dance

With a choppy little backwash the Spirit Island canoes thumped upon the beach. Down tumbled the sails as the Miriam-le surrounded the vessels in welcome.

A different type of men these, their long straight hair arranged in shaggy coils, their bodies thinner, but expressive of sinewy strength. Their eyes were deep-set, under eyebrows much shaggier than those of the Miriam-le, and gleamed with an animal wildness. Their chief, Kara-Kara, exceptionally tall, with catlike step and body all whipcord and muscle, was greeted by Bogo, who almost immediately escorted him towards the Zogo-house. Amid greetings and laughter the warrior visitors were chained with flowers and drawn towards the palms, where steam from the *kop-maori* ovens made the evening smell tantalizingly keen. The people sat down in chattering circles, where a broad banana-leaf was spread in the sand before each person. On each such platter the attendants spread a portion of steaming food. The evening was given up to laughter and song and pleasurable excitement, for it was the Dance of the Maids to-night, and there was to be a dance every night until the Dance of the Skulls; then the great voyage, the event of the year, was to start. A veiled uneasiness was over all the Strait; who would not be excited among all these events?

In front of the Zogo-house were being discussed serious matters affecting the destiny of the people. Rugged as a grey Wongai-tree C'Zarcke stood with his face as sombre as the black cloud shadowing Gelam. Beside him waited expectantly the two others of the Zogo-le. As Bogo and Kara-Kara appeared in the Sacred Grove, the Maid-le in pairs proceeded to carry their packed baskets into the Zogo-house.

C'Zarcke knew that the flotilla of Kara-Kara was only at half strength. He knew that the chief bore bad tidings, and realized the cause.

Kara-Kara made obeisance, then the two interchanged the sacred recognition of the Bomai-Malu. "Report everything!" commanded C'Zarcke briefly. Kara-Kara looked him straight in the eye. "This season my canoes and trade are at half strength," he answered in a cold hard voice, "because the Lamars are become masters of the sea. All through the year they have interrupted my trade with the Great South Land. We have killed some, but they have killed many of us. Now I and my people dread them, we elude them, and are confined more and more to our island. We have learned that their thunder-weapons are invincible, our arrows the toys of children. They are coming faster in ever-growing numbers; this year they swarmed like pigeons at Wongai time. Ships and ships, and many ships, passed between us and the Great South Land. Ships and ships and many ships passed between us and the open sea. On this our trip to Mer, we sighted the first flotillas returning. We dodged them among the islands, like kingfish when the sharks are ravenous. The sight must have made the Spirits of my forefathers weep!

"Had I collected more trade, I should not have dared to bring it, for so many of my men must needs remain to guard our villages. Continually this year the Lamars have landed on the mainland where they cut much wood for the fires of their ships and drain the springs of water. On handy shores they erect houses where they smoke the big worm-fish of the sea. They have contact in many places with the savages, and though some have been speared, still the Lamars kill many more and terrify the rest, thus again interrupting my trade. And—" he paused, and glared searchingly at C'Zarcke, "the savages have failed me in much trade usually collected from the tribes of the far inland. They tell me that those tribes are too busy with fighting or making friends, yes, *friends*, with Lamars whose number is uncountable. These land Lamars have come up from they know not where, and along a great river, over solid land which could reach from Mer to Murralug, they dig the earth for a yellow stone. And with the Lamars come yellow Lamars, who also dig, and these yellow Lamars are not fighters, so the savages ambush and kill many of them and feast on the bodies and the goods. They are countrymen of the yellow people whose ships search our waters for the big slug of the sea. And the savages far inland are so intent on what is going on around them that they have taken no thought for the trade of the year."

Kara-Kara paused, staring at C'Zarcke. Suddenly he thrust his right hand towards the sky, and abruptly stepped forward. "What is the number of the Lamars, C'Zarcke? How can we keep off these hawks of the sea? Oh, C'Zarcke, whence come they, and how far will they came? C'Zarcke, I am afraid, afraid!"

His chest heaved; the glare left his eyes; his arm dropped. Sullenly he stared at the ground. For some moments C'Zarcke gazed into the drooping shadows of the Wongais. A bird of ill omen shrilled from the Sacred Grove. C'Zarcke spoke tonelessly: "Take your food with Bogo; we will talk later."

He turned and disappeared into the Zogo-house. A line of Lamars stretching from Mer to Murralug!

If Jakara had known, he would have cried aloud in astonishment; the distance was over a hundred miles!

Fierce resentment dulled by fear burned in the heart of C'Zarcke.

Little knew the diggers of the big gold-rushes of Queensland that the picks of their northward-tumbling thousands helped to swing the death knell of the Island nations.

Under the torchlit palms of Maiad chatted many people not yet tired after a week's ceremony and feasting. This was the night of the girls – their great night. Suddenly a silver tracery trickled down the palms, while rippled light caressed the sea. The people crowded into one massed circle, leaving a barely distinguishable opening down towards the beach, where from the shadowed palms the dancers came slowly, singing a plaintive melody. The circle was held by dancers until each fresh squad arrived. Those of the spectators who were not applauding or laughing or eating, chorused to the rhythm. They were astonishingly happy, those hundreds of people, throwing away dull care as lightly as a white man discards a soiled garment. The circle was enlivened by animated girls in sets of four advancing and retreating alternately, swaying in sensuous rhythm to the song and the hypnotic drone of the *wasikor* drums. Once heard, never forgotten, those drums of Mer! The blood-boiling throb of the war-drums, the compelling roll of the secret drum of Bomai, the evil in the distant throb of Waiat, down to the drums of the *wasikor* ceremonies and the dances – every drum throbbed, droned, or crooned a distinctive tone of its own, uncannily insinuating the reason of its song. Now in a line at the upper side of the circle, with their backs to the village houses, the drummers sat, and evenly and in perfect time the drums throbbed forth seductive, hypnotic waves of sound which, as time dreamed on, made all sway unconsciously to the expressed and unexpressed meaning of the dance.

There came floating a pretty song, a haunting melody which drifted nearer. Excitement fevered the throng. For coming was the Dance of the Virgins, and Eyes of the Sea, that incomparable dancer, had added new steps of her own, and was taking the leading part. Gracefully the grouped dancers already in the circle began swaying backward, still facing the spectators, still singing, still dancing. Into their wilder song now drifted the song of the oncoming dancers. It swelled as they entered the shadowy circle and swayed up through the lines of the retreating performers, the light sea breeze carrying the pleasant voices up among the listening palms.

There emerged one dancer through the rows, there emerged lines of girls behind her, all in perfect formation and step and song. The silence of complete delight overwhelmed the crowd. These girls were strikingly attractive, and their dance expressed a beauty which made itself felt and subconsciously understood. Jakara drew an appreciative breath, for Eyes of the Sea was lovely. The crowd stared at the sparkle upon her breast, for those fire-stones they had never seen before. The black feathers of the Bomai-Malu leaned forward, their wearers astounded: they knew!

Eyes of the Sea's light-brown hair was airily puffed, and upon it floated gorgeous butterflies: cunningly held captive within the strands, they yet could flutter their velvet wings. Knobs of gold encircled her forehead. These were the big green beetles that gleam with a golden phosphoric light at night, and in this captivity they continually outspread their wings and vibrated them with a loud, angry whir. Her breasts were cupped with scarlet hibiscus banded with yellow crotons, a broad armlet of mother-of-pearl glistened upon each arm. Daringly she wore a short skirt which dissolved and re-formed rhythmically into many colours, all silken strands of fibre, teased as fine as hair and brilliantly dyed, interwoven with jet-black horse-hair-like threads of cassowary feathers. Her ankles bore musically arranged bangles of nautilus pearl, while her daintily proportioned body was like living bronze under torch and moon. The excited little face all illuminated by eyes of intense blue.

Beizam had sight only for the Pretty Lamar. She was worthy of the son of a powerful chief. Right-corner dancer of the leading rank, tall of figure, she had cunningly emphasized by her adornments a whiteness heightened by the brown and chocolate skins of her sisters. Her hair was fluffed six inches high above and around her forehead, to be combed back in a heavy compact mass and fringe out, fantail fashion, from her neck. A head-band of yellow croton-leaves emphasized the paleness of the forehead, and across the coal-black crown was a bridge of latticed tortoise-shell. Behind the small ears there peeped an orange Cusack. On her upper arms were spirals of mottled tortoise-shell carved to represent snakes. Thanks to the elasticity of the material and the cunning of the workmanship, these snakes writhed with a lifelike "hiss-sss" to the movements of her rounded arms. A treble-row necklet of tiny black shells showed sombre round her throat. Her breasts were perfect, and she wore no flowers upon them.

Instead of the usual all-round skirt, she had fashioned a masterpiece which accentuated her light skin and striking form – a broad belt of metallic blue, composed of a band of fibre over which were sewn hundreds of wings of the broad blue beetle whose wings shimmer by night. Extraordinary thought and patience the girl had used in planning and collecting material and arranging that belt. The sacrificed beetles had been beautiful too. Under the front of the belt were massed long soft feathers of birds of paradise, plush black. These she had tucked in between her legs and spread out to tuck up again under the belt behind. Then, drooping from the belt in front almost to the knees, and similarly behind, was an eight-inch-wide plait of feathery plumes splashed with scarlet, free to sway as she danced. She was a chief's daughter, and he was of the Bomai-Malu, otherwise she would never have dared to wear such feathers without at least C'Zarcke's permission.

Above her ankles were broad bands of tortoise-shell, in lattice-work carving. Her face was ablaze with vitality, striking in its expression of determined purpose. One felt instinctively that, what this girl wanted, she would scorn hell to gain. Her thick, bow-like eyebrows she had slightly blackened, to emphasize them in the uncertain light and movement. Her lips were full and curved, and ripely red, but these too she had enhanced in colour, staining them with the crushed petals of a flower. Nature had made her eyes perfect, and she left nature to add fire to them now. They flashed forth beauty and an invitation to one man only.

The girls had each expended months of thought and ingenuity on their dresses and ornaments. None rivalled Eyes of the Sea and the Pretty Lamar, but all were ripe with a barbaric beauty which stirred the throng to a throaty approval that swelled to a shout and burst into a thousand-voiced roar. The drums beat stolidly on, the crowd took up the chanting song, the goa-nut rattles shrilled a quickening chorus. This dance, like all the dances, was symbolical. The movements illustrating each sentence of the song had a definite meaning. It continued for hours.

For one exultant moment the heart of the Pretty Lamar stood still as she noted the astounded admiration on Jakara's face. But his gaze wandered, and presently he had forgotten all but Eyes of the Sea. And the Pretty Lamar, though she smiled while her body merged into the perfect spirit of the dance, had feet of lead, and her heart ached far worse than any physical pain. Her teeth flashed as she laughed, and she sang the louder to stifle her craving to scream.

Imari saw only one girl. He was so intent on her that he had no thought for this noisy crowd of fools who saw many girls. Sabiki was third girl in the front row, and Imari was certain that nothing ever born was so beautiful. He edged along the inner ring of the crowd so that the light breeze would fan across his heated body towards her. She was deliriously intent on the dance, her heart and body and soul glorying in its subconscious meaning as she pirouetted and swayed in rhythmic accord with the girl directly in front. Her head-dress was of scented, blue-coloured grass, and it drooped in rustling tassels about her big brown eyes. Presently she glanced sideways, pouting her full red lips. Again she peered, wonderingly, and swirled on with the dance, to glance again and meet the staring eyes of Imari. Sabiki *knew*. Fire that was not alone of the dance warmed through her breast. She sang wildly, she looked again, long and daringly, and Imari's eyes met hers, staring eyes, meaning eyes, asking a great question, urging a steady command. Presently Sabiki was dancing only for him. The tone of her voice, the promises of her body, the gift in her eyes, were all his. Imari seemed to draw still more erect, he folded heavy arms across his chest, triumph thumped in his heart, his eyes fired with conquest.

From time to time the dancing ranks exchanged, the front ranks stepping sideways and back, and their place being taken in a reverse movement by the ranks behind. And so on, and so on, until the last rank was first and the first last, after which, all in perfect rhythm, the ranks changed place again, to the continuous shrilling of the goa-nut rattles.

Presently Beizam, standing eagerly gazing at the dancers, heard a sigh from someone close beside him. "Why, Pretty Lamar," he exclaimed in startled happiness, "I was watching for you to come up from the rear rank. No girl on Mer has ever danced as you have danced to-night!"

"I am tired of the dance," she replied shortly. "Do you think she is beautiful?"

"You are more wonderful than the beauty of the moon," he replied abstractedly.

"Bah!" she said. "It is Eyes of the Sea that I mean."

He glanced towards the dancers. "Yes," he admitted, "she is pretty, but," and he turned hotly on the girl, "she is only a butterfly, and yours is the grace of the sea-gull, Pretty Lamar. The sea-gull is the queen of the air and the sea and the land! Nothing could be more beautiful."

Across the mist of faces the girl looked wistfully towards Jakara, and then gazed into Beizam's eager face.

"I think she is like a girl smiling by a pool, Beizam. See the torchlight on her limbs! They are wonderful!"

"Not so wonderful as yours!" answered Beizam emphatically, as he grudgingly weighed up Eyes of the Sea.

"Watch her body," whispered the girl. "How firm and round and warm! Her breasts would scarcely fill a strong man's hand."

Beizam gazed more intently. Apparently he had missed something.

"She is all life and joy," whispered the Pretty Lamar. "Would you not like to crush her in your arms, Beizam?" She stroked the tough muscles of the man. "They are arms that were made to hold a girl," she insinuated.

Beizam drew a long breath. The girl was tall, but he was taller, and the splendid turtle-shell *dari* fitting almost down to his neck like a Roman helmet, surmounted by the busby-like paradise plumes, made him appear a veritable giant. He had filled out, every inch a man now. He stared hard, gripping his shark-tooth sword.

"You mean—?" he whispered.

The girl gazed up, but did not answer.

"She is Jakara's," he said gruffly, and looked away.

"Is Beizam afraid of Jakara?" whispered the soft voice.

Instantly his powerful hand gripped her shoulder, his distorted face glared into hers. In unshrinking defiance she awaited the blow.

"Beizam is afraid of nothing, neither of man nor of Lamar!" he snarled, and, whirling her from him, roughly pushed his way towards the shadows.

Beizam was deeply offended, but the Pretty Lamar knew that the insinuation had sunk in. She would tend it, oh, ever so craftily, and in due season it would bear fruit. She bit her lips, glaring towards the dancing ring where smiled Eyes of the Sea.

Presently Sabiki stood by Imari – quite naturally, as if she had become exhausted and had stepped out to join the crowd and look on. Imari did not move. The girl leaned towards him, nearer, dangerously nearer. She pressed against him. Still Imari did not move, except his heart, and the girl thrilled to its thumping. She sighed, and her hair brushed his cheek. He shivered, and whispered hoarsely, "The big palm by Las!"

The girl moved leisurely away. Imari did not even watch her go. On the outskirts of the crowd the girl hurried, then ran into the darkness. Under the big old-man palm of Las, a shadow awaited her. It was Meiti, bosom friend of Imari. Here they arranged matters, though Sabiki's girl friend should have been intermediary. But she had thrown to the winds all regard for etiquette. To-morrow night Sabiki would feign sleep until her parents were well abed. Imari and his friends would creep close to the house. The signal was to be the thrice repeated cry of a night hawk. The girl would creep out, and the lovers run away into the bush.

Sabiki laughed softly. Meiti smiled sympathetically. They separated and stole back to the dance.

Of course, the day following would bring a hullaballoo. The parents would seek the girl. Eventually the friends of Imari would tell. The parents and relatives, armed and furious, would approach the village of Imari. But peace would soon be restored, negotiations commence, and presents be given. The lovers would finally return from the bush, a feast and dance would celebrate the wedding, and everything would end happily. Such was the custom.

Next day, in the jungle gloom, Beizam sat all alone fashioning himself a love-stick. Dreams shadowed his eyes as he carefully whittled the stick, and some of the dreams were good, and some were bad. But some were not of love, and his fingers grew quiet, his handsome face stern and hard, as he sat motionless, thinking far ahead of the greater things of life. Not a sunbird came near him to trill of love and luck.

RAVI HOUSE, GULF OF PAPUA

INSIDE A DUBU HOUSE

CHAPTER XVIII

The Trouncing Of Kebisu

That same night they danced at distant Tutu. A war-dance! Kebisu, weary of awaiting the trade fleet, had decided on a little expedition to kill time. He grinned in anticipation the pleasure of C'Zarcke at an unexpected addition of heads. The Coconut Islanders would supply the heads, for their entire flotilla had recently chased a Tutu canoe when it was head-pirating in Massig waters, and the canoe men were justly indignant. Such a thing was unprecedented. The Coconut Islanders, those insignificant people on a sandbank, actually chasing Kebisu's men!

So, to wipe out the insult, and incidentally the insulters, with derision, Kebisu grimly decided to take only two canoes, the *Skull Chief* and the *Raider*. Full well he knew that the terror of his name combined with two of the huge war-canoes packed with Tutu warriors, was sufficient to vanquish a larger population than the Coconut Islanders.

Kebisu sailed, and at red dawn his warriors, full of fight, beheld a magnificent sight which they did not appreciate except to appropriate the omens to themselves.

"The sun is like a ball of blood," said Kiari.

"Coconut Islanders' blood," grinned Golge, and the warriors applauded the wit.

The island was beautiful, the encircling sandbank all gold. The palm-tops were gleaming and spilling the light on the brown roofs below; the sea, flower-blue, was lightly ruffled. The canoes glided like bat-like hawks under the broad mat sails. The savage warriors with the blood-lust under leash, were resplendent in head-dresses of magnificent plumes, necklaces of sharks' teeth, strings of crocodiles' teeth intertwined among their beards, crescent ornaments of pearl-shell upon their chests, *kadik* guards with drooping plumes upon their arms.

The village slept, just one pretty village alone in the heart of the sea, but as the canoes skimmed in with the high tide right over the reef, men, women, and children ran from the houses down to the beach.

Kebisu smiled grimly. Toik laughed uproariously: "Coming to welcome us," he shouted, and waved his left hand with the fingers all lopped off. The Islanders carried no bows or spears or clubs. "They would much rather make friends with the Shark than tickle his tail with an arrow," said one of the Beizam-le. "If they caught our canoe, it would have been different," said another; "they would have arrowed the Shark's body as well as his tail, and we should never have known who did it. These people would have looked so innocent then!"

"Their women appear to be lagging behind," remarked Arus suspiciously.

"The more fun in chasing them afterwards," said Tarao.

Young Nari pointed, while eagerly exclaiming: "There are some fine heads among that lot on the beach!"

"Do you notice that they seem to have only one hand?" said Malili suspiciously. "One hand of every man hides behind him."

"Holding his *gaba-gaba*," grunted Deboro. "They do not trust us. Pity they did not all have weapons; it is a shame to take their heads without the pleasure of a fight."

The crews laughed heartily, a trifle too boisterously. By now they could see the little shells upon the beach, and in two minutes blood would be spilt, skin and hair flying. The crowd ashore had divided into two groups, one awaiting each canoe. The vessels closed together as Kebisu guardedly ordered them both to skim straight up on the beach. The opposing groups walked casually to the water's edge and merged together. Kebisu's men, with twitching hands under cover of the deep canoe-sides, were fingering bows and arrows.

Suddenly Kebisu's eyes widened, for the beach had misted over; a strained and agonized expression creased his face. The Islanders, the very island itself, were fast fading away. C'Zarcke was violently calling him. Too late!

The group on the beach suddenly spread out, weapons flashed up, every head was bent. Kebisu's amazed men gazed straight down the barrels of carbines. Some did not hear the thunderous volley or see the smoke belch out to drift over the water in a little black cloud. In the packed canoes at point-blank range those bullets were deadly.

Kebisu came to earth suddenly. He roared: "About!" Too late, for the canoes had spitted the beach sand. The Coconut Islanders bolted backwards, reloading as they ran. Kebisu did the only thing, the wisest thing. "Charge!" he roared, and leaped ashore. "Charge! Quick, you sons of dogs, quick!"

But his warriors had received an almost supernatural shock: some stumbled up to obey, but Kebisu charged alone fair into the mouth of a second volley. He heard shrieks behind him, splintering wood, a voice screaming the fateful words: "The Lamars! The Lamars!"

Kebisu raced back. "To sea! To sea!" he roared, and swung his great strength into the launching of a canoe. More easily said than done! One third of his company down, the remainder stupefied, within the space almost of seconds! In vain Kebisu roared to his warriors to float both canoes. The dead were in the way and the wounded, unnerved at this new manner of being wounded, clung to the canoes and the out-riggers and howled.

Bullets thudded among them, but mostly whistled wide out to sea, the enemy having become so excited that their carbine muzzles were waving in the air. Shrill above the medley were the hysterical screams of the women and children hurling coral rocks at Kebisu's confused warriors.

One canoe was rushed off: Kebisu turned to rescue the other but his terrified men, howling "Lamars! Lamars!" scrambled into the canoe that was already afloat and the maddened chief was compelled to rush in after them. The sails took the wind, a bullet tore through the matting followed by another splattering rip. Then Bariki sprawled across the bows with a bullet through his head.

Screaming in their ecstasy, the Coconut Islanders rushed into the water, firing in such excitement that they forgot to reload their weapons while some even hurled them like clubs out after the fleeing canoe.

Kebisu sailed over the reef, swaying on the canoe stern, a figure of berserk rage shaking his fists at the shrieking victors behind. He raved, he snarled at his men; with vicious taunts he urged them to return now that the enemy was disorganized, and fight it out. But he realized, as he glared at their blanched faces, that his picked men had received a fatal thrashing.

The Coconut Islanders splashed back while in frenzied haste the women and children rushed the stranded canoe into the water. The men stayed only for a few minutes to club the wounded, laughing while Kebisu raved. Then, over-filled with men, the pursuing canoe set off while the overflow on the beach raced to launch their own vessels.

But Kebisu had a flying start, though he cursed the speed of his canoe that day. The greater sails of his vessel outpaced the pursuers: Some among them who had grabbed ammunition from the women, fired, and Kebisu howled as each bullet splashed the water farther and farther behind.

Kebisu the Mad, Kebisu who had lost half his men and a great canoe, and to the Coconut Islanders! Kebisu who had received his first defeat! He glared over the sea towards invisible Mer; the left side of his face as hot as fire; Kebisu, who did not know what he talked of, what he even thought of!

On Mer the people were happily excited. There was the interest of packing the trade goods, the visit of the Spirit Islanders, and the excitement of last night. For no less than thirty couples had run away into the bush. It was that dance, of course. But, well—

And now many villages were in an uproar. Angry fathers, with weapon-flourishing relations and sympathizers, hammered at the doors of the abductors.

But a something cooled the pleasant flurry on Mer, some whisper of disaster. They of the Bomai-Malu knew it first in the early morning. By midday the higher classes of the Beizam-le and the Zagareb-le knew it. In the late afternoon the noise of the villages ceased, and the people formed in speculating groups.

Something had happened, something dreadful. C'Zarcke was behaving like a hurricane unleashed. Even the Maid-le dared not enter the Zogo-house. The Sacred Grove was ominously silent. And a black cloud, seemingly now ever present over Gelam, was spreading and sinking as it spread, until it threatened to envelop the whole of Mer.

Kebisu, now in sight of Mer, held his arms to the skies as a symbol of revenge. Soon now he would have command of the canoes of Mer, of a thousand warriors; he would return on the wings of the wind and wipe out every man, woman, and child on Coconut, and every Lamar, though they possessed all the thunder weapons on the ocean.

For although Kebisu had been too desperately busy to see them, his men swore that the Lamars had sprung from "everywhere!" And the farther the canoe slipped seawards, the more Lamars had the dismayed warriors seen.

Jardine's letter to the Colonial Secretary of the day, complaining of Captain Walton having entered into treaty with and armed the Coconut Islanders, explains exactly how those gentlemen came to be armed. But as to the white men present on the date of Kebisu's disaster, they existed only in the distorted imagination of his men. Jardine himself knew but little of the real facts of the case. He did not know of Kebisu's repulse. He would have chuckled with delight, had he been told. He was only afraid of what the Coconut people would now do to any unsuspecting white vessel that might anchor beside their reef. Neither did he know that the Coconut Islanders, eager as children to try their new toy, had stolen to their old enemy the Dugong Islanders, and – having by the devil's luck and to their very great joy chosen a day when every young man was away on a turtle-hunting cruise – rounded up the main village and shot every soul in the place. Such a day the Coconut Islanders could not remember in the chequered existence of their tribe. Almost invariably they had been the hunted. To be for once the hunter was a taste of paradise that had gone to their heads, and now Kebisu the mighty had so obligingly come along with only two canoes, not in the least understanding that he was sailing into the midst of men well armed with rifles, men who had tried and gained experience of their new weapons, men who now had implicit confidence in themselves and who were frenzied at the turn of the tables and eager to try the new weapons on any living person who should come along. After Kebisu's defeat they would willingly have challenged the whole world, if only it would have come to them.

It was evening when Kebisu landed at Mer. An ominously silent crowd lined the beach. As the canoe sighed up among the shells, the people clustered around it, not talking at all, with no laughter, no calls of welcome, just waiting to see and learn. Kebisu's warriors all spoke at once, their eyes bulging while they emphasized the invincibility of the weapons, the overpowering number of the Lamars. The crowd grew more silent, gazing on the bullet-holes in the canoe and the three men dying of wounds, and they listened to others who moaned with shattered limbs. Beizam, listening with eager eyes, hid the joy that was pounding at his heart. So Kebisu, the great Kebisu, was vulnerable! And now that he had received one defeat – where might it not lead to! And Beizam, afraid that the crowd might read his thoughts, hurried away into the shadows of the palms, to walk off through the night his fever of excitement and ambition.

Kebisu waited for none of the talk of Lamars and their weapons. He pushed straight through the crowd across the beach and through the village on to the path that wound along the hill-sides to the Zogo-house, his great form doubly menacing in the dusk, his fierce resentment boiling over with what he should say to C'Zarcke – the hurried explanation, the demand for reinforcements, and then—

His eyes lighted furiously as he pictured the warriors of Mer tumbling into their avenging canoes.

At the Zogo-house a Maid-le silently admitted him. Kebisu's mouth opened for the torrent of words. It remained open.

C'Zarcke stood there. C'Zarcke the terrible! An iciness touched Kebisu's spine, for he was afraid of a man. C'Zarcke's face was distorted with passion, his terrible eyes looked as if possessed with the power of a fiend. Kebisu was fearful that this man, nay, this Zogo, was about to take his life and torment his spirit for ever.

"Cursed dog!" hissed the priest. "Why did you not let me know that you were going to make the raid?"

Kebisu was speechless.

"Brainless clod," snarled C'Zarcke, "what think you your puny club can do against the mystery weapons of the Lamars? You are fighting the very gods, until we understand them. Idiot! You put aside the brains of the Zogo-le and risk the future of all the Island peoples. And at the very time that the people are becoming unnerved at the Lamars you pile fear on fear; you know the essence of our plan, that every Island group must unite against the Lamars and then patiently wait while we see and learn. It is our one hope of survival. The people, and such as you – wonder that you think yourself to be – have no knowledge, and it is with brains alone that we may fight the Lamars. And now you help to spread the helpless terror which we know will end all chance of unity and discipline. Far worse, you have destroyed the one great chance that the Lamars gave us: for they taught the Coconut Islanders the secret of their weapons; the Islanders could have been prevailed upon to teach us, and we should have been on equal terms with the Lamars."

Menacingly he stepped towards Kebisu. "Cursed pig," he cried, "why did you not first submit your intentions to the Council of the Zogo-le?"

Kebisu was speechless. C'Zarcke pointed to the door. "Go!" he thundered, "and count yourself wondrously lucky that you are a fool who has his place in the scheme of things."

And Kebisu went.

CANE CUIRASS, NEW GUINEA
(Native armour against arrows.)

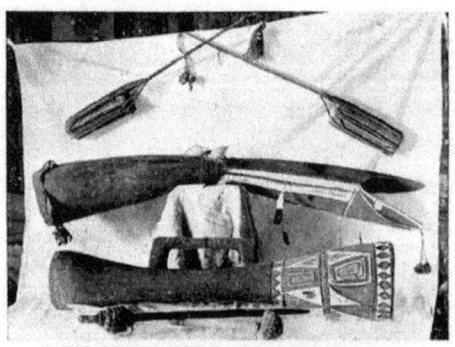

KADIK GUARDS, DRUMS, AND PINEAPPLE CLUB

CHAPTER XIX

The Sailor Of The Fleet

It was the night before the sailing. Such a quiet night, such a quiet people. Surely they could not have dreamed that this would be the last great fleet to sail from Mer! And this the last Dance of the Skulls! And that soon would come the last time when the *booya* would flash upon the Eastern Islands nation! The people vaguely feared calamity in the coming of the Lamars. C'Zarcke read the sails upon the sea, his was the breadth of vision, the great understanding, and he possessed a psychic power which is only now being realized by our advanced thinkers. C'Zarcke saw the inevitable passing of his people, and with them the uncompleted knowledge which had taken the strivings of generations of Zogo-le to attain.

The people rested upon those sacred grounds which were taboo except during this one night of the year. In massed formation they faced a black cliff enveloped by the shadow of Gelam. Jakara had never satisfactorily solved just how this dance was managed. He imagined the details. But even now he experienced the weirdness, almost terror, which this dance had inspired in him during his first years on the island. He strained forward to see and understand just what properties of the imperceptibly changing moonlight the cunning Zogo-le made use of in this masterpiece of deception.

The cliff had a natural stage of rock some five feet above the ground. Then rose the cliff, which at fifty feet sloped outward and upward, leaning over the stage to rise a hundred feet sheer, and finally bend in again and slope on up the mountain. Jakara thought that the moon's rays at some particular time struck the topmost wall and was reflected down under the roof to strike the rock forming the back of the stage. Straight along this rock at the height of a man's head ran a ledge jutting out some six inches. Jakara felt sure that to catch the moonlight playing on this ledge helped in the secret of the dance. And yet all through the performance the face of the rock never varied from an inky black, cross-shadowed by grey. He had never been able to decide emphatically how the Zogo-le danced the puppets.

To-night there were present many Black Feathers. For this was a sacred dance of the Bomai-Malu, to be witnessed in a spirit of intense reverence. To the ordinary people it represented a Malu dance, for none save the highest in rank dared more than whisper the sacred name of Bomai. Bomai was the "secret" name, Malu the cloak for it. It was Bomai to whom the people prayed when in sore distress, Bomai, apparently son of Ad Giz, "the God of the very beginning of things." Jakara knew that the great Au-gud was but the emblem of Bomai; it was something definite that the uneducated people could reverence, believing it to be the vehicle of that Power which they could not understand nor see, but which directed life.

Jakara sat among the front row of Black Feathers. Behind him sat the Beizam-boai and the Zagareb-le, then all the people according to their rank, class, and district. Fronting the Black Feathers were the Maid-le, in two standing groups with the big baskets arranged symbolically between them. Fronting them again, stood the three Zogo-le. C'Zarcke wore the monstrous Bomai mask. The other two of the Zogo-le wore the mask of Malu. At a sign from C'Zarcke the Maid-le took from a special basket sixty skulls. These had once belonged to noted men. The Maid-le carried them to the rock platform, placed them all at equal distances upon the jutting ledge, and then retired. The onlookers drew an audible breath, gazing at the obscure skulls which so unappreciatively returned their stare. After ten minutes of tension, Jakara felt almost certain that the greyness of the skulls was becoming distinctly white, while the black greyness of the rock became more vague and shadowy. As he strained forward, a faint unearthly music floated down from the mountain over the crowd. Jakara heard it distinctly, and yet felt that, if he did not strain his ears, he would lose the fleeting sound. He felt that, if all the spectators together did not concentrate to hear, then collectively they must lose the sound. Jakara had never seen the instruments which breathed that music. He knew well the bamboo flutes and reed instruments that crooned such plaintive music at certain of the ceremonial dances, and he guessed that these instruments must be delicately made of similar materials.

Presently, as if in recognition after death, the skulls faced towards one another; then, nodding a mocking acknowledgment of the spectators, they floated through the air and lined up on the platform as if possessed of invisible bodies. Jakara could distinctly see the rock; there was no mummery – and yet there *must* be. The skulls formed into four rows of fifteen. The silence was acute; Jakara's skin crept. They danced a triumph to Bomai, because through him had Death been overcome. For death was life. They swayed in unison from side to side, and bowed towards the floor as if their vanished finger-tips coldly touched the rock. With dreadfully accurate rhythmic movement they pirouetted from side to side, to front and rear, then bowed again, to float erect and glide on with the dance – and with what a sneering expression, in what lifelike time to the whispering music! Presently, standing motionless some twenty yards back and in line with the natural stage, C'Zarcke held the *booya* longitudinally towards it. Immediately a circle of greenish-blue light flamed up, to dissolve in the sky. While he thus held the *booya*, its rays fanned up so that the audience were staring through a curtain of greenish light. Jakara glanced to where the curtain spread up with its rays like that of a setting sun flowering the crest of Gelam. He spied on the dancers, for this part also interested him intensely. Though the rock was quite distinguishable, it was now of a colour unrecognizable, as if the light sprayed upon it some property forcing the impression that the rock was slowly creeping. Plainly, and yet waveringly, now stood out the dancing skulls, the strange light not only playing upon, but gripping, the bone. Devilishly lifelike appeared their eyes as the jet-black pupils swam menacingly in the irradiation of the pearl-shell disks.

The music sighed into silence, but the dancers swayed vehemently on with a keen impression of enjoyment. Finally the lines stayed motionless for some minutes, then the second and third line wafted themselves to right and left of the front line. Minutes later, the two rear lines formed up on the flanks, making one straight line. Minutes later again, the complete line, still facing the spectators, floated back to the ledge and grinned in deathly silence.

The *booya* flashed out. The dance was over. A sigh of intense relief rose from the people. The Maid-le walked quietly forward, collected the skulls, and carefully cradled them in their basket. The priests then grouped together and remained statuesque.

It was the signal. A strange noise like the rustling of a million leaves as everyone stood up. Quietly they dissolved in vanishing groups, all making towards their different villages. There was not even a whimper from a child. The Zogo-le, the Maid-le, and the main heads of the Bomai-Malu alone remained.

Jakara sought out Eyes of the Sea, though he knew there would be very little talk on the way homeward. Always this dance had the effect of making talk distasteful to the people; somehow each individual wished to think within himself and remain secluded until the light of another day.

Sunlight, and the chatter of birds. Waves, with a rolling hint of strength, smacked the shores of Mer. Circling seabirds, at the height of the palms, were gracefully confident of a good day's fishing. Every man, woman, and child on the island thronged the main beach, huzzaing towards the fleet. Up shot the big brown sails, the bows creamed, and to rollicking song and echoing farewells the fleet sailed.

Yet the boisterousness was much less noticeable than in former years; also the fleet was smaller. There was a seriousness, an anxiousness, oppressing the people. That confident farewell which anticipated the triumphal return was missing. Instead, parents seemed loth to part with sons, whereas before it had been an honour to be picked to sail with the fleet. Jakara, waving a laughing farewell from the platform of the *Skull Chief,* stared with upraised arm as he saw the face of the Pretty Lamar smiling to him from the beach. In that moment he realized what the smile cost her. She waved palm-leaves, waved to him alone. Feeling suddenly unhappy, he answered.

Kebisu, very glad to be away, headed for the open sea and Eroob. Never once did the big chief look back. C'Zarcke was overlooking the fleet from high up in the Zogo-house. Kebisu shivered. His trouncing at the hands of the Coconut Islanders was a bitter, bitter disgrace for him. But when he thought of C'Zarcke's words, he felt like diving overboard deep down to depths from which he could never return. That Kebisu, Mamoose of Tutu, Conqueror of the Strait, Chief of Western New Guinea, should have to swallow such words! They represented, of course, not the scorn of a man, for C'Zarcke was a Zogo possessed of powers which could affect the destiny of a man's spirit after death. Kebisu knew that he could thrash Mer if he so desired, and Eroob and Ugar, too, if it were only a matter of fight, but the terrible reputation and spiritual power of this priest could wither Kebisu the great Mamoose and all his material power. Kebisu tried to brush the unalterable from his mind, then snarled. Not at the memory of C'Zarcke – at that he dared not snarl – but at the knowledge that he commanded only twenty canoes from Mer. Such a puny number had not been known to leave Mer for the yearly trade within the memory of man. True, the goods were packed to the gunwales and the platforms were lashed high with goods and food-stuffs, so that the big crews found it awkward to find a place to cling to.

A steady south-easter bellied the sails and danced the giant canoes towards the north-west. Eyes of the Sea laughed for the very joy of life. She was very happy now, returning to Tutu to her people. Jakara intended to take her back on the homeward voyage, and was determined that afterwards the first sail of the returning Lamars that should come near Mer would take them off and away to civilization, whether the girl would or no.

So he lazily ate bananas and clung with practised toes to the bulwarks of the outrigger platform, leaning back against the pile of food-stuffs on top of which the girl was perched. She laughed at his jokes and, when he was not looking, leaned over and dropped scarlet necklace berries on his brown hair. Presently all gazed in surprise, for upon the shark-jaw bows of the next canoe stood a splendid figure of a man who, as his vessel suddenly shot out from the line as if to cross the bows of the *Skull Chief*, dived into the sea and with powerful strokes swam towards them almost with the speed of a shark. Grasping the outrigger, he swung himself up on to the platform and leapt in a shower of spray up beside Eyes of the Sea. At the sound of his ringing laugh all joined in, for what can be more infectious than the joy of life and youth and strength and laughter?

Kebisu did not laugh: he stared amazed while Beizam openly made love to Eyes of the Sea. Beizam was now second in command of a canoe and expected soon to captain his own, but thus to leave his post was an unprecedented crime. The eyes of the big Mamoose were rolling mad: his teeth gritted, the left side of his face blushed a blood-red. He roared like a bull and crashed across the platform. Sullenly Beizam dived. A silence fell on the canoes. And Jakara began to remember. He had welcomed Beizam's swift swim as a joke, but why had the man left his command to make love to Eyes of the Sea? It looked as if this joke was deliberately planned. Jakara remembered then many strange glances from Beizam at Eyes of the Sea. Why, the fellow always seemed to have his eyes on her. Jakara now remembered other things: words of disgust and hate against the Lamars which he had overheard from whispering groups; and dark, meaning looks in his direction. Jakara put two and two together. This had begun definitely about the time of the trip to Murralug, just after all those whispers about the shadow of the Lamars. Since then, the hostile, ill-defined feeling had steadily grown. He had hardly noticed it, so delighted was he with thoughts of the quick spread of his countrymen, so full was his mind of Eyes of the Sea.

For the first time for many months, the old dreadful feeling stole over him. What if he lost his head after all! What if Eyes of the Sea—? He clasped the girl's arm with a warmth of feeling. She smiled tenderly. Jakara determined to watch, to see and hear by day and night, and craftily to break away at the earliest opportunity from this ever-present threat of death.

Beizam's heart, as he gazed out across the sea, was an inferno of passion. To be thus roared at, to be compelled to give way – and in front of the allied warriors! To be bullied by the Mamoose of another race! Might the curses of the demon world fall on this one-eared pig of Tutu! Beizam's eyes were bulging while silently and deeply he cursed this man who had organized and led a band of warriors powerful enough to browbeat even Mer. But there surely would come a day—!

Presently he grew frightened. What if Kebisu should rescind his command! The big Mamoose was undisputed commander-in-chief, and would certainly leave Beizam without compunction at Tutu, if his anger had not calmed down by then. A cold fear of icy disappointment as strong as his previous passion, took possession of Beizam. He felt that he would die of shame if deprived of his place in the fleet. He made up his mind to placate Kebisu quickly in every possible way.

Then came a mad fury against those two cursed Lamars. They were the cause of all his troubles, the cause of – everything! Jakara the Fighter, a hero of Mer – far worse, his brains had made him a pet of the Zogo-le. The beloved of the Pretty Lamar!

Beizam sprang up, then knelt down hurriedly, as if tightening an outrigger strut. All eyes throughout the nearer portion of the fleet were, he knew, covertly watching him.

When he calmed down again, he gazed out to sea – smiling. But his brain was racing with clever thoughts. Why was Jakara invincible? Was he? Beizam would watch, and make sure! Jakara was only a man – even though his sword of marvellous metal was terrible. Beizam felt his chest expanding, his muscles swelling. He drew a deep breath. He would like to have Jakara alone, without weapons, and crush him in his two splendid arms. Then he began to think again, and to plan coolly and well ahead.

When they were passing Eroob, fifteen canoes sailed out and joined the flotilla. The men of Mer cheered, and sang their welcoming songs. The *boo* shells brayed from the hill-sides, which were covered with people. But Kebisu scowled. Fifteen miserable canoes!

At evenfall they glided up the beach of Ugar. The people were ready with the feast, and had manned ten loaded canoes. Maros was there in great fettle, resplendent in towering head-dress and crescent *mai*, nursing his pet *gaba-gaba* in the crook of his arm. He laughed, and rallied Kebisu on his solemn face. Maros, the Ugar people's idol, a thorough-paced scoundrel, a bad man! Beizam smiled with a quick joke at Maros's expense. For the ugly chief wore, conspicuously chained round his neck, his love-stick. This was of Wongai wood carved to a certain design, and in Maros's case carrying plentiful notches. Each notch on a love-stick represented a man's conquest of a girl. The Strait Islanders were very proud of these records; they are so to this day – especially the wives, for, the more notches on her husband's "stick," the prouder the wife for having bound such a terror in the bonds of matrimony. After death, it is the love-stick that the widow keeps for remembrance of her husband: the little ornament signifying so much is always buried with her.

Maros took the joke in good part. Smiling-eyed girls were pressing close around him, all surrounded by grinning warriors. He twisted his love-stick within his luxuriant beard and roared that he would not return until the nicks were as many as the hairs on his chin.

Next day they sailed past Campbell Island, and Damut and Umagar, and other pleasant isles, and at late afternoon sped within sight of the most famous, and most dreaded coral islet of the Strait surrounded by dark green mangroves and waving palm-tops. This was Tutu, called by white men Warrior Island, on which dwelt the fiercest and most determined tribesmen in all Torres Strait. The canoes glided along the edge of the great Warrior Reefs and slipped into the little channel which has given to this tiny island such a strategic advantage. The beach was thronged with roaring warriors, and many women quite as demonstrative. Shadowed behind the crowd stood the tall Maid-le. Kebisu frowned as he noted questioning eyes searching his own canoe. For the first time in his life he dreaded his home-coming.

As the canoes grounded, Kebisu's vessel was rushed. "Where is the *Raider?*" cried many voices. Kebisu shrugged his great shoulders and without a word walked right through the crowd towards the village. "Where is Arus?" screamed a woman.

Imoki reached down into the canoe and fished up a cleaned skull. He placed it in the arms of the mother. "Oh Nari, Nari!" wailed a wife. His skull was placed in her arms.

The father of Ramaru held out a dumb hand.

The wife of Deboro screamed when she received his skull, but the sweetheart of Vulala gazed at hers silently.

But more bitter was the wailing of those whose loved ones had been left behind on Coconut Island.

"Their spirits have flown to the Isle of the Blest," said Toik gruffly; "we that are here are all that are left."

Softly there arose the wail for the dead, taken up by mother after mother, sweetheart after sweetheart – a mournful sound, rising and falling, rising to sob almost to silence, to wail out pitifully as a mother bowed her head and cried to Bomai for her son.

Beizam, watching this people's distress, his ears alert, laughed happily but silently at the Tutu warriors' quiet dismay at this first deep blow to their Island pride, this first disillusionment as to the invincibility of their idol. The women wailed throughout the village, but the men of Tutu, in sullen groups apart from the men of Mer, Eroob, and Ugar, stood along the beach, or among the mangrove shadows. To these in turn Beizam quietly went, with the most careful regard to etiquette, sympathizing with them as warrior with warriors: Beizam, young chief and proved fighting-man: Beizam, son of the Mamoose of Mer: Beizam "The Shark."

Up in his village house Kebisu cursed deep, walking the bamboo floor with the tread of a tiger. "What omen is this?" he snarled to the smoke-browned roof, "The start of the voyage, and they greet me with the wail for the dead!"

That night Jakara, coiled upon his sleeping-mat in Kebisu's house, sought sleep in vain. For above the sighing of the palms came continuously that haunting dirge, women's voices rising and falling under the moon, crying back the spirits from the dead.

MAINO, SON OF THE GREAT KEBISU, LAST MAMOOSE OF TUTU AND YAM
(Holding his father's famous *gaba-gaba*.)

CHAPTER XX

The Looting Of The Lamar Ship

Dawn saw the beehive astir. C'Zarcke had warned Kebisu not to waste the favourable weather, and Kebisu was anxious for the open sea. He felt that he could hardly breathe here, for he had brought home the skulls of his first defeat.

Almost at the breath of dawn there echoed a thunderous crash – and an excited howl from the beach: "Lamar-Nar! Lamar-Nar!" (A spirit ship! A spirit ship!)

Men snatched weapons and rushed seawards. Women grabbed children and stared wildly through the mangroves. Jakara instantly sought for Eyes of the Sea. Were the whites about to attack the place? A triumphant shout reassured him. He raced for the beach. Warriors were tumbling into canoes. When clear of the mangroves, he saw five large surf-boats, their people pulling desperately, while others were frantically rigging masts. Jakara's heart almost wept blood. He understood why those people were straining their hearts out at the oars, he could realize the agony in the hearts of the women as they clung to little white children. He turned to throw himself at Kebisu's feet, to hold fast to the man, to beg for the lives of his countrymen, to kill him if necessary. But Kebisu was already in his canoe.

Jakara sprang into the water, screaming at Kebisu to stop. The Lamars, directed by an officer in the bows of the leading boat, were shouting with united voices the one word "Ship! Ship!" and pointing. Jakara looked. Fast on the reef was a big three-masted ship, all sails set; but the foremast had snapped and now hung overboard in a confusion of ropes and sails.

Jakara instantly guessed: his countrymen were praying that the natives would rush the vessel for loot and thus afford them one forlorn hope. Jakara ceased swimming, and drew breath to ease his panting heart: he screamed to the warriors to tell them of the rich loot awaiting them aboard ship. Already the bait was drawing. Every canoe was racing out towards the prize, confident that they would overtake the castaways when they wished. As the canoes definitely headed for the vessel, Jakara raised trembling arms to the sky, crying and laughing. A little brown girl swam out beside him, all blue eyes and wonderment. Jakara ducked her, and swung her high out of the water, pointing: "Look there! Look! No, not at those cursed cannibals! Look at those boats, at your own countrymen and women and children! See, every boat has hoisted a sail, and see, each is feeling the wind! If those niggers will only maul that ship about for half an hour, all those white people will be saved. They will have such a start that they will never be caught."

Excitedly he laughed to the girl. She was quite silent. "Aren't you glad, Eyes of the Sea?" he demanded. "Wouldn't you rather see your white brothers and sisters sailing safely away than see their dripping heads thrown on this beach? Wouldn't you?"

"They are Lamars!" said the girl quietly.

Jakara dropped her. "Lamars!" he shouted, "*I* am a Lamar. *You* are a Lamar. Haven't you got any human feelings at all? Are you just as much nigger as those black swine you call your parents?"

The girl's eyes blazed: she turned into a mad thing of the wilds. "You miserable Lamar!" she hissed, "I shall see *your* head thrown on the beach yet! When Beizam comes back I will get him to club you before he sails out after the other Lamars."

She swam back to the excited crowd on the beach, leaving Jakara speechless. Kebisu's canoes neared the ship. She was wedged firmly upon the reef. Nimbly the warriors climbed the towering sides, laughing like schoolboys to whom has fallen a heavenly prize. They rushed across the decks, but stood as if petrified when a man leaped up the broad companion-way, a wee man, all brown hair, clasping a coconut under one sinewy arm. He glared angrily at the invaders out of two bright brown eyes, then with a hoarse bark of rage raced across the deck and swung up the mainmast with a skill and speed never possessed by humankind.

With a patter of feet the warriors sprang overboard. There were splashes and gaspings and coughs as they plunged from the water and fought for paddles. Kebisu, the one man left on deck, keeping his eyes aloft, edged superstitiously towards the rail. Angrily he called to the fleeing warriors, but they were yelling to those coming on that "the spirit of the ship" was loose!

Kebisu had run only once in his life, but he was sore pressed again. Only one man in all the world did he fear – C'Zarcke! But this was not a man, it was a spirit, an evil one, and what human being can contend against the powers of evil? He stepped aside to the rail, shook his fist at the clustering canoes, and roared for them all to return aboard. They noted his red ear, and so, between the devil and the deep sea, a hesitating few dipped their paddles – when instantly the thing in the yard-arm screeched a stream of foreign curses. It shook its fist at them in maniacal fury. Kebisu found himself half over the rail, glaring up at this man that was not a man. When the thing quieted a little, Kebisu ferociously beckoned to his own favourite bodyguard. They, singled out from all the rest, much ashamed but abjectly frightened, paddled nervously to the ship's side. Beizam, from his canoe away back among the cluster, suddenly sprang overboard, and with long powerful strokes rapidly overhauled the *Skull Chief*. He clambered aboard, laughing, and, standing in the bows, shouted the warriors onward in a bravado of good fellowship. The thing up above careered along the yard-arm, sneering at them, but saying nothing.

Gingerly the warriors climbed the vessels' sides, Beizam in the lead. Immediately that the first scared head poked itself above – "Bang!" and a simultaneous crash, as sixty men hit the water. Kebisu found himself clinging to the rail by his fingers and a foot. Too bewildered to recall the fleeting canoe, he cowered, looking up at the triumphant thing that gibbered from the yard-arm, running along at that great height as if independent of a hold, swinging by its tail, and chuckling in fantastic glee. Kebisu's braves had heard of New Guinea hillmen who grew tails, but this was the first man they had ever seen wearing one. They stared aghast, expecting every second that the devil thing would transform itself into a malignant demon.

Kebisu regained his breath. He concluded that, so long as the thing only threw a coconut, no harm could be done. He drew himself up in a dignified fashion, then step by step advanced warily across the deck, with his eyes turned up to where the chuckling thing was now indulging in ribald sentiments. It was enjoying itself mightily, shaking its fists and screaming at the huddled canoes three bowshots away. Maros was pummelling his warriors with fists, feet, and tongue, but when he roared among them with swinging *gaba-gaba* they sullenly turned the *Headhunter* towards the ship. Beizam, trying to cover up his fright by bawling at the Tutu warriors, urged them forward again. Kebisu resolutely shrugged his shoulders, strode heavily across the deck, and roared again to his picked crew. Under the sting of his reproofs they paddled hesitantly forward, gliding along beside the canoe of Maras. The thing above displayed interest. It scampered to the extreme end of the yard-arm, adding its harangue of stinging invective to the hoarse insults of Kebisu.

Fearfully both crews climbed the vessel's side, Beizam noticeably in the lead. He hopped smiling over the rail as Kebisu snatched the first man's wrist, while Maras got a vicious "half-Nelson" on a Ugar man. The cowering wretches were flung across the deck while the chiefs threatened them with clubs, Beizam shouting across the water to the men of Mer to "Come on! Come on!" The men stared up in abject fear. The Mamooses seized two more, and were encored by appreciative clapping from above.

In knee-knocking fear the warriors grouped together. Throwing out his chest, Kebisu strode across the deck shoulder to shoulder with Maras, Beizam advancing deferentially behind. Finding themselves alone, the chiefs turned, and with berserk howls rushed upon their warriors, who scattered like frightened sheep, to the delighted jabbering of the fiend above. Kebisu mustered his braves and faced them towards the mainmast, while the club of Maros threatened the stragglers from the rear, Beizam advancing proudly as the lone man of Mer. At each faltering step, the devil above worked itself into demoniacal fury. It even somersaulted by its tail and shrieked at them while swinging upside down. Finally it turned its back and made the most insulting gestures.

But the turning away of its hairy, bright-eyed little face was its undoing. Beizam's bow twanged, and the monkey screamed, a five-foot arrow through its body. It turned an agonized face towards them. shook its tiny fists, and slowly toppled over. The warriors dropped their weapons and rushed overside. to be brought up short by Kebisu's roar. The monkey's tail had caught a rope, and it hung half-way up the mast, but only for a second, and then it fell with a swift thump at the feet of Kebisu, gazing up with accusing, dying eyes.

Minutes of tense silence: the thing was dead! It had not transformed itself into a vengeful being! Kebisu's men rattled their weapons and stamped the deck in the triumph-song. From the water echoed a roar as the canoes raced for the ship. In an instant its broad decks were swarming with men: pandemonium broke loose. They smashed the deck-houses and squabbled over the wonderful things inside. Maros became greatly annoyed when he tried to crawl into a woman's garment upside down: the pink lace caught in his beard and nearly choked him. Kebisu took command. With his now brave warriors pressing behind him, he paraded below decks and found himself descending a broad carpeted stairway. The silence below brought back a touch of nerves. They trod gingerly with their big bare feet, making for the saloon, though they did not know it. The stairs turned round a bend, and Kebisu fell over himself in the effort to jump backwards: his head loosened Maros's teeth, while Beizam nearly fainted with fright. Instant panic spread: the men threw one another backwards, struggling for the open air, while the hundreds descending behind, not understanding, pressed the mob forward into hysterical confusion.

Kebisu, on peering around the corner, had seen a huge savage sneaking towards him with murderous intent! With threatening club and blood-curdling whispers Kebisu rallied his nervous men. Shoulder to shoulder they crept back down the stairs, weapons poised, chests heaving, thirsting to commit atrocities on these sharks who would steal their prey.

Vengefully Kebisu peered round the corner. Yes, there he was – a heathen with a thunderstorm face brandishing his *gaba-gaba* and glaring like a crouching baboon. He had no ear on one side, but the other was indisputable. Kebisu bared his teeth: his antagonist showed his: each twitched the remaining ear, while the opposite side of the face grew desperately red. Kebisu crept forward, viciously swaying his club. The huge savage did likewise, promising bloody murder. Then Kebisu hopped back upon somebody's toes – hurriedly, for two fierce savages had momentarily glared over his antagonist's shoulder: one of them was the image of Maros. Kebisu had never had such a fright in his life. He snarled abuse at his warriors in his relief when the strangers disappeared. "What turtle-backed devils had come over his men! Ducking back like women in a thunderstorm!" Kebisu rapidly spoke unprintable things, and one side of his face reddened again. His harangue cleared the air. Maros breathed heavily: he had caught just one glimpse of the ugliest man he had ever seen. He almost felt scared; he gripped his club menacingly.

There was going to be a fight! A bloody fight! The air fairly hummed with it. These savages had sneaked the ship that was rightfully theirs: what number were they? Kebisu neither knew nor cared. He snarled at his warriors to cluster around, to charge when he charged. Maros was ready to single out just one man: he twisted the thong of his *gaba-gaba* until it bit into his muscular wrist: the order of the fight was hissed up the stairway: the air became electrical. The crowds on deck packed down the stairway, and their pressure spilled the leading forty warriors into the saloon. Instantly they roared a war-cry to the tune of clashing weapons. Before them forty warriors crouched in open-mouthed defiance, flourishing clubs, setting arrows to bows, shouting, though their shouts made no noise. Kebisu's roar shook the saloon. He charged: his warriors charged: all charged. Hundreds tore down the stairway; clubs whirled; arrows whizzed; a *doab* thrummed. There was one grand ear-splitting "crash!" A million splinters sparkled through the air.

Instant silence. Petrified warriors gazed into the empty walls of the saloon. Amid the heavy breathing a dreadful, superstitious fear gripped them all. Their enemies had vanished – disappeared into the air! Slowly Kebisu reached out his hand towards a splinter of glass. He gazed earnestly into it, then laughed. It was a weak little laugh, but then everything was unnatural on this accursed ship. "It is the Lamars' 'see-my-face,'" growled Kebisu. "Look! It is what they shave in."

Gingerly the warriors crowded round. They stared at the glass; they examined pieces. An odd man broke into a chuckle which confirmed

Kebisu's guess. Beizam laughed a loud unnatural "haw, haw!" Soon they were laughing like relieved children. A shame that those fine ships' mirrors had been smashed into ten thousand fragments!

Then started the exciting work of raiding the ship; but they went steadily and quietly until convinced that there was not a soul on board but themselves. Two severe shocks were enough for superstitious people.

In the meantime, on the beach at Tutu, a man stood watching the fleeing sails of his compatriots' boats. He sighed with relief; the sails were visible now only as handkerchiefs. What treasures were in that ship! Casks and cases and bags; bales and boxes without end, carried up to the deck with shouting and laughter to be smashed until the broad decks were littered two-feet deep with salted meat and sugar, salt and potatoes, clothes and onions and bed linen, and a thousand and one mysteries that the Lamar carried in his ships. Many were the contemptuous guesses at the foolish Lamar things spilled on deck. The raiders spat upon broken chests of tea, and dressed their big black or brown figures in the queerest of ways with dresses and bedclothes and curtains. As they waded ankle-deep through spilled flour, they laughed contemptuously at the Lamar men's foolishness in bagging up "ashes." The rice they mistook for ants' eggs, but they claimed as a treasure some big fat barrels of soap. The women swam out to the ship, and the soap was handed to them with grave instructions just how to cook it. Back on the beach the women broke it all up, and, wrapping it tenderly in young banana-leaves, placed the packages in the *kop-maori* ovens to roast.

As the sun went down, Kebisu's canoes unwillingly pulled away from the ship. Every canoe was crammed with a motley cargo. The big Mamoose would have dearly loved a week aboard that ship, but he dreaded C'Zarcke's anger. If the wind should change to the north-west, as was likely any day, the delay might be disastrous to their trade voyage, and Kebisu could not have faced the consequences. He compelled the men to feast and work alternately all through the night, finding room somehow in the already overpacked canoes for much of the looted goods. He would return with a better trade than C'Zarcke expected, and Kebisu very much desired C'Zarcke's favour again.

Amid the heat of their labours a smiling girl brought Maros a junk of roast soap, tastily served on a banana-leaf. He winked and bit off a great mouthful. At the astounded expression on his face, Jakara broke into joyous laughter. Some seconds later, both he and the serving girl were fleeing for their lives. The laughter was hilarious until others of Kebisu's greediest braves began to foam at the mouth.

Just after daylight the flotilla, reinforced by seven canoes of Kebisu's arrogant fighting-men, sailed for Boigu – not Boigu Isle of the Blest, but a low-lying island just off the south-western New Guinea coast.

CHAPTER XXI

The Raid Of The Tugeri

From Tutu, Kebisu sailed north-west for Boigu, the flotilla passing Giaka Island, then Muka to the south, then Gaba. It was a breezy day, with the warriors in rollicking humour over looting the Lamar ship and in gleeful anticipation of completing the job when they returned. Time sped merrily in songs of love and fight. Maros, having spat out the last of the soap from between his teeth, was bursting with energy, and his lusty love-songs received a whole-hearted chorus away down through the fleet.

But Jakara had been deeply hurt by the scornful face and bitter words of Eyes of the Sea, and now the insinuating smiles of Beizam embittered the ache at his heart. He felt hopeless of ever teaching the girl that she was white; her environment was too strong. Leave a baby angel among savages, and it must grow up tainted; and this blue-eyed savage was no angel. Jakara wished miserably that he had never seen her, had never heard of her. He could have taken his freedom, and wealth too, long ago but for her. By staying he was risking his very head. Was she worth it? He was beginning to doubt.

Before midday the massive hill of Dauan loomed skyward, straight from the sea. In early afternoon the great grey rocks were plainly visible, hugging its shrubby sides. Shortly afterwards, like a monster grey cloud pressing the sea, appeared the island of Sabai. For diplomatic reasons Kebisu stood clear of that hornets' nest. Then Jakara saw the coast of New Guinea, limitless miles of trees, with columns of smoke ascending inland and betraying either many villages or hunting-parties. A big, flat, grey-green land from this particular approach, a mysterious land, and within the unknown interior invisible mountains raised snow-caps to the heavens.

Jakara began to recover his spirits; the voyage began to savour now of interesting things. Towards sundown they espied Boigu as a flat grey cloud, water-spattered. Sailing level with the New Guinea coast, the flotilla melted into the cloud, which enveloped them when they came to the four islands almost embracing one another as if for mutual protection. Jakara had never seen such a thick growth of trees, nor such luxuriantly tall mangroves. Cruising among these twisting waterways to locate the big village of Boigu was a difficult task to those who did not know. The feathery tips of the palms, after a twist in the waterway, finally betrayed its position.

The flotilla came to rest on the low tide. The warriors jumped out, and, knee-deep in blue mud, pulled the heavily laden canoes as near to the mangroves as possible. A crowd of excited people plunged out towards them, carrying long mangrove stakes. To these the canoes were tied.

Jakara studied these folk interestedly. Not so heavily built as the men of Mer, they were agile fellows with woollier hair, like the Papuans. Intellectually they were a much lower class than the Eastern Group Islanders. Jakara was puzzled to notice among them a scattering of natives almost white, much resembling the Samoans. The majority were nearly black.

All was bustle as the sun went down. Along the grass-grown sand which runs by, the mangrove edge numerous *kop-maori* ovens were smoking, and the smell was appetizing. Here one half of Kebisu's force sat down to eat, supplying much of their own food, as was necessary with such a large force. The remainder followed the villagers through the trees, among which loomed portions of a mighty circular stockade. Jakara was delighted. He was in a new country, among a different people practising interesting customs. The stockade was made of rows of large mangrove poles, with the points sharpened. All were lashed together into an impenetrable barrier by twisted cables of lawyer-cane. The stockade leaned sharply outwards, defying the most agile palm-climber to scale it: the sharpened ends were fourteen feet above the ground. The walls were loopholed for arrow-fire, otherwise there was not even a crack in that massive stockade that a man might peep through.

The surrounding country was flat and swampy, sombre with gnarled trees, low and peculiar-looking, with odd giants that reared rugged limbs high above their fellows. Farther out, beyond the little swamps, were low hills which were practically only mounds. The night opened to a deafening chorus of frogs.

Jakara could see nothing of what might be inside the stockade. He pressed forward curiously with the crowd that were shouldering between the beams of the one narrow gateway, guarding his eyes against the cruel barbs of the nasty weapons, and sneezing violently when his nose was tickled by the flowing plumes of a chief's head-dress.

Night came like a falling blanket. Inside the stockade, Jakara stared at packed houses built high on piles, some exceptional buildings being two-storied. Made of grass and palm-leaves, they were built well back from the stockade walls, so that from outside the strongest bowman could not shoot a flaming arrow into the dry fibre of the roofs.

Pandanus torches flared inside the stockade. Then even Jakara was startled, for in the centre of the village stood (and stands to-day) a huge gnarled tree with scaly reddish bark and broad green leaves, its trunk covered with knobby protuberances. Far up its butt it spread into two massive limbs. Most of the side branches were kept chopped off, enough being left of each branch to form a stout peg. On every such peg, as if on a hat-rack of civilization, was a gleaming skull. It was only in 1927 that the Anglican missionary nailed to this dreadful tree a plate inscribed "Sibui Pui" (The Tree of Skulls). The tree now shadows the little palm-thatched church in which the missionary teaches.

Jakara, carrying himself as a chief of importance, sat upon the handsome guest-mat with Kebisu and Maros. Bogo had remained in charge of the company on the beach behind. For the guests of honour pigs had been roasted whole, and the flavour added keenness to Jakara's sea-livened appetite. He set to hungrily, and did not spare the roast sweet potatoes and yams and roast bananas. He washed it down thirstily with coconut-milk, and at last sighed contentedly as he lolled back in comfort. His comrades would eat methodically for an hour yet.

Inside the stockade were packed busy groups eating hungrily. They were almost quiet, except that now and then some joking warrior would cause a torrent of laughter among mischievous-eyed girls. In scurrying crowds were pot-bellied children, all clamouring for their share, the boys hurrying off, clutching a chunk of yam, to touch with reverence some particularly murderous club among the weapons scattered upon the ground. Quite unexpectedly the flare of the torches dimmed as a light flooded the stockade. Jakara glimpsed a silver tracery on the tree-tops of the outside world, with the blue velvet sky in between. Then a swimming moon floated up the heavens. Something else caught Jakara's eye, for in the centre of the stockade, high in the air, was a clump of moon-bathed houses. They were built high up in giant trees, and the black shadows of the houses now blotched the diners below. Big houses they were, with strong platforms around them supporting little pyramids of stones. Drooping from each house was a slender ladder of lawyer-cane.

"What are those?" asked Jakara, in delighted surprise.

Kebisu was gnawing a dugong bone. He grunted: "Houses. In trees. Protection against the Tugeri. The people here climb up to save their heads."

"What are the Tugeri? Where do they come from?"

"Savages. Nearly as ignorant as the South Land savages. They do not understand the Dance of Death. They only take the heads. They smoke-dry them; they mutilate the dead too, women as well as men. They do not understand the life after death, either; they believe that they live again when they die, but they cannot understand that we progress to greater things. They come from New Guinea-somewhere away up the Kussa rivers. They sneak down in canoes, pulling themselves along by the mangrove branches, using a sago-palm pole in deeper water. They do it very fast and quietly, like shadows of the night. They have to sneak by many villages on the way. When they get to the river-mouth their troubles begin, for they have five miles of sea-shallows to cross, and their canoes are only river canoes. If a sea springs up, they drown! If a strong current catches them, they are swept out to sea and we collect their heads! They hate the Boigu people, and have done so ever since Ad Giz breathed life on the earth. They creep along the waterways, hide their canoes in the mangrove creeks running up into the island, and then sneak through the bush and attack from the inland side. If the Tugeri cannot be resisted from behind the stockade, the Boiguites rush up to their tree-houses and fight from there. The Tugeri can then only fire the village. It would cost too many men to take the houses in the trees, though with luck they occasionally roast a tree out. They make their raids mostly in the calms between the north-west, returning before the south-east blows. The Tugeri depend mainly on surprise to collect their heads." And Kebisu, grunting the close of his speech, reached for a lump of turtle.

Jakara lay back, gazing up at those silver houses. The moon showed him how necessity had built them. Their foundations, criss-crossing on the longest and strongest limbs, were of tough mangrove poles, supple bamboo, and lawyer cable; with care as to balance, they were firm against the strain and stress of the wind. Imposingly large too, each house with its platform would shelter a surprising number of people. The floors were reinforced against the penetration of missiles, heavily loopholed, and armoured with ant-bed cement against blazing arrows. Eerily beautiful was the scene, though Jakara wondered what awful tragedies those giant trees had witnessed. Strange that these people are the merriest Islanders in all Torres Strait!

The moon rose higher, drawing away her silver and leaving Jakara to gaze at those weird black blotches up in the air.

Suddenly he sprang erect. A tattoo of shark-jaw drums startled the night. Instantly the Boiguites leapt up and raced towards the big trees, the children scampering as if hell snapped at their heels: a frenzy of screams put the fear of death into a thousand hearts. Arrows whistled like blazing rockets: warriors tore through the open gate with clash of bow and club, stamp of feet, and grunt of close-packed bodies: the tips of climbing poles jerked above the stockade, and down from these sprang howling savages.

Kebisu's men snatched their weapons. Confusion supreme! – the feasts overturned; men trodden on; youngsters diving between hurrying legs; the rasping twang of bow-strings on *kadik* guards, the shrill of rattles!

Flame shot skywards when an arrow hissed into a thatched roof. There came the wailing groan of men stricken in surprise, Kebisu's bull voice roaring the rally, Maros bawling a war-song, swinging his *gaba-gaba* towards the struggling gateway: furore of painted figures, swaying plumes, swinging clubs: Jakara with Lightning gleaming like his eyes: fleeing Boiguites yelling "Tugeri! Tugeri! Tugeri!"

Jakara laughed derisively at those strings of monkeys swarming up the ladders, until a slim warrior leapt at him and both fought for life.

Tugeri drums throbbed faster and faster: the air raved with shouts and screams, or sobbed with gasps while sweating men fought death: there was splintering of wood as club clashed against club: the hoarse "Ah!" when the pine-apple knob thumped home: the definite scream when a barbed spear bit deep. The air hissed with flying snakes that came stinging down from the sky. Kebisu roared curses in accompaniment to Jakara's snarls while they struck and cut and hacked and thrust, for the Boigu people were shooting arrows from the houses above and were likely to pin both friend and foe in the struggling crowds below. The Tugeri raved their triumph at the complete surprise and puzzlingly open gate, not yet realizing into what a hornets' nest they had come.

Kebisu's men recovered nerve after the first shock, and now, though split into groups, fought with the unholy fury of trained savages. Though the Tugeri were over a thousand strong, they presently began to fall throughout the length and breadth of the village.

Another house blazed, then two more. A breeze rustled the palms – the village was roaring pillars of flame. The scene was one of satanic beauty, all furious movement of flame-splashed men, shadowed by the wall of tree-tops far out around the mighty stockade; amid it the nodding of the great plumed head-dresses; the shimmer of crescent *mais*; the swing of the feathery *kadiks*, as shark-tooth sword thrust home; eyes that flamed green and red like a dog's at night; white teeth in the last hard laugh; the glowing reflection thrown back from the inner stockade; the writhing mass choking the gateway; the swarms of violently active men fighting back from the flames inside. Above all rose the hysterical screaming of women, the shrill of the fighting-rattles, the whizz of sling-stones, the maddened boom of drums, the shattering thrum of the *doad*, the howling of dogs!

Jakara, in a lather of sweat, fought away from the heat and saw amid the inferno what manner of devils clawed for his head. These were tall and illusioned into sinewy giants, for their hair stuck out from the back of their heads in erect grass-bound tufts two feet high. They were light-brown in colour, but splashed with painted bars. Grease gleamed from their wild-cat bodies while from well back they fought with a snarling spring upon their adversaries. Their eyes were circled with painted white rings which produced a terrorizing effect. Through a hole in their nose dangled crooked eagle-talons. They bared their teeth as they screamed. The effect of their appearance, apart from their peculiarly ferocious form of fighting, was well planned beforehand to produce panic fear in the enemies whom they surprised. Jakara was amazed that many of the warriors had the heaving breasts of women – for the Tugeri amazons fought beside their lords, screamed louder, and were the more treacherously quick.

Like a flash from a side-show Jakara saw Toik hit the ground, roaring like a bull calf; his claws were tearing at a woman who had fastened her teeth in his groin. A stampede in the fight swirled Beizam into fighting shoulder to shoulder with Jakara. With wrinkled brows and gasping breath they smiled swiftly, for the terrible joy in fighting makes even enemies friends.

Came a curious lull, and then, like Valkyries above the din, screamed the Tugeri leaders, and instantly their men began to fight their way backwards towards the stockade wall. Realization of their position had dawned upon them; the chorused war-calls ceased. Stubborn hand-to-hand fighting is the hardest work of man; every breath counts; every muscle, every nerve, and every sense, every instinct in Jakara's being was straining in this gloriously tough fight. When the earth darkened under rolling palls he sensed the wind-wafted smoke from the village; when it blazed, he knew that the flames had triumphed again; at such outbreaks the eyeballs of his adversaries bulged like the eyes of wild beasts, their teeth shone white like fangs. Stones thudded around him, hurled by the screaming women and children from the tree platforms above. These aimed for the tufted head-dresses of the Tugeri, but, now that the throwers were uncontrollably excited, they hurled their missiles into the rolling blackness where smoke blotted out both enemy and friend.

Then Jakara saw a dreadful weapon used upon young Musa of Eroob. The isolated lad was hard-pressed and he turned to run towards friends. Instantly a Tugeri thrust out a looped cane, like a long-handled tennis-racquet. It slipped over the lad's head to his throat. The Tugeri jerked back, then sharply forward. Two spikes on the handle inside the loop penetrated the base of the boy's neck. As he fell, the Tugeri were slashing at his head.

The strongest and most accurate bowmen of the Tugeri had grouped round the trees, and, as the flames blazed in sheets of light, the maddened people above became targets for the finest bowmen in the world. Feverishly confident in the strength of Kebisu's men, and becoming almost imbecile from the stench of the fight below, numbers of the householders forgot cover and fought silhouetted by the flames. A triumphant scream from a Tugeri, and the sound of a thud, signified a hit. But few fell from the platforms, for immediately that a long arrow pierced into him, the victim would sling his leg round part of the platform or branch, as the stricken possum grips with his tail.

A woman, tall and slim, with a Samoan whiteness, stood silhouetted in a lurid glow. Her body was entrancing in the dancing light; her eyes were blinded with smoke – she was quite mad, hurling stone after stone and screaming piercingly all the time. A lean bowman crouched, and quite steadily took aim so that his arrow-point would just sear the nipple of her breast. The arrow hissed up, its head blazing; it passed straight through the massed waves of the woman's oil-soaked hair. Instantly it blazed, a living torch. Her wail rose above the sounds of all the fight. Before friends could club her, she had leaped across the platform and, rushing into the house, dashed her head against the coconut matting: the dry walls blazed, flame leaped high above the lower inferno, a roar of complete understanding came from all the Tugeri. Some nearer ones actually broke from their own engagements and rushed towards the bowmen to be in at the death.

The tree roared like a flue. From those crowded platforms such women and children as could no longer stand the heat leapt with desperate cries. Their heads were slashed off almost as they hit the ground. Showers of sparks sprayed the fighting village when the house crashed in: as their hair caught alight, men, women, and children flared despairingly down, like gigantic fire-flies. The survivors walked like cats along the hot branches, their eyes turned upwards so that they might dodge the blaze of falling timbers. But the arrows from below hissed to work.

Again Jakara found Beizam fighting beside him. Some deep inner instinct told him that it was neither accident nor a desire to protect his sword-arm that kept the Shark so near. With a snarl Jakara leapt forward and hacked a startled wretch with all the fury of a blow that he would have loved to thrust into Beizam.

Kebisu was anxious. Again and again he leapt aside to bellow into the air. With rolling voice he cursed the Mamoose of Mer who was making too sure that all the Tugeri were trapped within the stockade.

There merged into the bedlam a curious sound – a murmur like the thumping hearts of giants, the muffled thunder of many feet. There was a triumphant roar as the men from the beach poured in through the gate. Maras whirled his club in maniacal glee: men fresh for the fight surged furiously forward. One instant of shrieking confusion, and the Tugeri, shattered from the rear and with a fighting barrier pressing them from the front, broke and dashed frenziedly for the stockade. Many got through, and, springing straight at the leaning walls, leapt away into the night. Yells of triumph mingled with the drums on high as the Boigu men swarmed down their ladders like singed ants.

Jakara panted forward to the slaughter which was surging back towards the stockade wall. Then he leapt and yelled, for a wounded Tugeri woman had fastened her teeth in his thigh. He instantly lost all interest in the surrounding medley: he yelled loudly enough to bring the dead to life while he gouged the jaws of this gnawing fiend: stumblingly he tried to reach the place where he had flung Lightning, but the woman's teeth met, and she chewed, and Jakara howled squirming to the ground. Toik, sorely maimed, came limping along, a mad light in his eyes. He knelt down, pushed one bony knee into the back of the Amazon's neck, lovingly clawed his great hands round her throat – the left hand with the fingers all lopped off – then jerked and pushed – quickly. An oily snap sounded, and Toik grinned in unlaughing glee. He would have loved to go on snapping women's necks! Jakara, sick and groaning, had a fellow feeling.

THE ZOGO-MAI
(Only three are known—one is in the British Museum.)

165

CHAPTER XXII

The Peoples Of The Auwo Oromo

From Boigu, Kebisu dispatched one-third of his fleet under Bogo for a short trip along the south-western New Guinea coast. They were to trade quickly, and afterwards to re-unite at Kiwai, for Kebisu was in a hurry. He sailed the morning after the fight. Those of his men who were badly wounded were to remain at Boigu until they recovered or died. Later, the Boiguites would canoe them, with the prepared skulls of friends and foes alike, to Moatta, whence they would be shipped to Kiwai, the general rendezvous. Kebisu had lost a goodly number of men. But there were no regrets; it had been a glorious fight.

In full sail the fleet followed the coast eastwards, past rocky Dauan rising sheer from the sea, and sailing clear of low-lying Sabai with its brawny warriors of the bow and arrow; past hummocky Mabaduan, which relieved the flatness of the south-western New Guinea coast; past Sogara and Malukawa and Dubuaru islands and the mouth of the Kataw River, calling in neither at the important Moatta trading-centre nor at Toori-Toori; past Daru and Bobo and the mouth of the Oreomo River, and, to the disgust of the fierce Paramians, passing their island without drawing sail.

Jakara could not realize that the fleet had turned into the mouth of a river, be it ever so mighty. The forty-mile-wide estuary resembled an uncharted sea crammed with timbered islands. Across the blockading bar heavy seas were rolling, foaming away into invisibility upon mud banks, islets, and distance. Upon countless sandbanks, extending miles out to sea, dirty rollers were creeping, to burst in booming sheets of spray. Clouds scudded under a blue sky. Ruby-eyed gulls circled down upon the fleet, their sharp beaks uttering piercing cries. Numerous channels, rippling passage-ways, and swirling currents were indistinguishable by Jakara from the hurrying masses of the sea. The fleet flew like golden-winged birds straight towards the crested waves crumbling on the bar. Jakara thrilled to the pitching of the fleet, the hiss of spray and slap of wave, the warm sense of comradeship, the knowledge that thousands of eager eyes were watching from the islands and mainland as they passed; he thrilled as the bar thundered closer with a threatening tossing of waters. Its magnetic power quickly absorbed him: he ceased wondering at the dirty yellow colour of this sea, forgot the tense feeling that they might at any moment crash upon a clouded reef, forgot the submerged danger of floating timbers: he lived for the great moment when the fleet would take the bar.

Magnificently Kebisu handled his vessels; never swerving in their arrow flight, in perfect formation they rose and sped straight into that tumbling inferno. Clinging to the fighting-platform, Jakara tingled to the powerful rise and then the shuddering plunge as the *Skull Chief* sheered through breaker after breaker. Thunder roared in his ears while he gazed down into the bubbling brown depths, to rise again and glimpse the spume-tipped cauldron snarling round the flying ships. He marvelled at the nerve of the steersman staring towards the serene steadiness of Kebisu's directing hand. Cross currents in choppy waves lashed the vessels, but they went on, on, up and down and through and up again, steady, sure, certain.

Amid the roar of welcoming thousands the fleet crested the bar, and to the blare of conch-shells in hundreds and the water-flung boom of drums Kebisu cruised towards the quieter waters washing the left bank of the river.

Later on, when Jakara knew that river just a little, it gripped his imagination. Though he did not know it, he could easily have understood how that environment was responsible for the travellers' tales which were to be told about this river in a very few years to come. Some of these reports were spread over the world even by a missionary – stories of tailed men, of rhinoceros and sabre-toothed tiger, of giant birds with a twenty-foot spread of wing, of buffaloes, and of men joined together.

As the islands closed in upon them, proof of the large population showed in smoke along the mainland and island shores, native coconut-plantations, peeping villages, and countless canoes dodging among the islets in hallooing welcome. They sailed up along Kiwai Island with the woods echoing to the long-drawn blast of the conch. On the large island of Mibu the Sumai people from their splendid gardens frantically waved palm-leaves. Crowds rushed from the numerous Kiwai villages and blackened the shores. In thankful relief Kebisu anchored his fleet opposite the main village of Kiwai. The weather had held splendidly.

Dense throngs welcomed the voyagers, canoes in shoals swarmed round the fleet. With impressive ceremonial the chief of Kiwai carefully introduced to Kebisu a group of leering sorcerers, shrunken of body but lust-bright of eye, their skull-like heads filled with wickedness. These relics of cunning evil were the most feared and most powerful men in the land. Then were introduced the chiefs congregated from many tribes, some from far inland and from east and west of the Fly River, though

Jakara only knew the name of this river as "Auwo Oromo." Jakara regarded these natives with an ever-fresh interest, but there were so many tribes present that he could mark but one such predominant type as distinguished the men of Mer and Tutu.

After he had been presented to the chiefs, the women crowded round him, bashful-eyed, intensely curious about this Lamar, the first whom they had seen in peace. For they had seen others, to Jakara's surprise and intense curiosity. For, as the days passed and they answered his many questions, he gradually realized that numerous wrecks and castaways had been drawn by the currents, as if by a magnet, into the great estuary. But all whites who could not fight their way to escape had been savagely attacked and massacred. For here, too, white people were believed to be Lamars, "spirits of the dead." Jakara was surprised that the Torres Strait belief should exist here also, but he was soon to learn that there were other similar customs. Some Lamars had put up a stubborn resistance, he was told; occasionally they had actually got away.

Jakara listened with melancholy interest to such recitals, but with a quickened beating of the heart at the few instances of successful resistance. He little knew that one was the attack on Captain Blackwood in 1845. They had quite a number of "Lamar heads" the chiefs proudly assured him, in the "Dairmu" House. They would point them out to him.

Jakara listened with unmoved countenance, though in his heart was a bitter hatred against these ruthless slayers of helpless castaways. They had, they eagerly explained, some queer heads, for all Lamars were not the same. One day a funny great clumsy canoe crashed on the bar. Jakara listened while they described a Chinese junk. The Lamars aboard, they said, were frantic with terror and threw things that went "bung" and smelt like many dead-houses. These Lamars' eyes were like a pig's, but not straight; their hair was one long rope. Their heads looked very strange when they were smoke-dried or stuffed. The people prized them highly.

Jakara silently sympathized with those unlucky getters of *bêche-de-mer* whose unwieldy junks had been blown into the mouth of the Fly.

Hours passed that first day with the chiefs in grave discussion while the people fraternized. Then all congregated at the feast, for there must be feasting and dancing for days before business was begun. Every moment fresh canoes arrived, until Jakara began to think that all the population of New Guinea had swarmed to Kiwai. He was intensely interested, but, though he was limping painfully, he would much rather have explored the villages than sit at the long-drawn-out feasts.

All that first night, as on many others, for a length of thirty miles the entire island feasted and danced. Thousands of torches flared among countless palms, the starlit waterways thrummed to battalions of dancing feet and booming drums, the night sang with massed choruses of voices in many tribal dialects. The noise of the insect world was entirely drowned by human revelry. Jakara thought of a black Babylon feasting under a wilderness of stars.

With a quiet interest he noted that Beizam, in his most flashy fighting regalia, was subtly worming his way into the confidence of the foreign chiefs, his arrogant bearing but winning smile impressing upon all the people that he was Beizam the Shark, already a distinguished fighter, and one day to be the Mamoose of Mer. He was a splendid specimen of manhood too, and looked every inch the chief. From the admiring glances of the village belles, Jakara knew that Beizam's maiden love-stick would carry a few notches before the return to Mer.

When dawn came and rolled the mist from the river, Jakara, sleepy and bewildered by the flaring fires silhouetting the ceaseless coming and going of dancing squads, was glad when the chief of Kiwai courteously invited the Mamooses into the Man House to rest. The festivities would continue for days.

Jakara climbed up the ladder to the raftered platform fronting the invisible doorway. Here frowned long posts carved into terrifying designs of wizard men, devils, and imaginary beings partly human, partly animal, partly fish. All were painted with a view to inspiring superstitious fear. Overhead were suspended charms of coloured fibres which creaked in the breeze. Two grinning skulls, in which were stones, revolved with a gentle rattling. Ferociously barbaric was the towering carving of the semi-god Marunogeri.

When within that great house, Jakara felt that he trod in a ghosts' corridor. Stretching ahead and on all sides was twilight space, quiet as the gloom of a church. Shadowed in lines to right and left were tree-trunks rising like pillars towards the roof. The wide floor was of split palms, grey-shadowed and brown with clay. Down the middle of the aisle lay evenly-placed mats of fibre vividly dyed in striking patterns. Coconut matting divided the sides into many cubby-houses, in each of which squatted a silent figure. At intervals were tiers of split palm reminding Jakara, with a quickening of the heart, of ship berths. In these were supplies of food-stuffs, ceremonial images and dresses, grotesque masks and drums.

There also were shaded erotic carvings of women, and hidden away were the "Maduba" and other things which it meant death for a woman to see. Apart from these, Jakara was shown things which curdled his blood. With an absolutely terrified feeling he wondered if, after all, the Dance of

Death was the most dreadful thing in the world.

The Man House would shelter hundreds of initiates. Along the aisle from the trunk supports leered weird faces which could only have been imagined in a madman's nightmare. The trunks themselves were carved with sneering faces of gods and spirits, the evil predominating, their totemic animals, birds, or fishes always near, like bats at a devils' meeting. As daylight strengthened, the walls were played upon by shafts of light through some invisible arrangement in the roof. The silence was sepulchral. The chief conversed in whispers while he took the Mamooses slowly towards their allotted spaces. Jakara felt chilled at the sight of three withered sorcerers, crouching like shadowed birds of prey. Their snakelike eyes seemed bent on probing the very secrets of his heart.

The leering faces on the pillars were giant masks, some of them over seven feet in height and over two in width, carved and painted in what appeared to be hieroglyphic signs, picked out vividly with feathers and shells, coloured clays, and tassels of dyed grasses. The faces were those of men of a cruelty personified. Some of the gaping jaws were furnished with rows of crocodiles' or sharks' teeth, and other parts were painted red to represent lust and blood-hunger. Others snarled with the curved tusks of boars.

Towards the warriors' quarters the support-trunks and cubicles were necklaced with strings of skulls like bunches of withered coconuts. Some of the skulls were jewelled with scarlet berries and inlay of pearl-shell. At intervals, mummified and sun-dried heads were suspended, hideous things, with the dusky skin stretched over the bones. The eye-sockets and mouths of some were plugged with clay. There were stuffed heads, too, bloated and beastly, though the inlaid tortoise-shell work which ornamented these bladder-like things was beautiful. Some of the mummified heads stared with fish-white eyes of shell. Jakara's fancy was gripped by two. One was a man hideously Asiatic, possessing a remarkable head-dress. Jakara immediately thought of the wrecked junk. The tresses were three feet long, twisted like the tentacles of an octopus. Each tentacle had been ornamented with infinite patience. Tiny rings of bamboo, microscopically carved, alternated with rings of polished shell right down each tentacle in ever dwindling spirals, like a whip-lash. The head-hunter who had bagged that trophy had gone to an artist's trouble in preserving it. The other was the head of a young girl. Her hair, delicately combed, stood out in a striking mop eighteen inches above and around her head, the circle at the perfectly trimmed tips measuring many feet. Her face was modelled into a tense mask of fear, and hate, and loathing. Jakara was given a cubicle with this girl staring down at him. Later, he had two quiet months in which to become acquainted with her accusing company.

The end of the house was barred by wickerwork of sago-palm. Only the sorcerers dwelt there, seeing without being seen. The secrets of that inner chamber were secrets indeed.

Jakara stretched himself upon the sleeping-mat, his pillow a block of wood carved to represent fighting crocodiles. The air smelt old and musty, the silence breathed of whispers. Almost immediately he sank into a trancelike sleep.

Jakara was the first white man who had ever penetrated such a Sacred House and lived, but then he was not regarded as a white man. He was a spirit chief, and, as such, was admitted as being already familiar with the spiritual beliefs and communal laws. Honoured chiefs were the only visitors occasionally admitted.

War canoe at Erub - Darnley Island - 1849.

CHAPTER XXIII

The Great Trade

To his intense disgust, Jakara was awakened in the early afternoon when the chiefs reviewed the goods for sale. Every village was a-bustle, and the house platforms were piled with trade goods including mats of sago, in rolls bound round with the midrib of the sago-leaf. Jakara grunted as he lifted one of those prepared bundles; he estimated its weight at a hundred and thirty pounds. Huge coils of hibiscus bark were there for the making of ropes, and numerous other articles.

Kebisu's men were busily unloading their canoes, surrounded by talkative crowds of envious natives. Kebisu's goods were stacked in seductive lines and pyramids, the packages and bales being partly undone, so that, before the selling, the cupidity of the buyers should be fully aroused. The string, possum, twine, and human-hair belts, and big shell cooking-pots were especially admired by the women. All wares were under strong guard. The waterways were thronged with vessels, from the raft to the simple dugout, and even impressive war-canoes, but none were such great vessels as Kebisu's, none had similar fighting-platforms or sails, or double outriggers. People from the mainland and the islands continued to arrive with the tides.

Jakara was amazed at the grace, variety, and strength of the canoes lined for sale on their log rollers. The war-canoes were built from forest giants hollowed out by fire, stone axe, gouge, chisel, and adze. Jakara was to notice later that the implacable hand of Fate had helped to fashion these vessels. Already she had inserted the thin edge of the wedge in favour of her petted white man, for stray tools were of iron, looted from wrecks, ground to axe-blades by one lump of metal against another with the help of water and sand and incalculable labour. The canoes were complete to outriggers and masts.

Proudly the chiefs exhibited their masterpieces: Jakara could have examined the vessels for days and continually found more of interest among them. Every chip, every bit of work down to the carvings and paintings, had been done by specialists: every design had a symbolic significance. For centuries these people had traded in canoes, and the builders had followed the particular work of their fathers throughout unnumbered generations. Beizam could not drag himself away from the vessels, for one shark-jawed leviathan was to be his own command.

In the days following, Jakara learned that the Kiwai people were the traders in, rather than the makers of, the giant canoes. These came from special tribes up the Fly; from the Baramura people, from Pisarame, Taitiarato, and the Wabadas. The greatest vessels of all came from the Dibiri River. Jakara was greatly interested, for apparently the Dibiri was another great river. The chiefs would tell him very little of the Dibiri – which white men later called the Bamu mysteriously shaking their heads in a wish to avoid conversation on the subject. Kebisu explained that somewhere up there, near great Siva, the god Sido was killed, the god of the Kiwai people. They believed that the river was accursed.

Kebisu also explained that the canoes were floated down from the Dibiri to Kiwai to be finished off. The vessels had no platforms, outriggers, masts, or sails. The Kiwai people put these in; the Torres Strait Islanders had taught them how to do it. But Kebisu had brought his own new sails. No New Guinea men, he proudly declared, could make the great mat sails of the Torres Strait Islanders. As to double outriggers, platforms, and sails, the river people and those of Kiwai very rarely ventured to make or use them for themselves. "They are only river people," added Kebisu contemptuously. "They are mud-turtles, not sailors."

But even Kebisu became wearied of satisfying Jakara's curiosity as to the names of the representative tribes. He had to be satisfied with distinguishing only a few of the local tribes – the Kiwais, the Moattans, the Kunini, the Masingaras, the Badus, the Toori-Toorians, and numerous nearby tribesmen living farther along the estuary. He was agreeably surprised, and to a large extent able to satisfy his own curiosity, when he found that throughout the estuary there was a common "trade" language used by all throughout this season.

Kebisu was secretly delighted. No price was talked of yet, but he knew that the price in skulls for some of these great vessels would be exorbitant. Well, he had the skulls, and had given strict orders to his men that on no account were they to mention the number of heads taken at Boigu. That was an extra account on which he could draw when Bogo's canoes arrived from Moatta. And before then he would know definitely the price of these vessels. He had also a fair reserve of armlet-shells, which represent very considerable money in New Guinea and were quite indispensable for bulk purchases.

It was after sundown before the chiefs returned to the principal village. Kebisu arranged by barter for the daily supplies for his warriors, and Jakara smiled at the big chief's annoyance when the eager droves of women flocked around him clattering such exorbitant prices for their staggering bunches of bananas, their yams and taro, their over-filled baskets of prawns and crabs, their fish and damp bundles of sago.

Then the long night's feasting and dancing began. As on many other nights, Jakara enjoyed the entertainment. This was a "woman's night." He ate leisurely, critically appraising the charms of the dancing girls in their constantly varying squads. All were dressed in their tribal glory, their skins shining from practised massaging with coconut-oil mixed with ruby saliva from the betel-nut. Their hair was their prize attraction, scarlet with hibiscus or starry with jasmine. It stood out in dense crinkly mops, and had been tended for these dances for weeks beforehand. Their bodies were smaller than those of the Torres Strait girls, plump and seductively formed, their faces animated and shining, their full lips blood-red from the betel-nut, their big black eyes feverishly bright. The first squad wore single grass *ramis*, prettily dyed, which swung from their shapely hips like the skirts of ballet dancers, swishing with their rhythmic movement. Their clinking armlets and anklets were of coloured corals or berries or shells, and they used, as a tambourine to accompany their song, a rattle of looped cane, on which were strung shells, polished bones, and the claws of the big mangrove crabs. The swaying bodies of the girls seemed as tireless as the monotonous influence of the drums which stirred them up to concert pitch. This particular squad was from an eastern tribe.

Jakara noted that, curiously, the women of nearly all the tribes were of a lighter colour than the men. Many girls wore their hair close-cropped, others in ringlets; all depended on their tribal custom. Some girls wore numerous *ramis*, some wore bark ribbons dropping from the belt in front to be tucked up under the belt behind, leaving the legs and hips bare. Some wore a tassel of coloured fibre.

Jakara spent entrancing days without even going off Kiwai. He found that in various places the island was so low as to be under water during the high tides. Between the villages were numerous creeks, sometimes even running through a village, and over these were built arched bridges of mangrove forks decked with split palm lashed together with rattan. All large timber had long since been utilized. Any exceptionally big material now required was floated down from up the river.

He soon appreciated Kebisu's contemptuous allusion to "mud-turtles;" the entire island seemed to be made of mud. Inland, the island was practically all sago-swamps, the thorny palms towering above the smaller forest timber and letting in splashes of sunlight to the gloom below. Jakara trod warily over the decayed trunks of gutted sago-palms and red-brown heaps of sour pith. All through any such swamp the trees would echo to the flails of the women as they beat the fibre to pulp. Often he came on groups of them busily gouging into the white pith heart, others kneading the pulp in the water-troughs. Primitive and often pretty, the young girls moved about with filtered light on their busy bodies; they left their skirts behind when entering the muddy swamp. Daughters of Eve were they all, and Jakara found each with a gay girdle of flowers adorning her waist; only occasionally did he catch sight of one unadorned. With laughing raillery, they sought to intrigue this bronze Lamar from across the seas.

In those quiet depths he padded into the village of Barosara, and a glance showed him that at one time it had been of great extent. He was canoed round to Saguan, Wiorubi, Sagasia, Isasia, and numerous other large villages. He would have liked to have had time to visit the large islands almost within hail.

He watched with interest the women "making sago," a work below the dignity of men. The principal food of all these people came from the great sago-swamps. The sago is prepared into rolls mixed with grated coconut, shellfish, bananas, yams, and other foods, and roasted in its own leaves. The women had to prepare all the food. They had buckets from the woodlike melon-shells, utensils of sago-bark, of bamboo, and of hollowed palm. Two meals seemed the order of the day, though now the nights were given to one continual feast. Jakara admired fine gardens of bananas, sugar-cane, sweet potato, yam, and tobacco. He was told that far larger tobacco gardens were grown up-river, for trade to the coastal tribes.

One afternoon he stepped noiselessly along that portion of the beach where the great new canoes were drawn up. Beizam was kneeling there, by the towering side of a shark-jawed canoe. The young chief's face was tense, his eyes dull with dreams. In that big vessel before him he saw Power, the power that could make him conqueror of all the Strait. If, in years to come, he could only prevail on the men of Mer to man such canoes against Kebisu's men – and defeat them! Then he, Beizam, would command the waters from the Great South Land to New Guinea. And then – all these New Guinea savages would have to pay rich tribute to Beizam, Mamoose of Mer and the Strait.

Jakara slipped away, leaving the dreamer to his dreams. He was uneasy, for he could not be blind to the fact that Beizam had both ambition and brains. In the near future, how would the maturing plans of Beizam affect the detested Lamar – Jakara?

He suddenly felt very lonely. Like a blow he realized as never before that his former enemy, C'Zarcke, was now his only friend.

What Jakara loved best, especially when he had one of the lesser chiefs of Kiwai with him to explain, was canoeing and walking about among the people drawn from so many tribes and gathered together under a truce at only this one great season of the year. The villages, from daylight until he fell into exhausted sleep, were full of clatter as noisy as if all the humanity in the world were turned into birds and caged on this one island. The overlords were the tall Kiwaians and Moattans, "the black Jews of New Guinea," as white traders were soon to call them. Jakara stared with fascination at the ears of the older men, which had no lobes. They had long shreds of leathery flesh which fell to the shoulders. The tops of the ears were punched with holes. In the dances, long coloured streamers of grass and fibres floated from these holes. The shredded lobes were caused by heavy weights gradually pulling the ear down until it burst. The septum of the nose was pierced, and ornamented by a carved bone or shell, a boar's tusk, or a crocodile's tooth. Moustache and beard were worn by many.

Jakara noticed young girls with their hair growing long. "Unmarried," grunted his guide. "After marriage some wear no hair at all, others only tufts, others ringlets, others mops, and others coil it in grass and mud; it depends on the tribal custom."

Many men and women had their bodies wealed and cicatriced across the back, shoulders, breasts, stomach, or limbs. Jakara saw part of the operation being performed. It was painful, and must have taken weeks to complete. A fanciful design proudly worn on a girl's shoulder advertised that her brother had killed his first man. "And a man is always anxious that his sister shall soon wear the mark," explained the guide, "for a head wins the love of a woman." The girlish bodies of one tribe in particular were walking art galleries. For in this tribe a father used his baby girl's body as a book on which to record the outstanding deeds of his life. Every time he cleared a new garden, built a new house, murdered another man, speared a pig, or fought in war, he came home and worked a design on the skin of the baby to commemorate the event. The young girls were very proud of these "pictures" of their father's life, and showed off their bodies accordingly.

This particular guide explained also with a patriot's pride that his countrywomen followed the men into battle with a screaming encouragement to the arrow-flights while they rushed between the warrior's legs killing the wounded and mutilating the dead.

Throughout his wanderings at the mouth of the Fly, Jakara soon realized that all these thousands of people were ever ready for instant fight. No village knew when it was going to be attacked; it was expected every moment of the night and day that men, women, and children might be instantly called upon to fight for their lives. The beliefs of many of these people concerning the spirit state after death were similar to those of the Islanders. They had a similarity of divination, too, but not nearly so advanced. They did not, however, know anything of the Dance of Death, nor of reading by the stars, nor of navigation, nor had they the deep inner culture of the Islanders.

In the nightly dances Jakara saw these various people in holiday mood. Some tribesmen sang excellently. Drums boomed monotonously, reed instruments and shell trumpets accompanied the drums both plaintively and stridently. As a protection against leeches, some of the men wore fibre leggings beautifully made and sewn up the sides with rows of tiny white cowrie-shells.

Their beards were plaited with flowers.

The day dawned when trade was to begin. It was spent by the Mamooses in a critical examination of the canoes, while the Kiwai chiefs exhaustively examined each specimen of Kebisu's most prized goods. And the people in surging throngs argued with the Komet-le around the trade goods. The Kiwai chief, with his tongue in his cheek, announced that, as an act of courtesy, the trade of people living far up the Fly would be given precedence, since the threat of heavy rains in the distant mountains made it imperative that they should return to their villages.

That evening some of "the goods" were paraded in an avenue of palms. They were eighty girls, all young and in good condition – a mixture; some belonging to the bartering tribe itself, the remainder a medley taken in war. All were dressed with extreme care according to their individual tribal customs. Some wore the up-river knee petticoat, some the grass *rami,* some the "bushmen's" petticoat of short dangling strips, some a waistband with a shield of clinking shells. Some were naked but for swinging tassels. Their bodies shone from oil massage. Their shapely legs were enhanced by berry and bone and shell ornaments. None were frightened, many were apparently shy, a few only were sulky.

Kebisu glared at the parade in silence, Maros in appreciation; twiddling the love-stick dangling from his beard. When a particular girl attracted his eye, he delightedly made her show off her charms to the fullest advantage amid the lively approval of the crowd. After a conventional appraisement, prolonged unnecessarily by Maros, Kebisu courteously declined to bargain, explaining to the tribal chiefs mostly concerned that his canoes, which, as they knew, were short-numbered, would be over-filled with produce and could not possibly hold the girls. Besides, they had abundance of women at home.

The Kiwai chiefs grinned, for they had fully anticipated Kebisu's answer.

Maros would have liked to do a little private trading on his own account, but Kebisu sternly refused further argument.

The visiting chiefs from far up the Fly took the refusal with a very bad grace, for it was an insult to their tribal honour. The girls took it more badly still. Their smiles froze to glares, they retired to their tribesmen, and, throwing discretion to the winds, harangued them to make instant war. But the sneering men had no intention of going under in what would have been a massacre of minutes. Next morning those tribes had vanished.

The following day was spent by the Mamooses and chiefs in arguing over the price of the canoes. Not until long after nightfall had a price been agreed upon. Next morning Jakara saw it paid.

For the ten largest canoes, twenty skulls apiece. Later on Kebisu would pay a lower but agreed-on price for smaller vessels. Crowds rolled up and encircled the canoes. Way was made for the chiefs, who were followed by the men of Mer carrying the skull-baskets. Standing defiantly by the bow of each canoe was a bound prisoner of war: beside each stood a tall guard of Kiwai in his war equipment and feathers. The chiefs halted, the basket-men stepped forward, and before each canoe solemnly built a pyramid of twenty skulls. Jakara recognized numbers, for each was painted to admit of identification. The basket-bearers stepped back; the crowd hushed. Then the chief of Kiwai raised his hand. Each guard swung his club; there was a sigh as with one accord the crowd stared forward; the clubs cracked down; the prisoners fainted across the canoes, christening each bow with crimson; a deep breath arose from the crowd, and the canoes had been dedicated to the war-spirit. Those prisoners greeted death philosophically, except the man who christened Beizam's maiden canoe.

THE SHRINE OF GOOD LUCK

CHAPTER XXIV

The Battle On The Fly

There followed days of happy bartering. The canoes from Moatta arrived, manned with the survivors of Kebisu's wounded, and containing many prepared skulls. The chiefs of Kiwai were piqued; they were certain now that they had sold their canoes too cheaply. Kebisu prepared to depart in continuation of the cruise along the gulf and up the eastern coast. But there arrived emissaries from far up the Fly River who completely changed his plans. They told convincingly of great trade up the river – the barter of many inland tribes congregated at one spot and delayed from coming down the river on account of war. Now that war was over, their light river-canoes were quite incapable of holding such an accumulation of goods: they bargained for Kebisu's larger vessels to go up for it.

The chiefs of Kiwai scoffed, declaring that the up-river tribes now knew of Kebisu's much depleted force in comparison with that of other years; they would ambush him and take his goods for nothing.

Kebisu realized the sense in this, but he knew quite well that, if the trade was really there, the Kiwai people had missed it and were annoyed. If he departed, they would hurry up the river, buy the goods, and on his return trip resell to him at a fabulously increased price. It was all in the game. As for an ambush! Bah! He knew the size of his fighting-canoes compared with the up-river vessels and he knew the fighting ferocity of his own men.

He questioned the emissaries closely, but they were apparently sincere on all points. He made his arrangements quickly. Bogo could not be expected back for another fortnight. Kebisu divided his fleet into two; one half he dispatched under the Mamoose of Eroob for the usual trip up the eastern coast, the remainder he quickly provisioned, loaded them with trade, and with bundles comprising thousands of purchased arrows, and one glorious morning, to Jakara's delight, set full sail up the river.

Kebisu hastened for fear the expected rains should flood the swollen waters irresistibly: the current was already murmuring. The messengers sailed with Kebisu as guides, except two, who travelled swiftly ahead to warn their people to be ready for a rapid loading.

For nearly a hundred miles the fleet bowled along under sail. When beyond the influence of the wind, they crept in nearer the bank and awaited the inrush of the tides, for to attempt to battle against the current rushing down the middle of the river would have been futile. Recourse was had to paddles; they were used mainly from the outriggers, to help while the uplift of the tide lasted. Those great canoes were built for the open sea, their big sails requiring a stiff breeze.

Jakara felt that it would take years of travel to explore this vast river and its mighty byways.

And a thrill was added to his interest that very night.

The canoes just dreamed along, almost as if waiting for something. It was the time of the full moon. And low tide, the yellow-brown water sluggish and quiet, no sound but the low murmur of the warriors' voices. His natural senses long ago keenly developed; Jakara waited for whatever was going to happen. A drum beat hollowly, muffled within the jungle. Silence again.

A low rumble-drawing nearer as Jakara turned and gazed downstream. But the rumble died away. As if obeying an unspoken order every warrior on every canoe lashed all his possessions fast, then the great canoes turned slowly about and with their bows facing down-stream – waited.

A low rumble growing threateningly as it grew from out of the night, a call from every canoe came through the semi-darkness: "It comes! It comes!" and the rumble spread, harsher, fast approaching. Jakara tingled, gazing from the fighting platform as a frothy white arc suddenly appeared with a moving yellow wall advancing through the moonlight. Jakara held his breath-that rushing wave was higher than the fighting platforms of the canoes! The crews cried encouragement as every vessel advanced to the wall which roared upon them as the *Skull Chief* rose up with her bows up, up, climbing, climbing right up to tremble on top of the wall. As Jakara gasped his intense relief the vessel shivered appreciably, then slowly, then quickly dipped down, down, right to the very river bottom it seemed where in a wave of sound it trembled to meet and climb again yet another wall of water, but a smaller one this time, then a smaller, and yet a smaller, until the river swept by broad and smooth again. It was the great "bore," the incoming tide from the sea, pent up between the converging banks of the estuary. At full and low moon that tidal wave oft times rushes up the river as a flood of water would rush up a funnel.

After a few days came the jungle in overwhelming patches as if determined on blotting out the habitations of man. Jakara gazed at this jungle for hours at a time; it gripped him with its sense of silent, remorseless life. There were two mighty walls of trees, their interlocked limbs forming a dense canopy between the sun's rays and the earth. Among the trunks, slender palms and ferns fought to live. For miles looping cable-vines in twisted strength linked the carpeted limbs. Tangled lawyer-canes trailed from countless inner jungles of palm-like leaves. Creepers in riotous profusion clothed the trees and hung veil-like from the cable-vines, apparently struggling to choke other masses of trellised greenery. Occasionally Jakara's heart glowed as he drank in the beauty of wondrous orchids with their tasselled flowers glowing down to earth from the green gloom above. Several were in fronds like chains of gold drooping from an unseen limb; one beauty flowered in purple bells with crimson hearts. The "ghost" flower enthralled Jakara. Its petals were pointed and waxy, with tiger stripes of orange. Some flowered like clusters of pink grapes, while others put all their beauty into just one hanging flower. Some trees were fragrant with their own flowers, while occasionally creepers in curtains flowered for miles, wiping out the riverbanks in vivid sheets of crimson and of yellow. Jakara one day held his breath when the whole bank blazed into a scarlet curtain stretching away up the river, from the tree-tops to the water. In a few short years that recklessly brave naturalist, D'Albertis, was to sail up this river for over five hundred miles and name the famous "D'Albertis Creeper." Next would stretch miles of sombre green, breathing a titanic strength, but with no sign of flower or bird. At a warning shout, Jakara would spy from the platform the ominous snout of a crocodile as a reminder that nature is not all beautiful. She is, in fact, a beautiful fiend.

The birds delighted Jakara – feathered things so beautiful as to cause intense reverence for their Creator in the heart, and a great wonder in the mind, of man. There were different species of the birds of paradise busily playing from branch to branch, generally only visible as a coloured flash upon the highest trees, while they conversed agreeably in their peculiar wild notes. These birds were beautiful in form, their peacock and rainbow colouring indescribable by man. He thought the Great Bird, as the canoe men named it, exquisitely lovely as it held its court on a branch overlooking the water, its gorgeous side plumes of gold quivering as its body moved in the dance. The less gaudy females always surrounded it, looking on with intense interest and admiration. This sight was only seen on a "dancing tree," where the birds had stripped a limb of leaves. Of these birds many were of a species quite unknown to Jakara. One beauty displayed streamers of a wonderful blue, twice as long as its body, another showing a brilliant emerald gorget and important ruff, its Joseph's coat sparkling with purple and black and chestnut and deep green. He thought it a shame that such beauty should be sacrificed to adorn the heads of savages.

Pigeons pouted in flocks and in pairs, many of them extraordinarily large, and each with a note and vivid beauty all its own. He could also hear the harsh voices of the great black cockatoo and hornbill.

Jakara found that Kebisu and the entire fleet were also admiring the birds of paradise and the occasional orchids. But not for beauty's sake. They looked upon them as so many pretty feathers and wasted flowers because they could not be put to ceremonial wear. Kebisu further explained that several varieties of the birds of paradise which they saw had been eagerly accepted as a good omen by the fleet, in as much as such varieties were seldom seen on the lowlands, but generally lived in varying heights on the interior mountain lands. Perhaps some failure of their food-supply in the upper lands had brought them down to the river. Some orchids also were unusual. The flotilla had seen more colourful life on this trip than on any before. The fact was accepted by all hands as a good omen.

A day before the arrival at the bartering village, the river unexpectedly broadened into a lake picturesque with islands, brown waterways rippling between. Kebisu ordered a lookout on each masthead. Jakara could not refrain from a thrill of pride at the discipline of his adopted tribesmen when, in answer to quiet orders, the big canoes gracefully formed a perfect triangle, with Kebisu's *Skull Chief* for the cutting edge. Each canoe shot up into place, until it travelled half a bowshot away from the next before it; thus each was guarded by its own fire and that of the vessels in front and rear, and one flank by its twin vessel in the side of the triangle. Every vessel was thus spaced with neat room to come about if necessary. This system of arrow protection gave each canoe the fighting strength of four, turning the flotilla, when properly handled, into a body of the utmost possible efficiency, both for fighting and for manoeuvring.

Jakara's blood quickened at this ominous move; he instinctively glanced to see that his weapons were handy: the canoes seemed to wake and breathe as if inspired by the brightening smiles and swelling chests of the warriors. Men had closed imperceptibly round the emissaries on the *Skull Chief's* fighting platform. Not by the faintest shadow did their faces betray the facts of their position.

Kebisu ordered the flotilla to steer for a waterway rolling between two islands, where the canoes could keep wide of the down-stream current and still be out of bowshot from the shores. The canoes glided along like prehistoric water-snakes, their lidless eyes glaring towards either bank as if they knew of the coming struggle. Jakara's hand itched to hold Lightning: he stepped to Kebisu's side.

"I do not like it," growled the Mamoose. "A fight against these bushmen will be pastime, but may the spirits of darkness seize the souls of those whom I shall slay if I have been brought up here on a fool's errand!"

Kebisu's ferocious temper showed in the glitter in his eyes, the snarl on his lips. The straining paddlers avoided his glance, but the whisper spread along the canoes: "The ear of Kebisu is red as blood."

Jakara peered from the platform at further islands opening out ahead. Two hours later, he saw that in the distance the river apparently closed in, to carry on again as a great tree-lined highway.

"I should have hated to be fooled," growled Kebisu with relief – and just then his lookout man shouted.

Instantly the emissaries jumped for their lives. One reached the water with an arrow twitching in his back: in a few seconds his mates were capering in the Dance of Death on the canoe platform. Their friends watched amazed as the flotilla emerged – their friends in canoes like clustered bees hiding round the points of the farthermost islands. It was the first time they had seen the Dance, and it caught their breath. Then, with a shout that rolled along the river, their paddles bit the water and they raced for the flotilla.

Kebisu's mind acted intuitively. He gave one glance behind at the empty river and guessed what must be waiting there, thought of the rushing current that gave an enormous advantage to light canoes, glimpsed the numbers of his enemies, and then gave a quiet command. Steady as the minutes of time, each canoe came about; Kebisu's vessel shot straight down through the middle of the triangle base, which was back-paddling. The two canoes nearest Kebisu followed him, and they in turn were followed by two, until the base was moving again and the perfect triangle was gathering momentum downstream, heading out for the centre of the current.

A triumphant howl arose from up-stream, with waving of heavy spears gay with coloured streamers and of pineapple-shaped stone clubs; flourish of cassowary daggers; menacing boom of drums and blare of conch-shells startling the river with a fiendish chorus as the light canoes, massed like a flock of ducks, came flying in pursuit.

An understanding howl shrilled from away down-stream. The big chief smiled grimly when he saw canoes racing to stretch in line upon line and join together the rear of the two islands up whose dividing waterway he had recently come, while the trees along both island edges sprang into life with bow-and-arrow men. Kebisu ground his teeth, "Dogs!" he growled to Jakara, "what fools they take us for!" He swept on into the middle of the stream.

As the current caught the flotilla, island after island swept past, and

Jakara rapidly surveyed the craft against them. It seemed that all the canoes of every village down-river must have followed them up for the slaughter. As far as the eye could see the water was black with dugouts striving to join their comrades who had already blocked the passage-way. Those canoes which were in the middle of the passage were paddling methodically but were stationary, just keeping bow on to the stream. Stretching out on either side, their massed comrades paddled less and less hard in proportion as the canoes reached out to the quieter waters touching the shores of the islands.

From that struggling bedlam arose shrieking choruses of encouragement to their rapidly reinforcing friends: startled parrots, in clouds of colour, flashed above the river that boomed with conflicting echoes as the drums and conches down-stream added their harsh quota to the infernal bedlam from above. Jakara's blood thrilled while he gazed astern, whence the very river seemed shrieking. Flying canoes chased them in numbers, which suggested that the tribes from the Snow Mountains themselves must have swarmed down-river to the rendezvous. Jakara glared towards these disorganized demons, Lightning naked in his hand, while he picked out their chiefs. These stood encouraging their men to superhuman efforts, right hand waving the club, left hand brandishing the cassowary dagger. Their gay head-dresses were of paradise plumes and cormorant feathers, and one tall savage with a splendid brown chest was brave in the feathers of the white crane. Jakara was startled to see men girded in cuirasses of basketwork cane; he wondered could this armour really stop arrows. But the rushing nearness of the fight drove all thought of the varieties of the foes from his mind, while a new sound sent a chill through his veins.

The island edges suddenly spewed forth women shrieking to their men to "Kill! Kill! Kill!" They incited their tribesmen with such berserk gestures that Jakara thought the viragoes of hell must surely have broken loose. Like flitting bats they skipped among the trees in line with the flying canoes, those not already stark naked tearing off their *ramis* and hurling them far out into the stream: the wildest men could not have worked the blood of human beings to such an hysterical pitch as did those mad women.

In a fleeting instant Jakara glimpsed the chances. Surrounding them were innumerable foes, confident of success, who had already manoeuvred an apparently invincible ambush and who would fight on the river which had given them birth. Against these, a tiny handful already apparently flying. Then Jakara gazed on the flotilla, and his veins raced with that glowing pride which is felt only by those accepted among a company of disciplined men. He saw every man's eyes flashing, lips wreathed in boyish smiles, chests heaving for the greater supply of air demanded by excitement, each man in his place knowing his allotted task, picked men of a fighting race bred to war on sea and land, under the leadership of a victorious chief, and classing their innumerable foes as mere savages; Maros, swaying on the platform of the *Headhunter*, guarded the middle of the base of the triangle, gently swinging his *gaba-gaba*, his broad body all rippling muscles as he controlled the lust for physical contact with the enemy, his ugly face peculiarly boyish, and the death-song on his lips. Beizam, a wild figure of young manhood, commanded the *Shark* on the flanks, laughing recklessly, his perfect limbs a joy to behold. Every man a powerful man, highly trained and disciplined, lusting for the fight.

Jakara laughed to the ribbony sky. He chose his position far out on an outrigger boom, whirling Lightning in a circle in order to gauge his fighting-room and avoid embarrassing the bowmen below in the body of the canoe. He laughed at the two long lines of their feathered heads down there glued to the loop-holes. From the outrigger boom he gazed far out and well over the mass of enemy vessels. It occurred to him that this triangle of huge canoes was a frightful battering-ram pushed by an irresistible current and endowed with cutting impetus by powerful rowers.

Among the enemy stood out numerous war-canoes, but they were river vessels, light and low compared to Kebisu's great craft. Not being built for the sea, the largest of the enemy had neither the depth nor the outriggers and towering platforms which gave Kebisu's craft such an immeasurable fighting advantage. The majority of the enemy canoes were only from twenty to thirty feet long, practically dugouts; they would be but shells when the weight of the triangle crashed into them. Jakara laughed mockingly across the water as he realized that the dense packing of the enemy canoes would multiply disaster for them. From the banks of both islands shot a cloud of arrows, which fell short. The bowmen raced along the banks to reach the blockading canoes: they would simply reinforce their fellows by using the canoes as a bridge: the fight was very close.

The bull voice of Maras burst forth into song. Instantly deep voices in unison swelled up through the howling air in the wildly beautiful war-song of the Torres Strait Islanders: the voice of Jakara joined in, tremblingly clear. The terrible excitement hurried the rowers to superhuman efforts: the massive triangle flew towards the blockade: the rowers leapt for their fighting-stations, to the clatter of discarded paddles and thrum of the big war-bows; the water was sprayed with arrows. In a trice the decks of the triangle were deserted, but arrow-heads peeped from the loopholes below. Only the fighting guards of the chiefs were visible on the platforms, shielded waist-high by crates of latticed bamboo. Deep down in the canoes were expert bowmen to guard the chiefs at close quarters, while others crouched behind the lattice-work, so placed that at any angle the farthest enemy sharp-shooter would be visible to them.

Then came the arrows raining on the flotilla at the renewed blare of conch-shells; quick roll of drums; howls of fury from painted men, hysteria curdling the note of some when the foaming wedge with all its fierce painted jaws and eyes staring from the beaks of those towering bows rushed down upon them.

Jakara shivered delightedly, expectant of the crash; Kebisu in his barbaric dress, a splendid figure, looked ahead with serene eyes, while the directions of his upraised hand were instantly obeyed by the steersman. For Kebisu, determined on striking a deadly blow, had no intention of having his canoes' bows split by the impact. He had the cool judgment that was needed for consideration of the current and for control of the great weight with which they would strike. Each canoe chief could pick his individual striking-point. The enemy, mad with excitement, bereft of reason, presented a seething mass of canoes.

A warning shout from Kebisu, and Jakara snatched an outrigger stay while, to the sound of a splitting crash, he was flung out over tumbling canoes when the *Skull Chief* rose high with a sickeningly invincible motion and groaned derisively as her bottom sawed over them. The stern of an up-ended dugout rose whale-like above Jakara's head. He saw her glistening bottom as the anguished crew slid down into the water. Waves slapped his face and blotted out the vision of interlocked canoes sweeping out sideways from the bows. Then came simultaneous crashes as the two following canoes broke into the dismayed mass, which, at succeeding angles, was crushed, while stinging waves rolled the helpless craft against, and right up atop of, their brothers. Then followed crash upon crash, spreading out along the line, while the river rose in spouting waves, spinning smashed canoes and drowning men.

The bellied-out mass was pushed bodily down the river, to the accompaniment of a harsh grinding of interlocking wood which dammed back the rushing current, while the pressing wedge now slowly crushed through, until, with the bursting of the dam, the whole tangled mass swept down-stream, a side issue of erratic whirlpools adding their quota of demoralization to the luckless river craft. The air whistled as Kebisu's bowmen shot death into the utterly demoralized target; sling-stones hummed, and the smack of their contact was sharp and clear.

The impact and resistance slowed down the triangle; the cross waves and irresponsible canoes inevitably bunched it out of shape; the *Turtle* and the *Shark*, to Beizam's maniacal fury, were slewed completely around. Kebisu calmly roared his orders; each canoe's leader roared his own when necessary; paddle-men sprang to positions and helped the current to right their vessels into position again. Quick hand-to-hand fighting followed, a blood-boiling medley of thrust and smash, to the accompaniment of a howling chorus extending as far as the women on the banks. Helpless canoes in scores were washed and jammed against Kebisu's vessels; drowning men clung desperately to the outrigger floats and swarmed up to the bodies of the canoes; the arrow-men dropped their bows and, leaping up to the bulwarks and platforms, smashed down with their clubs while shouting heart-delighted cries, ripping in the daggers with hissing breath, thrusting, stabbing, biting, throttling, in a howling crescendo of blood-thirsty ferocity. The pursuing fleet spewed itself straight into the battling cauldron and fought like despairing furies, for their pursuit had been too swift to allow of retreat. And through it all rang the calmly shouted orders of the chiefs, and their well-protected steersmen, with mind and eyes concentrated on their leaders' directing hands, worked the flotilla swiftly and surely into the triangle again, while great numbers of enemy canoes, extricating themselves, fled, their occupants bemoaning the many that had gone to the bottom; others, overturned, drifted away, interlocked with still others whose entire crews were transfixed with arrows, while swimming men dived deep to dodge the hail of missiles. The current grasped the wedge again as an entirety, and away it sped, with the enemy faster and faster disengaging himself from the greatest native debacle ever enacted on the Fly.

The flotilla suffered only a trifling loss. It swept down-stream many times faster than it had crawled up. Jakara landed in Kiwai with a dose of malaria. While they laid him in his cubicle, he raved that the girl's head accused him; that her eyes were those of Eyes of the Sea. He took no further part in the voyage until after long weeks, when the voyagers picked him up on the return trip to Mer.

CHAPTER XXV

The Cyclone

With a red dawn Kebisu sailed from Parama Island. The Paramaians had delayed him; there was intense rivalry in trade between them and the Moattans. Jakara thought the Paramaians fine men intellectually and physically, and he admired their tall strong-willed women. It was these very people, now waving a palm-branch farewell to the fleet, who a few years later massacred the teachers of the London Missionary Society.

The fleet looked very brave, one hundred and seventy great canoes blazing with barbaric designs, the masts right to the outrigger booms gay with streamers of dyed grasses, the mastheads crested in rattan-work designs of sheeny pigeon plumage, the "flash" paddles tilted skyward and decorated with black cassowary feathers picked off with jets of golden paradise plumes. The "beards" at bow and stern flopped heavily in their feathers and painted coconut matting; the "eyes" of each craft were startling in their circlets of brilliant parrot plumage. The warriors were garlanded with feathers and flowers and spoils of war and trade, their massaged limbs glistening, their oiled hair pulsating colour from imprisoned butterflies. Their massed song kept time to the rise and fall of the crocodile-jaws and vampire-heads of the war-canoes as they reared to the waves. The sails glinted golden, and a stiff wind creamed the spray from the arrogant bows as the sea made trial of these new revellers upon her breast.

Smaller canoes were to follow; they would arrive at Ugar and Eroob and Mer months afterwards, passed on from island to island. Such bought goods always did arrive, always would arrive, if – Kebisu frowned – if the cursed Lamars did not choke the seas with their own ships.

They sailed quite close to the spot where a few years later Jardine's brigantine *Lancashire Lass* sheltered from a storm and her diving "boys" recovered some thousands of pounds worth of old-time dollars from a long-forgotten wreck. They cruised by Maubiag, where John Cowling found tons of copper ingots in the skeleton hold of a long-forgotten ship. But Jakara sailed over those coral-cemented Don Carlos and Ferdinand dollars without knowing of others who had gone that way before.

Kebisu divided his crews among the newly acquired vessels, and equalized among them the goods that had been purchased. The fleet travelled fast. Kebisu was like an eager boy anxious to get home with his prize. True, he had lost many men, but all in unavoidable fight, and his warriors had killed far more than had been lost. Trade had been very successful despite the lessened purchasing power.

Previously the big Mamoose had started home from these trading ventures with regret, but this time he was very anxious to hand over to C'Zarcke the fruits of the voyage. With each homeward plunge of the *Skull Chief 's* bows a presentiment of coming disaster weighed more strongly upon him, sickening him mentally, for to the elect of Bomai these presentiments invariably rang true.

The wind was propitious; should it keep in this quarter and strength, the fleet would be safe at Tutu by nightfall. He gazed back over the fleet sailing· in brave array of following V's. The crews sang happily of victory and love and home-coming. He searched the sky; it was cloudless. He stared anxiously at the playful sea ahead. What could possibly go wrong?

Jakara sat back upon the lashed-down bales of feathers, of sheathed cane, sago, and hibiscus fibre, contentedly puffing at his *zoob*. The sky smiled, and the wind kissed his bronzed body. He was thinking, in a coolly methodical way, of love. He was confident that Eyes of the Sea would be awaiting him with tears and kisses and clinging arms and that sweet little smile of hers. He had quite forgiven her, but he intended to guide the reins for the future. He had allowed her too much of her own way, with disastrous results. She was a slave to her environment; if he could not teach, then he must drive her out of it; it would be better for both their sakes. When once in civilization, and when living among white girls, she would forget all her illusions about these coloured people; she would soon *want* to forget. He would take her back to Mer, keep C'Zarcke to his promise, and canoe off to the first white sail, then away to Sydney. After that, the future could take care of itself. Having settled the matter to his complete satisfaction, he let the *zoob* gradually slip from his fingers while he dreamed – and he had dreamed often of late – of those iron-bound caskets deep within the crater of Mer. Gold of the Aztecs might lie there, slumbering among those other relics of ages past. Who knew but that one of Cortez's continent-seeking captains had fallen on Mer? Many Las people were almost unquestionably of Spanish extraction. Why, he could name four in G's alone, Gesu, Geaz, Gehasu, Geasa, all indicative of Spanish influence. Who knew but that a royal banner of Castille had temporarily waved upon Mer? Perhaps gold and jewels from the temples of Itzapan lay among the treasures he had seen deep within the crater of Mer. So Jakara dreamed; but at the present day there are data which somewhat support his dreams.

Within three hours Kebisu was running parallel with the great

Warrior Reefs. They were on his lee, and would continue with him all the way to Tutu. At low tide the vast reefs glistened like a chain of yellow-green snakes, ominously distinct from the blue of the deep water. On this course Kebisu was running along the eastern side of the reefs. It was miles shorter than the western side, and quite safe with the wind in its present quarter. And to Tutu was only one day's run.

Before midday the wind dropped considerably. The sun glowed with blood-red heat. The waves sobered to a sullen heavy roll. The water surged oily and warm. The fleet slowed down to a crawl, its flowered pinions drooping. By midday the men were slipping overboard from the platforms, hanging lazily in the cool water.

They passed between Pierce Cay and the larger of the Warrior Reefs. The cay, of shallow depth, seemed burnished like water-dimmed glass. At midday they sighted Damut Island and glided along between it and Moon Pass. Kebisu gazed lingeringly at Moon Pass. It is a narrow opening between the two greatest of the Warrior Reefs. If he sailed through, he could then turn and sail so as to place the reef as a buffer between him and any possible dangerous weather – although the only wind that could hurt him would be a hard blow from the east, and a blow from that particular quarter was unusual at this season of the year.

Uneasily Kebisu walked the platform, cursing himself for entertaining unrecognizable fears. He was on the right course, the quickest course, the surest course! Why, if he had sailed through Moon Pass, he would have done exactly the wrong thing. For this was the tail end of the north-west season, and, although the winds were uncertain, if a squall did come up it would almost certainly blow from the west, and that would throw him right on the reef. Whereas, now, the reef was a protection between him and the weather.

He stared moodily ahead. If he could only define this dread taking possession of him, this warning from his spirit fathers that he was doing wrong when experience told him he was doing right. If they could only impress him with what to do, so that he would understand! Why could not that cursed priest send him light in his bitter need? He could worry him with warning; why did he not explain the facts clearly to his mind? Not do the thing by halves and then hold the Mamoose responsible for working out his own salvation? He searched the lowering sky and prayed to Bomai for wind, wind for only a few hours longer, a steady north-west wind.

Very gradually Damut Island became dim in the distance, and far ahead there appeared a haze denoting hilly Moa. The breeze died, like the lingering sigh of the dread Sea-witch. The canoes lapped to a breathless calm. Here and there a lighter vessel began to drift out of formation. Kebisu shouted to "Out paddles." In the quietness his voice boomed across the sea: the warriors dipped willingly to the paddles: they were only a few hours from home. The sun was half-way down, sinking unusually fast this afternoon, it seemed; turning into a fiery ball strangely early in the day. Up to the skies floated melody from hundreds of throats, the canoe-song of the Torres Strait Islanders. The air was so still that individual voices were distinct.

The vessels glided ahead, but such great craft, lightly manned, were ill served by paddles. Two hours later, and the sun balanced on the horizon: still the canoes rippled on, while the song drifted musically over the sea. Kebisu was sweating from mental distress; silently he called upon his spirit fathers to help him; from his heart he prayed to Bomai to avert any disaster that might be. As the sun sank, he spied a distant blur ahead. The tops of the trees of Tutu! Sighing with intense relief, he turned troubled eyes to the sky. A tiny black cloud like a tentacle was reaching for the canoes. The cloud was in the east!

Kebisu looked away, lest the warriors should note his glance. Sick at heart, his voice joined thunderously in the song, and under its influence singers put renewed energy into their paddles.

Night fell, and the cloud, no longer to be denied, cloaked the whole sky black. The song ceased: the heavens were brooding: hundreds of paddle-blows smacked the water distinctly; then from westward came a sucking murmur as the tides began swirling over the great reef: a flaming fork pierced the cloud from the heavens to the sea: intense darkness followed – and a sigh as from men afraid.

Kebisu called all the V's into closer formation, lest they should become separated in the dark; he cheered them with the assurance that Tutu was very near. They strained with the sweat of fear oozing upon their chests: fear gripped Kebisu, for the turn of the tide was neutralizing their efforts – it was almost dragging the vessels broadside on towards the reef. He roared for the leading V to paddle steadily while the rear lines closed up. They thrashed on again into a darkness almost felt, a sinister night awake with an uncanny moaning of the sea which was swallowed by the sky, a night that was breathless. One yellow star, only one! But it was the Zoogobar star, and so Kebisu directed his course and prayed Bomai to keep its brilliance unclouded.

Beizam, staring hard into the darkness, saw the threatening reef abeam, and suddenly urged his rowers forward with frantic actions and words. He just managed to manoeuvre the *Shark* dangerously close behind the *Skull Chief,* and with superb seamanship kept his vessel there.

Fiery tongues licked from sky to sea, illuminating the canoes with ghastly clearness. Green phosphorus splashed from the toiling paddles: the water sucked viciously against the vessels: men breathed heavily. Kebisu strained eyes and mind toward Tutu, so very near.

It came from the east – an icy breath from distant tortured seas. It travelled with a shriek that shrilled from the water and whipped the air and eddied to the heavens. Following it came a groaning sound which thrashed and sucked the water into cyclonic waves. "Down sails, luff up!" roared Kebisu just before the canoes reeled. With perfect seamanship their bows turned to the wind. The reef was now directly astern; they must fight it out. The paddles dipped in unison, driven by slaving arms to hold them against the wind. The ocean shrieked: twisted spray slapped the canoes: wave-crests were lifted and flung past in stinging sheets: the outrigger struts vibrated like a giant's orchestra to the lead of the wind: a roaring growl, fast coming, thundered the heart of the storm. Speech was impossible: the men strained their very hearts just to hold the canoes stationary and prevent them from being blown back upon the reefs. Waves arose cold as the heart of the Sea-witch, swelling and growing with the seconds, huge black rolling things lifting high the canoes, to thump them down into darkness. The great reef broke into the song it loved, a low croon extending into the distance, a heavy murmuring, a gentle roar, a loud roar, a far-flung swelling roar, then a continuous thundering that rumbled into crash upon crash! Demons shrieked past on whistling wings, sheets of rain bit like fiery wires as, like an inferno roaring through a funnelled sky, the cyclone struck them. It thrashed the canoes as if they were live things with heads bowed to the blow. It pressed them down into the wave-crests, pushed them into the swirling troughs: it merged them as shadowy grey things into the blackness of the combers, it illuminated them with flying sheets of frothy spray.

Then showed the marvellous workmanship of those canoes, the triumph of the mind of man fighting throughout the centuries against nature's storms of moments. For the huge cigar-shaped vessels were perfectly buoyant, they were really tough hollow tubes filled with air, while the outrigger floats made capsizing practically impossible, and every movement of the waves against them forced the canoe still more certainly upwards. Held thus, teeth on to the wind, the canoes were merely long thin torpedoes, against which the waves could obtain no purchase. They could not be swamped, for the shape into which they had been cut made them practically decked-in, and the narrow gunwale of planks made them still closer. It was the big broad platforms that felt the breaking weight of the waters. Presently these began to go, timber by timber.

The majority of the men were in the bodies of the canoes, but standing half-way up, so as to lean over and get a paddle-grip in the water. That was the great weakness. Those vessels were meant for sails, not paddles, but now the direction of the wind blowing them on to the reef astern necessitated the strongest of paddling as their one forlorn hope, and occasionally a paddler was torn from the canoe and his wailing shriek was the last of him in the darkness.

Human endurance could not withstand those masses of water all rolling to burst upon the reef. Yard by straining yard the fleet was driven back: minute by minute disaster became more certain. Kebisu, a giant of the dark, clung to the main platform with arms outstretched to Bomai. In the blinding flashes the crouching Jakara stared at this madman who prayed to his god to steady the storm. Jakara, with the fear of death in his heart, strained to plunge a paddle in the swirling power beating upon them, strained lest he lose his manhood and give way altogether to death. With frightened mind he wondered if *his* God could steady this fury from the shrieking skies. Then in gusts triumphant above the cyclone rose a song, the Death Song! It wailed up from the rear line of canoes, behind which the night was a ghostly shroud with hurrying masses of foam. Voices pregnant with meaning sang that song, most of them quietly resigned, others in submissive terror, all going the one way.

Kebisu raved. Jakara heard and was afraid. Death was so near that his senses fully understood while his straining ears heard the men of Bomai, of Malu, of the Au-gud, men of the different classes worshipping the Great One under different names:

O Bomai, O God of Life, of Soul, of Eternity,

Of man, of star, of all that is,

O, take thou the soul of me to Spirit Land.

The day is done and the night has come.

The sands of life are spilling fast

And earth my body claims: but to thee at dawn,

O Bomai, receive thou the soul of me.

Simultaneously the voices ceased. Was it imagination, or did he really hear above the wind a whining crash upon crash as the canoes were dashed upon the reef? Jakara shuddered. The wind howled. One line of Kebisu's canoes was gone.

With gritted teeth, straining every limb, with muscle, with mind and body and grim fear, the warriors fought to keep their canoes into the wind, hysterically joyous if only they could hold them stationary. Beizam screamed in a frenzy of encouragement, mad in the fear that he might lose his first command. Unceasingly from the darkness rolled up black waves that hurled high the canoes under their fearful momentum. And again, weirdly above the wind, wailed the Death Song:

O Au-gudeem! O Au-gudeem!
Spirit might of all that is and was and will be!
Deathless Power whose dreams are reality,
Smile on me O Au-gudeem, O Power, O God!
I give my spirit clean to thee
And thoughts and love and all of me:
Let my body rot and die;
Treasure my spirit as of Thee,
O Au-gudeem! O Au-gudeem!

Jakara, straining at his paddle, ground his teeth to stop his ears. Salt that was not of the sea alone stung his eyes. In a lightning flash, as at a devil's picture, he saw splintered canoes and men and foam flying upwards together. Kebisu bit the wood of the mast, screaming mad. His second line of canoes had gone. The night howled, men fought even for their breath: minute by minute that grinding roar came closer in the eardrums of Jakara.

Once again rose the Death Song, so plainly sung, so close, so full of the heart of men to whom now life was almost a memory:

O Malu, Maker of me, O Father, O Mother!
Maker of star-edged eternity!
Thine the life thou gavest me:
Receive it back to the deathless shores
On Boigu's blessed isle.
Clean I've lived, so judge thou me,
Malu, O God, O Malu, take thou my spirit back to Thee,

The song died as the men died. And suddenly came Kebisu's maniacal roar "Up sail!" Jakara felt the wind biting his cheek; it had whipped around, as it frequently does in the tropic storms. Would it last?

A frantic scramble in the darkness: a heaving of the canoes out to sea, a sickening falling away as the waves caught them broadside and sucked them back towards the reef. Would the sails hold under the terrific strain? The forlorn hope was to chance it. They plunged into moving darkness, with a maddened giant in the leading canoe screaming up at a star.

One hour later Kebisu swung what remained of his fleet into Basilisk Pass. As they came close into the quiet anchorage of Tutu, from the black island there rose from many people the forlorn, wailing cry for the dead.

CHAPTER XXVI

A Girl's Plan

Jakara luxuriated upon his sleeping-mat after hours of listening to wind-tortured trees. The seaward reef still mumbled its thunder song to the ghost-like voices of human beings wailing for their dead. Jakara heard them still, those forlorn voices rising and falling, ceasing only to cry again, mournful, and utterly abandoned. He sat up. He wished heartily that the wailing would cease, it was so despairingly human.

In a corner Kebisu crouched in ferocious misery. His world had crashed. Kebisu the Undefeated, thrashed at Coconut! And now he had returned with only one-third of the grand fleet! Kebisu was a figure who dominated the Island world. The time was coming when the very Lamars whom he hated and feared so much were to recognize him as a great native chief with whom it was advisable to be on the best of diplomatic terms. Kebisu little dreamed that he was destined to be laid to rest on Tutu wrapped in a Union Jack, which flag he would serve so well. That flag once flew on H.M.S. *Basilisk,* sent out later during Jardine's regime to clean the Coral Sea of blackbirders. In the days when Captain Moresby cleaned up the *Melanie* and *Challenge* and *Woodbine* and *Krishna* and others, he met and esteemed Kebisu and treated him accordingly. But Kebisu as yet knew nothing of this. And now – his world would condemn him as a tragic failure. With a hoarse oath he sprang from the house and hurried through the village, clapping his hands over his ears, to hear only the voices of the sea. He saw miles of foam and the blackened ribs of what had once been a big ship. He stared while the waves billowed in play, and then turned and rushed to the nearest house. His arm clutched in through the open door and dragged out a wailing woman.

Dragging her by the neck as a dog would a pup, he flung her on the sand and pointed to the sea.

"Who burned the Lamar ship?" he roared. The woman cringed at his feet. "The New Guinea men came down like the leaves of the forest," she breathed; "they took everything and burned the ship."

Kebisu rushed out on the reef until the insolent waves picked him up and dashed him upon the coral and rolled him over and over, far up on the beach. He staggered up bleeding, and thrashed his arms at the miles of oncoming waves. He shrieked to Bomai to flatten the billows, to throttle the wind, to dry up the sea and wither its power.

Back in the house, Maros sat up lazily and yawned. He had wonderful teeth. "I wish those old pigeons would stop howling," he grunted in Island slang, "I should like to stretch their necks."

Jakara gazed at those muscular fingers working in anticipation. "Tutu has lost many men," he answered; "the mothers are wailing for their sons."

"I would make them wail, if I were Mamoose here," said Maros grimly. "Their task now is to breed up other sons, and be quick about it."

"How about the girls whose sweethearts have gone?" inquired Jakara.

"Let them find others," said Maros promptly, "there are plenty of good men left. What's the use of their wailing for warriors whose spirits have flown to Boigu, where they will find plenty of girls anyway? The women are making life miserable just because of Death. One death at a time will do for me. Who knows how many more each one has before him? But where's the breakfast? Hasn't that gossiping old woman brought it yet?"

Jakara smiled. "I am hungry too," he confided, "but Kebisu has vanished, and the Maid-le isn't here."

"If they are going to moan all day on an empty belly, well, I am not," grumbled Maros decidedly. He poked his shaggy head through the doorway. "Hey, Ke-wa!" he roared. Jakara knew that breakfast would arrive quickly. It did.

Jakara ate hungrily. A bitter night and escape from death bequeath a man a keen appetite. Presently he hurried away, and eagerly searched the village, peering among the houses and clustered groups for Eyes of the Sea. He stepped inside the gloom of Babelu's house, his eyes very eager. Old Babelu crouched forlorn in a corner, his head upon his knees, for his only son had flown to Beig. Siau and her daughters crouched with hair disarranged in abandoned grief: the death-wail moaned through the house. Jakara stood silent, uneasily surprised that Eyes of the Sea was not here and wailing too, for Babelu and Siau were her "father" and "mother," and young Babelu was her "brother." Puzzled, he turned away. It would not be etiquette to interrupt here.

Anxiously he searched among group after group. To all inquiries he received a downcast shake of the head and a mumbled "She is not here." To his surprise, some of the people would hardly answer at all. Naturally he put such discourtesy down to grief.

With a growing anxiety he entered, without invitation, house after house, until he searched the entire village and among all the people. The girl was not there! Becoming half frantic, he ran along the beach, searching all the tiny island.

But he found only Maros, all alone, standing like a statue by the headstone of Captain Banner. That black-bearded giant from the South Seas had pioneered the pearl-shelling industry, opening up untold wealth for future generations of Australians and work for English mills. Hard luck that he had died soon after finding the first pearl-shell around the Warrior Reefs! A strange semi-tolerant regard had sprung up between Kebisu and Banner, two strong men of action in a wild life and age. On Banner's death Kebisu had allowed him to be buried on Tutu, and further, when later a stone had been sent from admirers of Banner in Sydney, Kebisu had allowed it to be erected above the sleeping face of the big white captain, on Tutu. The fascinating story of Kebisu and Banner would require a book to itself.

That smooth white stone with the intriguing black marks possessed an irresistible fascination for Maros. With a strange eagerness he measured the spent waves that came quivering in from far out over the reef. Each wave was surely reaching for the grave, certainly the heart of the mother sea clutched out for her child. Each wave, as it was spent on the tiny beach, smoothed out its waters and crept farther and farther up towards the grave. So persistently did those creeping ripples strive to reach the white man's resting-place that they became too exhausted to recede and sighed back into the sand.

Maros sighed. He saw that years must yet pass before the waves could undermine the stone and make it fall, and a tribal superstition forbade him to take the stone until it fell of its own accord.

Years later, the patient sea gave to the savage Mamoose that which he craved, and to-day on Ugar Island there lie the stone's broken fragments on the grave of Maros.

Maros started from his reverie as Jakara spoke. "Where is she, Maros? Tell me! They have not hurt her, surely! Where is Eyes of the Sea?"

Maros grinned heathenishly. "She is all right," he said soothingly. "Get a knobby sapling and give her a taste of it. It would be a kindness."

"Why?" asked Jakara. "Why?"

"She is only pretending, boy. She is hiding. Beat her, beat the hide off her, and she will crawl and kiss your feet."

"But why?" asked Jakara helplessly. "Why on earth should she hide from me?"

Maros screwed up his ugly face and waved a hand as if to exterminate a fly. "Why," he grunted, "why? If you get whying about women, you will why all your miserable life. Beat them, hard and often. That's why."

"But why should she hide from me?"

Maros glared, then shook his head, while the big black curls rolled about his shoulders. "Poor fellow!" he growled in mock sympathy. "Poor Jakara the Why!"

Jakara talked furiously back along the beach. Maros smiled to the marble stone. "The boy loves the little wild-cat," he said aloud. "Spirit of the big white Lamar, watch over the two Lamars as I watch over your stone. Give them their love, and give me the stone."

He folded his thick arms, musing at the stone. "We all want something," he whispered, "want it in a hurry, something that will vanish in a breath. And yet we all have the sea, and the land, and the sky, and the life everlasting. Yet we fear death, that will vanish in a breath, and we have no time for those things which will last for ever and for ever."

In miserable uncertainty Jakara searched among the trees fringing the island edge. He gazed down at the root-ribbed sand, dodging the broken lumps of coral, subconsciously watching his toes. His anger had given way to anxiety. What possibly could have happened to the girl? He longed to sit out here with her among the wind and spray, and just talk. He had so many things to tell her, and so much to ask of her. Why was she purposely shunning him?

Towards sundown, Jakara walked sullenly through the village, glancing neither to right nor to left. But a commanding figure, earnestly talking among a morose group of Mer warriors, instinctively drew his attention. His hand flew to Lightning. He would kill Beizam here and now! See! The fellow was sneering that he knew all about Eyes of the Sea, that she was his!

Beizam's eyes gleamed: he stepped forward. Jakara's neck tingled; he saw Beizam's head-mai, saw his powerful body tightening for the spring. A ghastly feeling crept up the base of his skull. The Dance of Death! Beizam was praying for the chance!

Jakara walked rapidly on, sick at heart. He would catch Beizam in a quiet place where it would mean man against man, with no chance of an arrow in his back for the victor. His brain raced, formulating all those vague fears that he had subconsciously noted of late, all the mishaps that were accredited to some evil influence on the part of the Lamars. The tragedy of the night before was inconsistently put down to the fault of the Lamars. This was Tutu! Here he lacked the protecting presence of C'Zarcke: one spark to the smoulder, and they might mob him. Beizam the Shark desired Jakara's head. Eyes of the Sea! She was a Lamar too! Ah, but she was a true Lamar of the natives, a spirit of their daughter visiting earth. She was passionately native. But Jakara always was, always had been, white. Very dispirited, he entered Kebisu's house just when Maros roared "Ke-wa!"

They ate quietly, except Maros. He was a noisy diner, and he liked to throw in a joke now and then. He received no response, so finally he grunted a world of meaning, and turned his full attention to his meal. Jakara ate thoughtfully, the Maid-le slowly and methodically, and his manner suggested that every ounce of food that he ate was going to do him the greatest possible good. Kebisu had lost appetite. Presently he turned to Maros and growled, "You will take the fleet back to Ugar, and Eroob, and Mer. I have done my part. There is no need for me to go farther."

Maros stared at Kebisu's sombre face, and then continued eating. Into each listener's brain had flashed the thought, "C'Zarcke!" Presently the Maid-le slipped silently away. Kebisu stalked morosely out into the night.

Maros leaned meaningly towards Jakara. "C'Zarcke will send different orders," he whispered hoarsely.

Jakara nodded.

Night came down. The Maid-le sat within the silence of his house. He reclined comfortably, his body at ease. He breathed regularly and easily; one would have thought he was asleep, although his curiously vacant eyes stared open into the darkness. He *was* asleep, in his physical body and his conscious mind. But messages from his subconscious mind were soaring over the sea to C'Zarcke, telepathic messages, of which the priests of Bomai-Malu have for centuries utilized a practical knowledge.

Maros poked his head out into the night, then sat back upon his mat and grumbled: "Nothing but a howling lot of devils! And the men as bad, squatting with heads dangling! Another night of it! Anyone would think the whole world was dead. And you moping for a slip of a girl! Did you hammer her?"

"How could I hammer her when I cannot even see her?" answered Jakara sullenly. "And I do not want to beat her either. If she does not want me, then she can go to the devil. I will not look for her any more."

"H'm," said Maros musingly, "you will not find her, anyway. She has told every soul on the island to put you astray. None will tell. You are up against hundreds."

"But *why* doesn't she want to see me?" asked Jakara in exasperation.

"Yah," sneered Maros, "why? Why do the stars shine? What is the good of battering your head against the reef? There are girls in plenty everywhere," he said, spreading out his big arms expressively. "And now that so many of us are killed, there will be twelve girls to every man. Take one, and see how quickly you will find Eyes of the Sea!"

Noiselessly the Maid-le entered the house. Maros gazed up at the thin ascetic face. "Where is Kebisu?"

"Prowling the beach like a lost soul," answered Maros.

"I will find him," said the Maid-le quietly. "Know that C'Zarcke sends word that Kebisu is to take the remnant of the fleet to their homes; and he, with you, must report finally to Mer."

Maros nodded at the glittering eyes which commanded his.

The Maid-le stepped outside. Maros drew a deep breath. "I would not be Kebisu for anything on earth," he mumbled cheerfully.

Heavy-hearted, and growing more angry every hour, Jakara answered nothing at all. In dull astonishment he could only think that Eyes of the Sea must have meant every word she said when last they quarrelled. Evidently she intended that they should never meet again; she had done with him. At the thought he became fiercely angry; his pride was hurt. After all, it was she who should have felt complimented, for he was a white man with a white man's ideals, while she was a primitive savage. And yet, he knew he could not leave her to her fate.

He brooded miserably far into the night; his overconfident plans had collapsed. As the still hours came, the wind moaned in dying gusts among the palms. Presently he was not sure whether it was the sighing fronds or the wail of voices that he occasionally heard. Wind and voices and hopes were dying, anyway.

Eyes of the Sea, in the quiet of a palm-thatched house, lay coiled like a possum on a warm sleeping-mat. She was sobbing in an anguish of uncertainty.

She wanted with all her heart to go to Jakara, to be with him always. But that would mean— For the hundredth time she puzzled over the reasonableness of her plan, her last desperate hope. Could it miscarry? Jakara would sail back to Mer with an unshakable conviction that she was determined to have her way. He would feel certain that she was prepared to give him up rather than leave her Island home. As time dragged on, he would become sad and lonely. He would inevitably come back to her, would agree to settle for always in the Islands; they would be happy all their lives. She would have attained her double object, for, with her by his side and all thoughts of the Lamar world growing fainter behind him, he would surely fight his way to become Mamoose of at least one island.

Eyes of the Sea was no Daniel, and to her the Lamar world was a den of fears, possessing terrors that grew more dreadful as the days wore on. For during these last few months the wise men had held many councils in the endeavour to combat this fast growing menace. The thought of the very name was frightening the people with the dread of national extinction, clouding the entire Island world with fears not understood. And now had fallen the blow of this great disaster of the night before. All the people were whispering that the Lamars were coming in numbers like the sands of the sea, and that the Island nations must perish. No, Eyes of the Sea felt that she would wither up with terror if ever she sailed to the inhuman world of the Lamars.

Nature and longing and loneliness would inevitably bring Jakara to her, she was sure. Something assured her that he would never sail without her, would never marry a native girl – and she was the only Lamar! And he loved her! Eyes of the Sea hugged her knees to her chin, and sighed, and with moist eyes whispered Jakara's name very caressingly, as if she would draw him to her by the very love of her thoughts.

Neither was there rest for Beizam. Feverishly he walked the dark beach with his eyes on the coral sands, living over and over again the wreck of the fleet. It had meant so much for him, for the future of Mer, if only Kebisu's vessels had gone down! But most of the big chief's vessels were in the van, and had escaped destruction. It was mostly the men of Mer, of Eroob, and of Ugar who had been smashed by the faithless sea. If only it had been the Tutu men's flotilla – with Kebisu! Beizam drew a breath of dismay, and stood with clenched hands gazing at the sky in an agony of longing for what had so nearly been. So near! If only Kebisu had gone down, if only Kebisu alone, the planner, the organizer, the great moral force!

Beizam swung his arms in futile rage against the gods of fate. In panther-like strides he stepped out again across the sands, thinking, thinking of how he could turn this great calamity to his advantage, thinking of how he could become Beizam, Mamoose of Mer and of all the Strait!

MEDIGEE BAY, EROOB

CHAPTER XXVII

The Duel

Morning dawned to a boisterous but favourable wind, a moderate sea, and sunlight undimmed by mists. The men of Ugar, of Eroob, and of Mer boarded their canoes. Kebisu took the lead with the *Skull Chief* filled with picked Tutu warriors. Quietly the remnant sailed with a silent farewell from the shore. Jakara, in black mood, scowled at Tutu from the *Skull Chief's* battered platform. When the lowlying island grew dim, he turned a lonely face towards the open sea. And back on the farthest limit of Tutu beach, a girl cried brokenly upon the sand. Gulls swooped down from above, intermingling their raucous cries with the sobs of the girl.

The canoes swept along in the sunlight like live things, bouncing through slithery spray in playful contrast to the quietness of their crews. Instead of returning with a huge trade and a fleet of canoes, they were but a funeral flotilla loaded with the skulls of their kinsmen and friends. On nearing Ugar, even Maros became morosely silent. In the peace of the afternoon they ran up on the beach, and the gulls shrieked to the wailing song of those gathered to receive them.

Kebisu remained at Ugar that night, wishing against hope that changeful weather would delay the sailing to Mer. But next morning dawned tauntingly bright, and a forlorn remnant sailed for Eroob. With a rollicking sea slapping their bows, they passed Attagoy, and the big bulk of Eroob loomed in sight, Lalour rising defiantly in the island centre. Late that afternoon they ran their canoes into Medigee Bay and skimmed high up on the village beach, which was black with people and weirdly musical with the high-pitched death-wail. Kebisu, barely acknowledging the quiet greeting of the chiefs, strode through the wailing crowd towards the house of the Mamoose, and stayed there.

That evening Maros raved. "Night after night, nothing but the death-wail! Is everyone dead? Are we all dead? Is never anyone to live again? Why, in the name of Beig, cannot the girls dance and laugh?"

His grumble was greeted by silence. "Ugh-gh-gh!" he grunted in utter disgust. His contempt was so expansive that he could frame no words to express his opinion of Jakara, sulking because of a mere girl.

Finally he ejaculated, "Beizam!" and laughed uproariously at Jakara's startled expression. "I thought that would wake you!" he growled affably.

"What about Beizam?" asked Jakara.

"Beizam."

"Yes, but what did you *say* about him?"

"Nothing," answered Maros. "But what I *was* going to say," he added with enjoyable anticipation, "is that he will be getting a crack from a big club if he is not very careful."

"Why?" asked Jakara, all attention.

"You know why, this time," answered Maros. "You have seen him sneaking about among the men of Mer, breathing things against Kebisu! He is out there now among the Erubians, undermining Kebisu. He is like the white ants in the Great South Land, that work quietly on the roots until they bring down a great tree. My own men tell me that he is working among them also, poisoning their minds against old One Ear. I can see Kebisu taking Beizam's head back to Tutu, or throwing it at Bogo's feet. He will whip it off before C'Zarcke can stop him, as soon as he hears what the pup's game is."

"I wish Kebisu knew *now*," said Jakara feelingly. "He is too busy thinking about what C'Zarcke will say to him when he takes the dead fleet back. He cannot see what is happening under his very eyes. But when C'Zarcke finishes with *him*, just what will *he* do to Beizam?"

Kebisu left Eroob lamenting. His deeply-lined face was unrecognizable as that of the man who had sailed from Mer so confidently but three months before.

The canoe men whispered, but became silent when grim Gelam reared above the sea. All were thinking of the reckoning that Kebisu must pay to C'Zarcke. In the late afternoon the canoes beached at Mer. An ominous crowd blackened the beach. A Maid-le signed to Kebisu and Maras, who followed him, Kebisu with the blanched face of one who sees beyond death. For the first time during the voyage Jakara felt sorry for the ending, as he glanced among these stricken people, many of whom had been his close friends; he felt the sadness of the home-coming. The air that he breathed carried the sighs and tears of those who had lost their men-folk. His eyes were attracted by the Pretty Lamar. She was standing among the crowd, eagerly talking to Beizam, but her eyes welcomed Jakara. Instantly he knew that she was not thinking one iota of those who were lost; she was in delight that he had come back – and without Eyes of the Sea. Beizam's face shone while he talked to the girl, but Jakara knew instinctively that her eyes were not bright because of Beizam and his great Shark canoe; they were afire with hope of Jakara. He turned away, angry, and yet feeling more pleased with the Pretty Lamar than he had ever felt before. She at least was genuine. *She* would follow him to hell, let alone to the land of the Lamars! He walked through the village and slowly up the hillside path that led to his house. He was miserably lonely, and his shoulders drooped.

Kebisu faced C'Zarcke at the Zogo-house. Behind the great priest stared out the Au-gud, the god of a people, judging the frailty of man. The Zogo-le stood ominous beneath the frowning god, the Maid-le like statues in the gloom. Behind them were ranged fifty Black Feathers, the whites of their eyes startlingly clear. The man who had failed feared a sentence that meant worse than death.

C'Zarcke stared at Kebisu as at a being accursed. A deathly silence filled the Sacred House. Surely the mummies were alive and accusing! The defeated man could feel the life in their death-grown hair. C'Zarcke spoke:

"Kebisu, Bomai has reserved you to live. Had judgment been mine, I would have cursed your spirit to wander homeless through all eternity. Twice, now, you have crushed the soul of a people. Now listen, for, if you and Maros fail in this your allotted task, judgment is to be mine alone: your spirits shall wander in eternal darkness through the limitless spaces among the great black stars!

"Jardine, chief of the Lamars, has sent a vessel feigning peace, with the request that the four Chief Mamooses of the Eastern nation shall meet and partake of the hospitality of the great Lamar Chief in their main village of Syd-nee. Jardine's object is to overcome us by peace. In Syd-nee they will show you wonders of their knowledge and power. In return they expect that we shall be dumbfounded by their might, and that in fear of their overwhelming strength we shall allow their ships to sail our seas and use our islands as foot-stools, unmolested. The Lamars have given us a miraculous chance, such as must have been breathed into their minds by Bomai. We can learn once and for all, at no risk to ourselves, whether the Lamars or we can definitely hold our islands. You and Maros only will go in the Lamar ship, and in Syd-nee spy out every detail in the life of the Lamars. And take great care in ascertaining the true number of their fighting-men and the strength of their ships. Find out everything, but tell nothing! On your wits hangs the destiny of the Island nations! If after events prove that your tidings have deceived us, I will cause your spirits to become dried like the body of a mummy, but possessing enough life-force to make them wander without a reasoning mind through all eternity. The Lamar ship will call for you both at Ugar. Go!"

The two chiefs, dazed and confounded, found themselves stumbling down the path to the beach. Without a word to the silent people, they turned the *Skull Chief* about and sailed away into the night.

The birds chirped cheerily at Mer, while the trees smiled up at the sun.

The sea rolled lustily to a south-east breeze. Three distant sail disappeared, and came again, and vanished, to rise to the big swell rolling in over the Great Barrier Reef. Smoke, just perceptible, told of a steamer voyaging to the Chinas. Jakara sat upon the slopes of Gelam, wishing for his telescope. During these last three months he had sighted more sail than he had ever seen in all his years on the island. They were flocking in droves to the Coral Seas, like the coming of the Torres Strait pigeons. Jakara knew nothing of the facts of the great pearl-shell rush, but he did know that, for every sail visible to Mer, there must be thirty or more farther west between Cape York Peninsula and New Guinea. But these sail never called at Mer. The island was far off the then known belt of shell, and the reputation of the Islanders was too bloodthirsty. The sailing directions of those days, even for big ships, warned mariners away from the vicinity of Mer.

Jakara was restless. He was burning to be away and doing something in the world of men – white men. Eyes of the Sea had not come back. She could not come, until some canoe of Tutu visited Mer. Jakara gazed seaward in sullen hopelessness. Meanwhile an occasional chance of escape was sailing past, all the more to be seized since this ever-increasing resentment against the Lamars was spreading fast amongst the Islanders and—

Jakara jumped up and strode down the grassy slope. He would walk about the island. This lying about and perpetually grousing at Fate would drive him mad. He pushed through a clump of bushes encircling a little flat knoll, only to halt in tense surprise when there appeared the plumed head of a chief, and then the broad shoulders of Beizam, as he stepped up to the knoll from the lower path. The effect on both men was electrical. They glared, with a violent throbbing at the heart. After the first shock came a thrill of joy, the gloating anticipation of killing this thing. Lightning flashed out. Beizam crouched; his club-head swung shoulder-high; with his left hand he whipped out a long bone dagger.

Jakara laughed. Beizam, club and dagger, against Jakara and Lightning! Ridiculous! Beizam's dagger, terrible in native frays, but against Lightning, bah!

The intensity of Beizam's eyes as he stared at Jakara's necklet connected the thoughts of the men. Jakara laughed tauntingly; he shook his head.

"Trophy of trophies," he mocked; "come and take it dog!"

Beizam gasped in open-mouthed rage. To call a chieftain of the shark clan a dog! Jakara was intensely surprised at the self-control which held Beizam from springing straight upon him.

Now that he was fighting for his head, he felt utterly confident. There was no one to interfere, there was no one man to be butchered by a crowd; it was just man to man in the sunlit silence. He crouched forward. "The master must whip the dog!" he sneered. Beizam shivered while curbing the demon that urged him to spring with a shrieking recklessness. But for long past he had trained his mind to this fight by impressing upon his consciousness that to defeat the dread Lamar and his terrible weapon he must fight with mind more than with physical strength. Straining as if upon the leash with the suppression of his animal passion, he crouched forward with a terrible eagerness. It meant so much to him, this fight – far more than to Jakara, who was only fighting for his life. Beizam was fighting to win an empire. If he could only win, could only kill this cursed Lamar, the news would flash over every island that Beizam had killed Jakara the Invincible – had taken his head. Alone, man to man, Beizam's *gaba-gaba* against Lightning!

What a roar of acclamation would follow throughout every tribe! And how pleased would the Zogo-le priesthood be at the vast moral gain against the Lamars that would ensue!

As for Kebisu – Kebisu was far away. In the wave of enthusiasm that must follow the slaying of Jakara, Beizam, son of the Mamoose of Mer, might well snatch the Mamooseship of Tutu.

Calling his every sense to a terrible concentration of purpose, he crouched forward – to win.

Jakara, not meeting the expected rush, lunged forward. Beizam instantly sprang aside. Lightning flashed back to the guard. Jakara smiled: "The Shark is wary! Or is it that the dog can only grind his teeth?"

He feinted again: Beizam slid warily sideways. Jakara lunged again, just to see. Instantly Beizam side-stepped. Jakara toyed with his blade and laughed. Confidently he met Beizam, lunging, swinging, thrusting, making Lightning hum viciously. To every movement Beizam instantly corresponded, slithering to right or left, leaping backward, or twisting his body a fraction of a second faster than the thrust of the blade.

Provided that he kept his head, Beizam was naturally well versed in dodging that blade, for his youthful training in the Kwod had been severe.

They circled: Jakara in sneering enjoyment, Beizam guarding his *gaba-gaba* with extreme care lest a slash should shear through his wooden handle. Occasionally, with a jerk of the wrist, he tried to snap the blade against the stone head of his club. Jakara played with his prospective victim until that phase of his enjoyment was spent. He stood, scowling. He would finish this dog now! A sunbird trilled sweetly; the grass wafted up a crushed odour. Neither man heard; neither smelt. Jakara sprang forward, hacking and thrusting in a whirl of steel. Beizam swayed in slithering movements, then unexpectedly crouched low and hesitated. Jakara thrust straight forward, astonished that his blade sped between the legs of Beizam, who had sprung into the air and screamed as his dagger arm sped down: the point slipped on Jakara's collar-bone and ripped through his breast as he bounded back. Both men trembled, Jakara gasping from the reaction of what had almost happened, Beizam's mind on the point of snapping against the iron control placed upon it.

At sight of Jakara's bloody breast he moaned in an animal lust to rush in and kill. He crouched low, sidling round and round his pivoting enemy.

Now Jakara realized that he was not fighting an animal, but a powerful, reasoning man. Grimly he crouched, watching this stealthy adversary, intuition telling him that Beizam had studied him for long, must have watched his fights closely, endeavouring to learn why it was that all his adversaries fell to Lightning. The warmth of his bleeding told of a coming weakening effect: tensely he watched for the slightest chance to run his enemy through.

Beizam leapt with a twist in the air and stabbed, while swinging his club for Jakara's ankle: he had sprung back even as his toes touched the ground: Jakara had thrust and dodged the dagger and leapt from the club in a second. Their chests heaving, eyes glaring, they flew at one another in a frenzy of cut and thrust, hit and stab, all controlled by red-hot instinct in parry and evading footwork. They sprang apart again, their straining minds concentrated, each against the other.

Beizam leapt with totally different tactics, and in a breath Jakara struck and missed, and dodged leap and dagger and *gaba-gaba*: but Beizam had no sooner leapt back than he sprang again, and Jakara almost somersaulted to dodge the blows that whizzed from every angle. Again and again Beizam leapt from right and left, striking upward from the very earth with his dagger while swinging his club. Jakara twisted like a galvanized eel to keep this in-closing devil at the rapier's point; finally he whirled Lightning with a desperate quickness. Sweat poured from the men, mixing with a running crimson down the chest of Jakara, and glistening like varnish over that of Beizam.

Beizam sprang only once after the whirl of Lightning and only by a breath missed being cloven in halves, but Jakara had flung up his left arm to ward off the dagger-blow which slashed a finger to the grass as a child flips off the head of a flower. Beizam had paled grey-green from his own narrow escape as he bounded back.

Both men crouched, panting, hollow-bellied, their body muscles swollen in sweat. Beizam snatched at the fallen finger, and his bloodshot eyes fiendishly watched Jakara while he thrust the finger into his mouth and chewed it. Jakara glared on, wholly unfeeling while he listened to the small bones cracking. Beizam swallowed the pulp, hoarsely whispering: "So will I chew the neck-bones of your head, Jakara, when I tickle your spirit in the Dance of Death. How you bleed! I must finish you before you are too weak to dance well."

Jakara sprang, and with a frantic thrust forced Beizam to leap in circles as he slashed and thrust and cut at the head and arms and body and feet; then he gasped when his rapier pierced the warm resistance of flesh. The point missed the stomach, but Beizam's twist was too late to prevent the cold steel from grating agonizingly along a rib. With a mad cry Jakara's hand clawed Beizam's hair while he wrenched in order to saw the rapier into the vitals. Beizam sobbed, and with maniacal strength jerked sideways. The rib snapped clear. In screaming rage Jakara attacked again, and Beizam in horrid pain swayed and dodged as the vicious steel snipped clean through the *gaba-gaba* handle; and, while the stone head spun to the grass, Jakara lunged again and again at the writhing form that leapt back and back and back. With death before his reeling senses, Beizam snatched Jakara's wrist, only to find his own dagger wrist gripped by Jakara's mutilated hand. Panting into each other's throat they clung frenziedly, knowing that whichever let go first would be killed. Neither cared. With bared teeth they swayed against each other's strength, breathing in panting sobs while each sought the other's weakness, straining for the least chance of a kill.

"Hold! Cease this madness and separate!"

The fighters stared, quite still, like children terrified in a nightmare.

"Separate, I say!"

That deep voice recalled the shreds of their reason to sanity.

Wearily they turned, and gazed at C'Zarcke: slowly the world came back. Trees formed, as if solidifying from a dream: hillocks took shape and grass waved as if coming from a mist into sunlight. They could not yet hear the chirp of birds, but the grim face of C'Zarcke dominated all their senses. A power that seemed almost above death was controlling them. Their stiffened fingers unlocked.

Birds sang, bees hummed, the waves below splashed musically on the beach, before C'Zarcke spoke again. "I forbid you men to fight. If you do so at any time, and one kills the other, I will reward both victor and vanquished with worse than death."

The great priest turned, and, striding across the knoll, disappeared down the hill-side. Beizam's head lolled like that of a sick child. His left side was a blotch of dark-red jelly-like blubber. Blowflies hummed upon it. Straightening himself in searing pain he tried to walk away, but sank to the grass. Jakara watched curiously. Two Beizams seemed huddled there. His own knees felt shivery, his thighs weak. He fell abruptly, so sick that his face could not avoid a patch of soppy grass.

And so old Passi the medicine-man, hurrying up with his assistants, found them shortly after.

THREE HEAD MEN OF MER
(Passi is on the right.)

CHAPTER XXVIII

The Coming Of Gareeb

Time sped by, and a night of hallowed silence came with a moon of silver set with stars all twinkling gold. The sea crooned to a breeze that was the whisper of God.

Jakara awoke as he had awakened at other times. On this dark island the very air by telepathic sympathy seemed to whisper to the minds of men when great deeds or tragedy were impending. Especially tragedy.

The house was dark. Jakara pushed open the door and moonlight flooded in. He stepped outside and glancing down the slope to the sea, held his breath – at first for very beauty's sake.

For there glided close along the shores a beautiful, a silver ship. Her decks star-splashed, her masts bellying sails of snow, the cordage vivid as ropes of silver-gold. Her spars queened the water as regally she glided along, disdaining the sea-kiss upon her bow. Little men, like goblins, stood upon the broad white decks; goblins clung high up among the spars.

Jakara cupped his hands to his mouth. A long-drawn cry of fear rushed out over the water. The goblins turned startled heads up towards the black mass of the island. Again that warning cry screeched superstitious fear into the hearts of men. Then Jakara screamed: "Keep off! Keep off! You are steering right for the reef! Luff up! Quick! Quick!"

Too late! though Jakara could distinguish voices in excited command floating up from far below. The bow slowly turned out towards the open sea; there came a long grinding crash, the bows shuddered from the water, and the gigantic bulk followed, as if the ship were about to leap to the stars.

The immense canvas spread dizzily backwards until a mast snapped with a report that awoke the hills. Another snapped thunderously and lurched with sickening swayings as tortured ropes jerked it back to masts and ship. Both remaining masts leaned slowly over, over, then splintered as if the ship's bowels were being riven. They went overboard to a rolling thunder while the canvases thrashed the air and volleyed on to the water.

As if ashamed of her nakedness, she immediately began to settle aft, her bow climbing momentarily into the air.

"Oh God," whispered Jakara, "the bottom is ripped clean out of her!"

The stern rapidly disappeared in a backward slide. Jakara heard faint shrieks as if coming from far away. The hulk dragged right over the reef edge into deep water. Her bows heaved upward, hesitated, then her copper-plated keel gleamed in the moonlight as she plunged backwards and vanished.

A shout of blended triumph and dismay arose from the beaches. The canoes had raced like porpoises for the stricken vessel, but she had sunk within minutes. Jakara stared moist-eyed while the leading canoes bobbed into the whirlpool: he could distinguish the warriors clubbing downwards. Thank God, the disaster had been so sudden that very few would be saved for the clubs. Those canoes had been ready waiting while he slept: he seized his weapons and raced down to the beach.

A crowd seethed there, lamenting the quick sinking of the ship, for now there would be no loot. They speculated as to the number of heads, and cheered in laughing derision when canoes collided while chasing an expert swimmer. All was finished in a few minutes. The dodging canoes grew quiet, several of them stole out and paddled toward the shore: lustily the triumph song floated over the water. Jakara sought for C'Zarcke. He knew that with the quickness of the catastrophe and the rivalry of the canoes it was scarcely possible that any survivors would be brought ashore. But if they were, only C'Zarcke could save them.

But C'Zarcke rarely appeared unless destiny demanded his presence. A medley of voices hurried Jakara back to the throng crowding the water's edge. The *Shark* was speeding inshore with Beizam in the bow waving aloft a Lamar head. Excited questions roared from the crowd. The canoe men called back in disgust. Only eight heads! The ship had gone straight down: Beizam had taken a head and was bringing back a heart to play with before he took another head.

The canoe slid into the thick of the crowd. Beizam whooped out, dragging a girl by the silky hair of her crown. Beizam's sinewy hand seemed to be twisted in Jakara's heart as the girl shrieked. He gazed in agony. A wet night-dress clung to her trembling form. On her knees she clutched Beizam's wrist, her head drawn back until Jakara thought the white throat would be torn across. The whites of her eyes gleamed, and her face was a white thing of unutterable horror. Beizam roared with laughter, and waved the severed head while twitching the girl back and forth. Steel flashed, and Beizam flung the head full in Jakara's face, making Lightning miss during that one blind instant, while Beizam flattened the girl and swung a pineapple club. Both men struck blindly, and the girl fainted under the trampling feet: they neither knew nor cared, for a claw that seemed neither of man nor beast, a bony black claw, was scratching at their eyes, at their nostrils: shrieks that surely were inhuman startled the onlookers: "Bomai, oh Bomai, I call on Bomai! Bomai! C'Zarcke! Oh, C'Zarcke! Quick!"

"Silence!"

Such utter quietness spread over the crowd that even the thumping of hearts sounded noisy. Beizam stepped slowly back, with a great fear in his eyes. Jakara stepped aside, feeling that vitality and power were being dragged from him.

On the sands, caressing the still white body in passionate endearment, spilling tears and kisses and mumbled tendernesses on the deathly face, was old Sasowari, passion-mad. Her claws dragged the girl's head to her breast, her awful face pressed upon the white one, she rocked the girl and crooned in a sing-song of love, "Gareeb! Gareeb!"

Ecstatic hope surged through Jakara; his eyes implored C'Zarcke, but the great priest ignored him.

"Explain!" he commanded harshly.

Sasowari's bleared old eyes were dancing while, panting in her feebleness, she dragged the castaway across the feet of C'Zarcke. She knelt with outstretched arms, her face transfigured as she cried: "Oh, C'Zarcke, blessed priest of Bomai! Our god has granted me the prayer of many years; he has brought me back Gareeb, my daughter, before I die. She is a Lamar; my Gareeb is now of the spirit people. Priest of the great Ad Giz, in the name of Bomai I pray you give me Gareeb, my daughter."

C'Zarcke gazed down at the girl. She opened terrified eyes.

"She is yours," he decreed at last. "Any Lamar of our own people who returns to us belongs to our people," he said, frowning on Jakara. "You should understand this, and not attempt to spill blood whether or no. If the girl had been a Lamar of the Lamars, then she would have been Beizam's prize."

He turned and strode away with the Maid-le. The people sighed with relief. Everything had been settled satisfactorily. Excited talking broke out, and Beizam smiled when some picked up the head and appraised it. The Shark was sorry he had lost his prize, but she had turned out to be a spirit-Lamar, and so was no prize at all. C'Zarcke had justified him – and above Jakara! He was exultant.

A curious crowd surged around old Sasowari. The girl in abject fear struggled to reach Jakara. "Stop that!" he said quickly in English. "Listen! Your life depends upon it: throw your arms about the old woman: she is supposed to be your mother. Act so, if you would live."

To the crowd he explained: "She is shocked with the suddenness of the wreck. After sleep she will realize that she is at home. She hardly knows Sasowari yet, so changed has the old mother become."

Murmurs of sympathy spread from this curious people, blood-thirsty, then lovable, one instant after another. "I will take her home," crooned Sasowari. "Come, Gareeb!"

The girl shuddered back from the hideous old figure. She sobbed pleadingly to Jakara, but he frowned as if angry. "Put your arms round her," he ordered sternly. "Pretend that you begin to recognize her. She is your mother, and you are her daughter Gareeb. Your very life depends upon it! She will take you home now: go, and don't look at me at all, or you might lose both of us our heads."

In pitiful bewilderment the girl shivered while skinny arms enfolded her, but she moved through the crowd with the old woman, who murmured to her as to a child. The people made way for them, some insisting on helping the feeble ones up to the lonely house.

With excited heart Jakara stayed among the crowd, laughing and joking, doing his best to keep all in a good humour. Then, as they drifted back to the main village for an impromptu feast and a talk about the events of the night, he edged back to the beach and ran, hoping against hope that he might find some survivors and hide them before morning.

Piercing screams broke out from the hill-side around him. He halted, horror-stricken, then bounded back the way he had come, to hear Sasowari shrilling: "Gareeb! Gareeb! Gareeb!" then "Jak-ar-ra!" He called in reply, and raced through the grass towards some mad thing tearing down through the bushes.

Old Sasowari had shut her door on the sympathetic ones. It was dark and silent as the grave inside, and smelt like it. The girl had clung to the skinny shoulders as the old woman bent low over the coals. She dared not look behind. Presently the fire blazed with the bright light of coconut-husks. Sasowari smiled at Gareeb. The girl caught her breath. Such a terrible old face trying to smile! To hide her feelings she gazed around, and nearly died of horror. Two shimmering eyes glared down at her from above the bared teeth of a demon; the shrunken naked body of a man showed her his ribs and the knobby bones of his thighs. With a cry that pierced to the summit of Gelam she sprang through the mat door and screamed down the hill.

Jakara caught her roughly to stop her clawings and bites and screams. Half smothering her in his arms, he hurried her back to the hut. Old Sasowari met him, her arms helplessly outstretched. "Warawa!" she explained. Jakara sighed with relief. As he bent under the entrance of the hut, the girl snatched at the thatch. "Gareeb," he said urgently, "let go! It is all right; I, Jakara, am with you. The man inside is dead! He is only a harmless mummy. They preserve them in every house. Let go, little girl."

He broke her straining hold, while Sasowari roughly patched up the entrance. Jakara knelt by the fire, tenderly sympathetic for this forlorn castaway whose presence he instantly foresaw would mean for him such terrible worry as would make his present trouble fade into insignificance. Whispering comforting words, he tried to quiet her convulsive sobs as he had seen mothers soothe children. Sasowari quietly put on some cooking-pots. It was dawn before the girl had quieted down enough to open her tragedy-filled eyes.

"Listen," explained Jakara earnestly. "You have fallen among savages, and must learn their customs very quickly. They will think it strange if you do not soon become reconciled, for you are supposed to have lived with them before. That man is Warawa, the husband of Sasowari here, believed to be your father. He is only a mummy! Every house honours its master in that way, triced up on that bamboo framework. He can do you no harm. It is only the live people that would hurt you, and they will leave you alone if you only play up to the belief that you are a Lamar."

"What is a 'Lamar'?" she whispered.

"A spirit come back from the dead. Try and understand this: Sasowari has claimed you as her dead daughter returned to human life. You must show a daughter's love for this old woman on every occasion when anyone is near. And, as a matter of fact, she saved your life down on the beach. I could have done nothing. They would have torn me to pieces. Always remember – and show – the fact that but for old Sasowari here we should both have been dead hours ago."

"But who are you?"

"Why, Jakara," he answered in surprise.

"But – you speak English. Are you an Englishman?"

"Yes, of course. That is, I'm an Australian." He smiled. "I have a long conversation once every seven days with a big old tree in the jungle. Otherwise I should have forgotten every word of our language."

The girl sighed in intense relief. "Thank God," she whispered. "Then how is it that these terrible people allow *you* to live?"

"Because I am a Lamar, the returned spirit of a savage who was once born on this island. I had the sense to accept and live up to their belief, although I was only a youngster when my ship was wrecked."

"Then all the white people are Lamars?"

"Yes."

"Then why-why did they kill those poor people struggling in the water?"

"Because they are Lamars of a foreign kind, and these people look on them as their bitter and supernatural enemies. You and I are 'spirit'

Lamars. We are supposed to have originally been *born* of these people, don't you understand? We are reincarnated, as it were. I was allowed to live because an old man claimed me as the 'Lamar,' that is, the living spirit, of his dead son."

The girl's eyes steadied, then widened, while she gripped him convulsively. "Oh, Jack-Jakara, it is terrible!" Her voice rose to a wail. "They struck down at us while we swam, oh, when we needed friends so urgently! They chased those who were swimming and struck at them with terrible things, and they laughed, and I tried to sink, and he – he reached down and caught me by the hair!"

She threw herself violently from Jakara and began to scream in hysterics.

He watched helplessly while Sasowari soothed her.

It was long after daylight before the girl lay, with long-drawn sobs, on Sasowari's sleeping-mat. Jakara regarded this countrywoman of his with mixed feelings. He had longed for the company of such as she, but now her coming was fraught with frightful possibilities. He turned to the old woman, who sat quietly regarding him. A warmth of kindliness, very near to love, welled up in the worried man's heart towards this woebegone relic. He smiled as he patted her bony arm.

"Well, Sasowari, your daughter, Gareeb, has come back. She is a beautiful daughter, and I wish you great love of her."

The lined old face smiled curiously. He wondered at the twinkle in the bleared eyes.

"Still unbelieving, Jakara?"

He stared. "Why, what do you mean, Sasowari?" he asked doubtfully.

"You never really believed that I should see Gareeb again. Now do you believe?"

"Of course," smiled Jakara.

"Oh, Jakara," she chuckled accusingly, "even now you do not believe that she is Gareeb."

He stared with a quickly rising fear. "But, mother, Gareeb is here," he almost whispered.

"You *know* that she is not Gareeb," replied the old woman deliberately.

Tremulous silence in the hut. The girl's sobs ceased. She did not understand a word, but she acutely sensed that something, something perhaps fraught with terrible consequences to herself, was happening here.

"But, mother, if she is not Gareeb, then *who* is she," he whispered.

"A Lamar!" said the old woman flatly. Jakara recoiled in ashen fear. Presently he reached out a trembling arm and stroked the claw-like hand:

entreatingly he whispered.

"Mother! you have made a mistake. Surely, mother, you would not say she is just a Lamar!"

She rocked backwards and forwards to an almost hysterical cackling. She leaned forward and put her arm caressingly, as a mother would, across Jakara's shoulders. Her blotched old face was trembling.

"Don't fear, Jakara: she Gareeb. She will always be Gareeb. But you and I *know*!"

Jakara hardly breathed. He clutched her hand urgently. "Oh, mother," he whispered, "tell me."

"Just this, Jakara. You have always had a kind word for me. Even when you were in a hurry you could always pass my door with a smile for me. And, Jakara, when my own people scoffed, you were kinder still to me about Gareeb. You would always listen when my old heart was breaking to speak of her. So, Jakara, last night I saw by your face that you would give your life to save this girl's. Your life would have been swallowed by the sands, Jakara, and hers too. So, because you have been kind to me, I claimed the Lamar as Gareeb."

Jakara flung his arms around Sasowari and kissed her as fondly as a lover would kiss his sweetheart – her withered cheeks, her gummy lips, her scraggy wisps of hair. At last she stretched bony fingers before his face, and leaned back with a queer old smile. She gazed bravely, with misty old eyes. "Why, Jakara, a withered old hag like me! What will the maid think?"

"That you are the dearest woman in all the world," he answered huskily, and kissed her again. "Sasowari, I can never never thank you for what you have done. Oh, Sasowari, your God is Bomai, but we Lamars call him Jesus Christ, the Son of our God, Who to you is your Ad Giz. Truly, Sasowari, our God Who is your God will bless you for to-night's work."

Tremblingly the old woman drew his face down to her. "Tell me, Jakara," she whispered passionately, "and this time the truth, by the God you have just claimed, you believe that I shall see Gareeb, my own Gareeb, before I die?"

And Jakara answered as he suddenly believed, for the words came out without effort of his own: "Yes, you will see Gareeb!"

The old woman sighed, long and tremblingly. Her hands could not hold the cooking-pots. With misty eyes and wonderful smile Jakara knelt over to explain to the astounded girl.

CHAPTER XXIX

In Which Gareeb Lear ns There Are Other Peoples, Other Lives

For weeks the girl was too terrified to venture out of the house. The shipwreck and its events had almost unhinged her mind. Many curious sightseers came to view the new spirit Lamar, but Sasowari volubly shooed them from the door. The girl trembled even at a voice. Jakara became alarmed for her reason. He comforted her in every way that he could think of, and then sought to distract her mind by teaching her the commoner words of the native language, impressing upon her the vital necessity of learning their ordinary manners and customs and points of view. Only by such means could she hope to be accepted as one of them.

A morning came when Jakara went whistling along the path to take the girl for her first walk. He pushed at the entrance-way, only to retire abashed at the chuckling of old Sasowari. Then a girl appeared – a very unhappy girl. Her breasts were clothed with the shreds of a white night-dress. She wore a skirt of soft yellow fibre, upon which Sasowari had worked all the week before. She was a little girl, with soft brown hair and tragic grey eyes. She would have been pretty but that she had grown very thin. Jakara smiled encouragingly. "Why, you look very nice, Gareeb. Just a sprig of hibiscus in your hair, and you are quite an Island maid!"

She smiled gratefully. Jakara felt intensely sorry for all that he knew she was going through – and must go through. He was very much worried, for he could not see a way out. As he looked at the girl, a lump rose in his throat, for these years of intensive study of native life had produced on his mind the effect of his environment. Was this grass skirt a symbol? Slipping backward! High civilization, no matter how unwillingly, on its first step to "going native"! Would she eventually look to the grass skirt and the sleeping-mat and the Au-gud as her all in all in life? No, of course not! She was too old now ever to forget, though it might be for the best if she could. For her, the years meant a slowly breaking heart, unless—

"Come," he said gently, "some curious villagers are loitering up the path. We can slip away while Sasowari holds them in gossip."

The girl walked timidly, nervous even of the bushes overshadowing the track. She stepped a trifle gingerly too, in the effort to get used to the fibre skirt. The path led up on to a knoll of grass and sunlight.

"Oh," she gasped, and jerked upright. Jakara instantly wheeled in fighting attitude. She smiled, with an embarrassed hand to her foot. "It is only a pebble," she explained.

"There are not many," said Jakara encouragingly. "They lie only along the forest patches. We will go by the Zomar-Mergar track, where the scrub paths are all loam and soft as a carpet. By and by your feet will become hardened." Presently, near Meket, they passed the Ziriam-Zogo, half-hidden by drooping trees, with its dais surrounded by creeper-covered posts helmeted by huge spiral shells.

"What a dear little face!" said the girl with a smile. "As comically serious as a native bear! How importantly he squats upon those huge white shells! I think the little stone images along the paths are the queerest things!"

"Um," said Jakara.

They walked up a grassy glade, with vegetation enclosing them from two hill-sides.

"What a pretty place!" said the girl. "So cool and quiet!"

"It is called the 'Glen of Dreams,'" said Jakara. "I brought you here so that you would know of a secluded walk when you wish to be alone. The islanders seldom come here."

"You have been the dearest friend to me," she said seriously, "in great things as well as small. I should have died but for you."

"You allow your imagination to terrorize you too much," he answered. "Come a little farther; it is a delightful spot."

It was a glade of ferns and scented creepers and peace. With an exclamation of delight the girl knelt by a large white flower on the edge of a transparent pool. It was a sublime flower, snow-white. The girl caressed it with her cheek.

"How beautiful!" she said. "Fancy such a lovely thing in this awful island! What is its name?"

"Gareeb!" murmured Jakara. She glanced up, puzzled.

"It is a lily," explained Jakara. "The native name is Gareeb. You are called after the lily."

"Why did they call the real Gareeb, Gareeb?" asked the girl.

Jakara sat beside her. "Because," he explained, "her skin was strikingly white. Tradition says she was the lightest-skinned girl they ever remember being born on Mer."

"But," said the puzzled girl, "her parents were black, or nearly so."

"There is an explanation," said Jakara, "but I cannot answer your question scientifically. Throughout the centuries odd survivors of shipwrecked people have been allowed to live on these islands because they were spirit Lamars. They intermarried with the natives, In the course of time their children merged into the native, but there have cropped up throwbacks through some strange trick of heredity, children with almost white skins, and brown hair and European features. It is a rather wonderful thing. In another instance a crew of shipwrecked Spaniards seized the villages of Las. They lasted quite a long time, and even to-day their strain is very noticeable among the Las villagers."

The girl was silent. Presently she said, almost in a whisper, "Shall we ever get away from here?"

"Yes," reassured Jakara earnestly. "It is only a matter of time bringing the necessary opportunity. In the meantime, put your whole heart and mind into learning the native customs; deceive them into believing that you are really one of them. By doing so you will make our ultimate chance of escape ever so much easier." But his heart was heavy.

"I pray God it may be so," she sighed, "and quickly." The strained fear left her eyes as she studied him; she smiled sadly. "It seems a dream," she said, "the shipwreck, this island of palms and savages, the big sea that hems all in, myself in this strange grass skirt, and. a bronze white man wearing a middle-ages rapier. I should hardly be surprised to hear a trumpet blare and see a troop of Crusaders riding out of that forest. I almost expect to see armoured men with battle-axes parading the battlements of that queer castellated islet down there. What is its name, again?"

"Waiar," answered Jakara.

"Nature is wonderful," she mused, while gazing down the hill-slopes to the sea. "She has built down there a medieval castle in solid rock. See, there is even the great arched gate running right into it under the walls. What really is that black opening? A tunnel?"

"You've guessed it," said Jakara; "a tunnel made apparently by the sea. It runs right under the rocky islet and comes out on the other side. All due to volcanic action in the dim ages, you know."

"It is an uncanny reproduction of a bad old castle in ye wild old times," she laughed. "And see, there blazes up their signal fire from the battlements. What that fire? I often see it. It blazes in such a furtive sort of way."

"Oh, it's a sort of sacrificial fire," answered Jakara offhandedly.

"Is it? That sounds rather horrid – here. Then are those shadowy forms that one occasionally glimpses, priests?"

"Yes."

"They don't seem to mix much with the people over here."

"No."

"What is that hollow drum-like sound that booms from there just occasionally after midnight? It scares me in such a queer way. It is as if a snake was in the room, crawling about in the dark! That sort of feeling."

"Oh," said Jakara, "just a signal drum."

"I see you do not want to talk of it," she said. "I should be thrilled if it were not for the terrible fear. What is that barbaric necklace around your neck, then?"

"Boars' tusks. All picked ones, and more valuable from an islander's point of view than a diamond necklace would be to you."

He leaned towards her and explained. "See the border of the necklace, these ebony bands in which the butt of each tusk is set. That border is really of human hair, a surprisingly large amount of it. Every hair is tightly compressed, and the compact strands are interlaced until every tusk is as firmly set as a tooth in a jaw. And notice how firmly those big scarlet berries are set in the band. And the border line of blue, yellow, and green. They are really the tiniest of brilliant shells, polished. The necklace makes a complete circle of a certain number of tusks, each one of which is symbolic, as also are the bands and the berries. It is really almost a majestic order, and represents more to the natives than any honorary insignia to our people."

"And how do you keep the tusks so polished?"

"Oh," replied Jakara airily, "any one of the girls does that. The job is an honour. You know," he smiled, "Jakara is quite a nabob on this island."

"I have realized that," she said meaningly. "In future, if it does not cause jealousy, *I* am going to keep the pretty necklaces polished."

"You will have me throwing out my chest like a Mamoose," he smiled.

"And what are those serrated teeth in the broad arm-band?" she asked curiously. "I must sound silly, I know, but those teeth affect me with a most baffling dread."

"Sharks' teeth. Tiger shark. I am one of the 'shark men.' They are similar to a Scottish clan. The Shark clan and the Zagareeb clan are the two most powerful clans on all the Eastern Group. This armlet is a symbol to all that I am a chieftain of the Beizam-le, the Shark people. They made me a chief long ago. I have been very useful to the Zogo-le. But I have had to fight with my body and brains; otherwise they would have kept me only as a slave."

"That peculiar basket-work with the beautiful plumes on your arm, what is that?"

"The *kadik*. You see, the basket-work into which the arm fits is of finely-laced strands of lawyer-cane. They protect the wrist from the cutting vibrations of the bow-string. And the plumes are the hair-like feathers of the male cassowary. But," he added with a touch of pride, "to-morrow you must come along to my house. I'll show you the fighting head-dress and the ceremonial *kadik*. Their plumes are magnificent bird of paradise feathers."

"I should like to come," she said. "I have not yet seen you in all the glory of a chief's attire."

Then Jakara again earnestly explained the ways and means by which the girl must become reconciled to her position until rescue was assured. She listened intelligently, for the first time actually beginning to realize the possibilities and impossibilities of her position. It was the lengthening shadows that caused Jakara suddenly to jump up. "My heavens, the sun is going down, and I'm jolly hungry. Gareeb," he smiled, "we must eat."

"I am hungry, too," she said in surprise.

"Good!" said Jakara enthusiastically. "You are on the turn! Get yourself in the best form, for health and strength are all-important in this life here. We'll start now by going to see what old Sasowari has got in the way of food."

"Turtle meat and taro," said Gareeb instantly. "The biggest bunch of bananas are ripe, too, and there's plenty of coconut-milk."

When they came out into the open forest, Jakara pointed far over the sea. "A steamer, Gareeb."

She gazed with startled eyes. "Just the smoke," she cried in disappointment. "Oh, are they coming this way? Please say they will come!"

Jakara shook his head. "Ships seldom venture close," he explained soberly. "Even if they did, we could not get off to them, at least, without C'Zarcke's permission. But I have his permission."

The girl clutched his arm. "You mean that they will let us go?" she breathed.

"Not *they*! But every soul in the Island groups is afraid of C'Zarcke's anger more than they fear death. And C'Zarcke is my friend."

His heart nearly cried at the sight of the intense relief on her face.

"Everything is all right, little girl," he said soothingly; "you will see the dear white people again. Come, let us hurry! I will go straight to C'Zarcke and get his permission to sail to the first passing ship."

While hurrying along, he felt that she trembled with eagerness. "Would you dare sail out to sea in one of those tiny canoes?" she asked.

He smiled reassuringly. "I have sailed hundreds of miles in them. They are perfectly seaworthy. Another, but a very hazardous plan would be, if C'Zarcke allowed it, to take the great risk of sailing at night when a favourable wind blew, and try to reach the Government settlement at Cape York, a hundred and twenty miles away. We should have to pass hostile islands. By day we should lose our heads, by night probably we should drown on one of the many reefs or sandbanks. No, it will be perfectly safe when a ship passes close enough for us to sail out and overtake her. The north-west season is coming soon, which means that most of the pearling-fleet sails south to Sydney. Their numbers have increased so much this season that probably the more adventurous ones will sail within intercepting distance of Mer. We shall not have long to wait now."

He left Gareeb with Sasowari, who with a twinkle in her eye was waiting beside a long overdue meal. He hurried up the jungle track, passed among the Sacred Wongais, and out on to the great grove. By the Zogo-house stood C'Zarcke, as if waiting.

Jakara half smiled at the man whom he desired above all things to remain his friend. "C'Zarcke, I pray you grant me my heart's desire – a canoe to sail away and land Gareeb on the first passing Lamar ship. I give my word as a chief of Mer that I will return."

C'Zarcke did not smile. But Jakara, gazing with his heart in his eyes, uncannily felt that the great priest was smiling, even though the grim face remained harsh and moveless. The Wongai-trees were very quiet.

"And Sasowari?" boomed the deep voice.

"She is willing," said Jakara instantly.

"You will return," said C'Zarcke slowly, and paused – "for Eyes of the Sea."

Jakara flushed. Despite himself, he was hurt.

The priest mused thoughtfully. Jakara would have given a year of life to know the thoughts behind those big calm eyes.

"I know that Jakara would return – if he said so – even if Eyes of the Sea never was. You may put Gareeb in any Lamar ship – while Sasowari agrees!"

Joy flooded Jakara's face. He stammered many thanks, and made a mess of it. "I wish you all the luck in the world, C'Zarcke," he said, as he hurried away.

Once through the Wongai-trees, he ran joyfully, but his pace slowed as he came out on the headlands. What, really, did the great Zogo mean! What did he *know*! Doubts and fears clouded Jakara's relief. The chilly dawn of a presentiment made him sick at heart. His steps lagged. When near the house he stopped altogether in icy despair, for there floated across the sea a wailing blast of sound like a giant's voice in pain. Jakara knew that it was the sea's voice cunningly forced through fluted columns on the isle of Waiar, just off shore. From the castellated rocks rose a sinister spiral of smoke.

"My God!" breathed Jakara; "the Waiat ceremonies! I completely forgot. They must be nearly due. But when?"

He knew that only one man in all the islands, nay, in all the world, could answer that question. And that man was the god Waiat himself.

Forcing a smile, he pushed through Sasowari's entrance-way – and scowled at the smiling face of the Pretty Lamar.

"Why, Jakara," she laughed, "anyone would think I had come to steal Gareeb! She is fairer than I am, Jakara, a real Lamar. But, oh, what will Eyes of the Sea say?"

Jakara scowled at the meal that Sasowari set before him. The presence of this girl had added to his worries. She laughed gaily, and stroked the white cheek of Gareeb.

"What a pity you cannot yet understand our language, oh Lily of the Glens! We could then tell you how gay our Jakara really is. But never fear, though he scowls ever so deeply, I see you have nothing to fear from Eyes of the Sea – until she finds out."

Leaning over, she mischievously rumpled Jakara's hair. She was enjoying herself immensely, but her sorrow would come when alone in the night. She tugged his hair, and he turned on her savagely. She sprang back with laughter that was sheer music.

"Why, Jakara, I believe you would even kill me. Poor little Pretty Lamar!" she giggled mockingly. "Why, what with Eyes of the Sea, and Gareeb, and Jakara, and Beizam, what is to become of me is a puzzle. And now even Sasowari scowls as if she would rend me limb from limb. And the sun has set – he scowls, too. Dark is the world for the Pretty Lamar." Smilingly she gazed at Gareeb. "You are lovely, Gareeb; no wonder Jakara has longed for a Lamar girl. Eyes of the Sea is the colour of the golden sands, but you are of the lily. I am in between, and my poor heart bears the crush. Very well, Sasowari, don't clutter so! I've done all the damage I can for the present, so good-bye!" She went, playfully tickling Jakara as she slipped through the doorway.

"Who is that girl?" asked Gareeb. "How strikingly pretty she is!"

"That is the Pretty Lamar," said Jakara.

"What is she?"

"A cat with claws – sharp ones."

Gareeb smiled. "I mean – surely she is not a Spanish castaway, a Spanish Lamar?"

"She is a native," answered Jakara emphatically, "stewed with nigger and curried with the devil and peppered with Spain."

He recovered his good humour at sight of Gareeb's puzzled face. "Well, how does the world go with Gareeb?"

"Growing very curious," she answered; "please satisfy my curiosity."

"Oh," replied Jakara easily, "she's a throwback. Away back in the dim centuries an ancestor of hers was a Spanish don with a face as sharp as her temper. She has inherited all his bad points – they are as numerous as porcupine quills, and sharper, and she has grown a lot of her own as well."

"That is a cruel way to speak of a girl who loves you." Jakara sat bolt upright.

Gareeb laughed. "You look so funny."

Jakara settled back again. "That's an unpleasant way to shock a man just after dinner," he grumbled.

"It *is* true," she insisted. Jakara glanced uneasily at Sasowari.

"You needn't accuse Sasowari," said the girl.

"Then who told you such a thing?"

"You both did."

Jakara sat puzzled, inclined to be sulky.

"Call it a woman's instinct," said Gareeb. "I know by the way her eyes softened when you came in. But I know that you don't love her."

"H'm!" said Jakara. He thought that the least said the soonest mended.

Cautiously he reclined on the mat.

"Who is Eyes of the Sea?"

Jakara looked troubled. Old Sasowari was noisy with her coconut-bowls.

"Tell me," Gareeb pleaded.

"Why," said Jakara quietly, "she is a Lamar, a spirit Lamar, a white girl."

Gareeb's eyes widened. "A white girl! Where?"

"On Tutu, 'Warrior Island,' down towards the New Guinea coast."

"But, oh, Jakara, why did you not tell me about her?"

Jakara spread out helpless hands. "There has been so much to tell; there are a thousand, thousand things yet to explain—"

"Tell me now," she asked eagerly. "Do you really mean a white girl living among savages?"

"It is very difficult to explain. You see, the worst insult you could offer her would be to say she is a white girl. She is really a pure white gone native. They took her from a shipwreck when she was a child. Old Babelu of Tutu claimed her as the spirit Lamar of his dead daughter, and she was adopted. She always has believed, and now still more wants to believe, that she is a real native. She loves the Islands and the people." And Jakara told the story of Eyes of the Sea.

"It is a wonderful romance," breathed Gareeb. "In civilization such a fact would hardly be believed. What is she like?"

"Oh," said Jakara almost proudly, "she is very pretty and quite nice. Got some catty little ways though, but she can't help that. Her environment, you know."

"Were you in love with her, Jakara? Oh, well, is she in love with you?"

Then Gareeb smiled. "You needn't trouble to answer, Jakara," she said, when he reddened. "You have done so."

"I've got great news," said Jakara, to change the subject. "C'Zarcke told me we can go. We can sail to the first ship that passes. Now *you* are surprised." Gareeb caught her breath. She touched him almost tearfully. "Oh, Jakara, he – he will keep his word?"

"As sure as the sun will rise," answered Jakara soberly.

Tears of utter relief welled to Gareeb's eyes. Jakara patted her hand. "There, there," he said clumsily, "it's quite all right. You'll get away, Gareeb; it is only a matter of waiting for a passing ship."

"And you—" breathed Gareeb at last, "will you—"

"Return for Eyes of the Sea!" said Jakara. "We shall get away – later."

"Couldn't you come with me?" suggested Gareeb. "Surely the captain would take us to this other island and pick the girl up."

Jakara frowned. "I had thought of that," he said miserably, "before I asked C'Zarcke. But you don't know Eyes of the Sea. She would not come. I have tried and tried and tried! The last thing she wants to do is to leave the Islands. I tell you, Gareeb, she is proud of being a native. She calls Tutu 'home,' and loves its people. She will never come," he insisted sullenly.

"Bring her to me," said Gareeb softly; "the poor little thing does not understand."

A warm wild hope flooded Jakara's heart. Of course! If only Eyes of the Sea could meet Gareeb, she would explain the big outside world and its life for a white girl far more convincingly than he could ever hope to do.

As if to dash his hopes, there came from across the waterway the booming call to Waiat. Jakara sat back despondently. "No," he said, "we cannot wait. For all our sakes you must go on the first passing ship. Eyes of the Sea and I will work out our destiny as the Fates decide."

"But the captain will know that you are here and the girl is on Tutu," said Gareeb. "Surely he will take you from the natives?"

"He can't," said Jakara decidedly. "Not the slightest hope in the world. A man-o'-war could not take us if the natives were unwilling and hid us away."

"What is that awful noise?" asked Gareeb, after a pause.

"Just practice for one of their beastly rites," said Jakara. "But let us talk of cheerful things."

He had been thinking seriously of telling the girl of the Waiat rites. But the knowledge might send her mad with anxiety. And before the rites took place, a ship might come. Who knows?

The silence of evening gave answer.

PALMS OF THE STRAIT

CHAPTER XXX

Virgins Of Waiat

During the following week C'Zarcke was locked in the Zogo-house, engaged in council after council with priests and head men of Island groups. Some came and went by night. All wore the black feathers. Something mysterious was being planned of which the people were not told. But at night, on the communal plots before each village, elders grimly discussed the now certain coming of the Lamars. All the tribes lived in a state of waiting fear against some unconquerable force which they could not understand.

One morning Sasowari was scolding. Gareeb was smiling as she gazed upon the looking-bowl. The old woman was brushing the girl's hair. Tastefully she twined a band of mottled crotons around the pale white forehead, and added a finishing touch with her own most prized tortoise-shell comb.

Sasowari was scolding because she wanted the girl to look well, for such an appearance would please Jakara and give the girl something pleasant to think about. But Gareeb was smiling because she felt a little easier in her mind, and also because the looking-bowl amused her. It was a shallow stone bowl, the inside of which had been coated to a dense shiny black with a mixture of coconut-oil and burnt charcoal husk. When filled with crystal clear water, it made the Islanders' looking-glass.

Jakara spent much of the time with Gareeb on his Lookout, but he would much rather that the girl had not come there. They saw only one distant sail, and as it faded away, the girl almost broke down. "It is not the time yet," Jakara reassured her. "They won't even begin to pass until the beginning of the north-west. They will remain fishing for shell until the very change of the wind. Then they must fly south, and some will certainly pass close."

He was very glad that he did not possess the telescope, otherwise the girl must have espied other disappointments. As time passed, she became resigned and more cheerful day by day. Jakara was very glad of this, he was so desperately worried otherwise. Over this island there always brooded death, grown imminent now as the people's fear of the Lamars increased. Passionately he desired life for Eyes of the Sea and Gareeb and himself. He realized that almost from hour to hour dangers were growing, but he was more troubled with guessing that perils threatened which he did not quite comprehend. One evening he determined that the time had come when Gareeb must be forewarned of things he could not guard her against.

Sasowari was teaching her the language. As Jakara moodily entered, she stepped forward and smiled from an anxious heart.

"Sit down and gossip. We have coconut-milk, sweet and cool."

Jakara dallied a while, asking questions of the lessons. Then:

"Gareeb," he said impressively, "now that you understand these people a little the time has come when you must more fully realize our perilous position. You have glimpsed what these natives can do, and love to do. To you, we appear safe now. But, Gareeb, these people have hated the Lamars with a superstitious terror, and at present over every Island group there hangs a heavy dread owing to the great increase of shelling vessels. Many expect annihilation at the hands of the white man cruising the Coral Sea. All fear the extinction of what is to them their national existence. They will know shortly when their emissaries, but really their spies, Kebisu and Maros, return. These chiefs are at present in Sydney, taken there on invitation by the authorities in an endeavour to reconcile the Islanders to the whites. When these two men return, the Islanders must learn for a certainty that they are really at the mercy of the whites. And, Gareeb, they may wreak their vengeance on us."

"But," said the girl slowly, "we are spirit Lamars, and C'Zarcke is your friend."

"Yes," answered Jakara, "and that thread has saved our lives. But you cannot realize all the risks, all the unexpected things that may happen from circumstances, from the smouldering hatred, from the inflammable temperament of these people. And always remember this, Gareeb; Beizam is your enemy; by the rules of these people he has a right to *you*, though always after Sasowari. And the Pretty Lamar is your bitter enemy. There are always ways of settling an enemy other than by public violence – an arrow in the back, a dagger by night, worst of all, the poison cup."

Gareeb went white. "Don't be frightened, Gareeb. Sasowari knows of all these things and guards you," explained Jakara; "but think these risks over quietly and realize that there are other unknown dangers, and your knowledge will guard you against them. You are surprised at the poison cup, but among the – shall we say – 'educated' of these people, there are adept poisoners. There is risk of poison not only from something that you may eat or drink, but from the mere scratch of a thorn placed in the path, from a breath of vapour blown from a reed across your nostrils while you sleep, from the petals of a beautiful flower which you wish to smell. There are other methods, and you could not possibly be on your guard against them all. But, Gareeb, there may not be any reason to worry over these things at all. Now that you know of them, half of any possible danger is gone."

Gareeb thought seriously, and then asked quietly: "Jakara, would not C'Zarcke allow us both to go for Eyes of the Sea? You say that the majority of the pearling-fleet are off Tutu waters. We could get the girl and be rescued at the same time."

"Even if I could get C'Zarcke's permission," answered Jakara, "the risks would be insurmountable in that direction. When we leave here, we have no further protection. We are simply two hated Lamars, an easy prey upon a coral-reefed sea. We should have to pass islands that are either neutral or hostile to Mer. Their canoes would be after us in a twinkling. All the large islands in the Strait have sentinels on every hill and mountain-top. They would see us hours before we saw them. The islands that are only sandbanks also have sentinels with eagle eyes. One solitary canoe, unless it were a huge war-canoe packed with warriors, would almost certainly never reach Tutu—"

He paused, his eyes staring as with fear. They listened. A dull throbbing came from across the water, drums soaked by the tears of virgins, the dreaded drums of Waiat.

Jakara sprang to the door. The night stole in, black velvet, with the heights pierced by stars. Plainer now, but muffled as with ill-omen, the drum-call to Waiat throbbed with horrid insistence. Jakara sent silent curses out towards the sinister islet whose rocky battlements sheltered the cavernous retreats of a devil's worship. He shut the door and glanced at Sasowari.

"What is it?" whispered Gareeb.

"The period of the Waiat ceremonies."

"What are they?"

"A relic of demon-worship of a thousand or more years ago. The isle of Waiat is their last stronghold. C'Zarcke has cut down their power a great deal, but every religion dies hard. It will take the whites to kill this one thoroughly."

Gareeb questioned him with calm grey eyes. "I can see that this Waiat concerns me," she said. "Tell me plainly, Jakara, as you just now forewarned me of other things."

"Yes," he said slowly, "a danger known is a danger met. This is a danger, Gareeb, against which no one can protect you. This Waiat was a god whom no woman could resist. His priests live on the islet that bears his name. At this season of the year, during any one week, for one night only out of that week his priests canoe over here, march through all the villages, enter any house, and seize any girl whom they desire. No one dare withstand them – not father nor brother nor lover: they may come tonight or any night of the week now that the drums have called. Once, they used to come every night, but C'Zarcke, after years of intrigue, reduced their authority to one night only. The girls chosen are carried off to Waiat to become his brides."

"But the god, if ever such a one lived, is long since dead."

"Of course, but his priests aren't; neither are his initiates, nor his memory," replied Jakara grimly.

Silence filled the house, made intense by that dim hypnotic throbbing. "It is the native girls whom they would choose," Gareeb almost whispered; "I should be of no account to them."

"Beizam is an initiate," said Jakara brutally. Presently he reassured her. "You will be all right, little girl. I will sleep outside the house, and I have the power of a chief of the Beizam-le, their most powerful clan. I can guard you against them all – if you are not chosen by Waiat himself."

At the door she stopped him, fear in her eyes. "If they came, and Waiat – insisted?"

"I will last as long as I can," he said quietly.

"Do not go outside. Stay here," she implored.

He looked straight into her eyes. "Gareeb, you are not in a white man's country now. You are bound by the laws of these people, which they enforce with a ruthlessness undreamed of by civilization. Let me go now. What is to be, must be. That is the inexorable law to which all bow here."

She stood staring at the door, terror in her heart.

Jakara walked swiftly to his house, meeting only one soul, a girl like a phantom flying from the arms of her lover to the dubious shelter of her father's home.

Jakara slung a lashed bundle of arrows across his shoulders, seized his bow, and hurried back to Sasowari's house. He camouflaged himself in the shadows fronting the entrance. He had hardly got hidden when another shadow slid along the path and merged with the butt of a coconut-palm opposite.

Jakara breathed with relief. He had recognized young Ormei, and, now that he came to think of it, the running girl reminded him of Magibi. He smiled; then his face set grim, for what hope did any man have, if his sweetheart should be chosen!

Night crept on. The echo of the drums floated up from over sea and bushes. Coco-palms, thickly grown, cast shadows that might not be their own. A rustling sigh betrayed the banana-gardens. Those broad leaves could shelter many men! A little farther along, under the densest palms, were patches of grey and black, where starlight through the trees partially splashed a house.

Jakara crouched. He had heard nothing, but his senses were growing "native." He sighed like a tired child, for he knew now, and was very glad that they were coming to-night. Long nights of watching when nothing comes torture the nerves.

A file of shadows glided along the path, their feathered heads moving above the undergrowth like flitting bats. Their tall forms joined with the palm shadows as they passed by into the village. Their demon faces were painted with a glaring white triangle on each cheek; a broad crimson band ran completely round the face: a red bar glimmered down over nose and mouth and chin: their forearms were a brilliant yellow with the palm of the hands, crimson. The rest of their nakedness was black to the knees. Then came a broad white band, then black again. These knee-bands gave a singular appearance of living phantoms treading the air on their knees. Fifty yards behind, with martial tread, marched a squad of fighting men. Scarlet and cream plumes swayed above their heads, horizontal bars of white crossed their faces, a crescent pearl-shell *mai* in phallic design gleamed upon their necks. A broad scarlet triangle, base uppermost, was painted upon their chests: dog-tooth armlets clenched their upper arms, and black plumes, set in scarlet *kadiks,* swayed to the swing of their forearms. They wore beautiful skirts of the snow-white feathers and orange yellow down of the Torres Strait pigeon. On each ankle shrilled a rattle of goa-nuts. A bone dagger in its lashing clung to their left wrists: the double row of sharks' teeth gleamed from their broad swords. They marched into the village, their firm tread measured to the shrill of the rattles.

Jakara heard a door burst open, a scream quickly stifled. Presently the rattles tinkled more faintly, growing dim along the jungle path towards the next village.

Jakara froze: so did the shadow at the butt of the coco-tree opposite. Back along the path a doubled-up man came breathing heavily, carrying something trussed. As he passed Jakara, the shadow opposite sprang and struck: the dagger pierced straight between the shoulder-blades. The man leaped while falling with a queer gurgling screech: the shadow snatched up the wriggling burden and plunged into the bush.

With laughing heart, but tigerish eyes, Jakara pulled back his bowstring to the arrow-head. For, as was the crafty custom, another man was following well behind the first. He came and halted, astounded, gazing at the huddled body at his feet. Then, throwing up his head, he listened, and caught a distant swishing through the bushes. He sprang in pursuit, pursing his throat for the long-drawn dog-howl of the Waiat: Jakara's arrow whizzed straight to his heart. As the man crashed, Jakara leapt to the path and threw the stabbed man into the bushes. Then he hastily knelt on the other's back and pushed the arrow-head right through, clear of the barbs, which were just protruding through the chest. Coming along the path from the sea was an uncanny clinking sound, a tinkling music that for some unaccountable reason raised any listener's hair on end. Jakara snapped off the arrow-head, thumped his knee in the man's back, and pulled hard. Away behind the tinkle-tinkle came the shrill measured rattle of other fighting-men. Jakara's brow beaded sweat: the arrow-haft came grudgingly out with a long, sucking gasp; the body seemed very loth to part with the telltale arrow. Jakara, breathing hotly, sprawled flat by the body. He could just see the path. To his ear on the ground there came plainly the thump, thump, thump of the feet of this second fighting-squad, still some distance away. The whispering tinkle was passing by with no sound of feet. Jakara clenched his bow, gazing with held breath. The shadow passed! Jakara nearly cried with relief. He sent a breathless prayer of thanks to God up there past the palm-branched sky.

It was a very tall shadow, and it glided by with the arrogant sway of a feared devil. On its head was a magnificent *dari* of turtle-shell flaunting black plumes which ran round the forehead back to the ears, where they were joined by another *dari* holding five splendid white feathers. The stems of these were trimmed and the quill itself split straight up the centre in such a way that each big feather vibrated electrically with the wearer's movement, and the air passing through these slits gave out a distinct, peculiar, hissing sound: a head-band of ebony sea-tree, in which was set one crimson *wada* bean, clasped the broad brow. In a half-circle jutting up from this were set alternately the polished white ribs of men and women (*eud lera bir lid*). Over his great chest and back fell a closely-knit cape of the ribs of women. These breathed music as he walked. For it *was* music. Each rib had been carefully picked from many, for its property of giving forth a clear musical sound at the slightest touch from its. fellow. And no one rib was out of tune. The man's magnificent body was unclothed, except that round his waist was a girdle of women's hair, beautifully interlaced with shimmering crescents of mother-of-pearl. From this girdle hung a pubic shell, fancifully carved in symbolic designs. His right hand grasped a *warup* drum, and under the armpit was a star-shaped club, the *saurisauri*. The left hand carried the *buzi le epei*, a red basket, dreadfully symbolic.

So passed Waiat himself, or rather the human representative of the super-god of centuries ago, the high priest who kept alive his name in the most erotic cult of all the Islands. It had come out of the west, a devil cult that had at one time almost overthrown the cult of Bomai.

Jakara laughed in silent joy as Waiat glided by without even glancing at Sasowari's house. Gareeb, then, was safe from the main devil. His hands took their strain off the bow, but his ears still strained for the tramp of the fighting-squad. Then he sprang round, staring with the mad eyes of a thoroughly frightened man.

"I have been behind your very palm: I saw you kill a priest of Waiat!" she hissed. "I hold your life in my hands, Jakara, like—" the Pretty Lamar snatched the hibiscus from her hair – "like that!"

Jakara drew a long breath. "Curse you, Pretty Lamar," he whispered tensely.

She laughed softly, but alarm heightened the excitement in her face. "H'st," she whispered. "Hark, Jakara! The tramp of feet! Quick, go! Run to your house!"

Jakara smiled cynically. "I will stay right here, Pretty Lamar," he sneered, "something tells me I shall never see my house again!"

She stared in quick dismay, then tried to push him back into the shadows, using a frantic strength as he stubbornly resisted. "Oh, go! go!" she implored. "Hear them coming! Trained fighters all!"

"Why should I go?" he sneered hotly, holding her back.

She listened breathlessly: the click of spear-hafts sounded from down the path, the thump of heavy feet. She snatched his arm frantically. "They are coming for Gareeb," she moaned. "Quick, go! Jakara, my man, they will water the palms with your blood. Oh, Jakara, Jakara, before it is too late. Nothing can save her! You know that."

He sneered insultingly. Subconsciously he was glad that he was coldly angry, for thus he would miss much of the sting of death. He drew out Lightning.

"As surely as you crushed that flower, so you have crushed my heart! I die to-night, Pretty Lamar, and it is you who have killed me. May the curse of Beig rest upon your heart!'"

She clung to his sword arm as the shadowy heads of men appeared along the path. "Stand back! Oh, Jakara," she panted, "I may be able to coax Beizam to forgo his choice. The son of the Mamoose may, if he will. I know he does not act for Waiat himself. Jakara, you would crush my heart that I have treasured only for you."

She sped across the path as the squad swung in and halted at Sasowari's entrance-way. Jakara thrust the rapier-point handy in the ground, fitted an arrow, and faced towards Beizam – waiting. He could just distinguish the proud poise of his enemy's head among the waiting squad. His heart thumped with an exultant hope, for instinctively he realized that the picking of Gareeb to-night was a private arrangement between Beizam and the Pretty Lamar.

What she promised the Shark, Jakara never learned, but presently the squad tramped by into the deathly silent village.

Jakara leaned back against a palm, unnerved with relief. The Pretty Lamar crept towards him. Jakara stared at her tragic face: her eyes were utterly miserable. Impulsively he put his arms round her.

"You feel like killing me, Pretty Lamar," he whispered, "dear girl of Las, forgive me. For what you have done just now I like and honour you more than I have ever liked you before!"

As she gazed at him, the colour drained back to her cheeks. Her tragic eyes softened, and she smiled with a tremble of the lips that touched Jakara's heart. "Jakara, the Never-understandable! I would give more than life for you – to be your slave for years would be joy to me. Oh, Jakara, I do love you!"

Her arms stole lingeringly round his neck, passionate entreaty shone from her eyes.

"For what you have done for Gareeb," he whispered as they kissed. She clung passionately, and Jakara did not resist.

A crash from the village startled them. Jakara became abruptly alert.

"The bodies," he whispered hastily. "I must hide them somewhere."

"The sharks' pool," said the Pretty Lamar instantly. Jakara laughed, picked up the crushed hibiscus, kissed it, and put it in his belt.

"The Pretty Lamar is as keen of brain as she is lovely of face," he said with a smile. "And," he added, "I like you very much, Pretty Lamar!"

He bent among the grass, seized a body, slung it across his shoulder, and hurried towards the beach, to the pool where the sharks mated.

Young Ormei had struck in the blindness of frantic love that sees only one object ahead and lets the consequences be what they will. Jakara would help the lad all he could. After that, Bomai, and the Pretty Lamar, would have to stand by both him and the boy.

One quiet evening, a month later, Ormei sought Jakara. The young man was obviously frightened.

"Oh, Jakara, I have only now learned what you did for me that night!"

"Who told you?"

"The Pretty Lamar. She said my head would look sweet upon the Sarokag pole."

Jakara laughed explosively. "That is just like the Pretty Lamar," he said. "But have no fear, Ormei, she will never tell!"

"Are you certain? Oh, Jakara, remember that I have slain a priest of Waiat!"

"So have I," answered Jakara cheerfully. "I wish I could slay them all."

Ormei breathed in overwhelming relief. "I wondered and wondered," he whispered. "I thought the Spirits of Evil must have flown away with the body."

"They would not touch it," said Jakara decidedly. "But tell me the gossip of the village. Only the Greater Council are sitting, and I have not been invited to attend."

"Waiat himself came over next day, and I nearly died. He demanded of C'Zarcke men to search every village and find his priests, or else slay one in every ten of all the people. We do not know exactly what happened," added Ormei in an awed tone, "but Waiat went away very quickly to Waiar and has been sulking ever since."

"Yes," said Jakara, "his dirty crowd have been sending up the smoke all day and chanting all night. Hear their drumming now!"

"Yes," whispered Ormei, as he gazed apprehensively down towards the shadowed outline of Waiar, "the people whisper that the Zogo-le have more to think of than the complaints of Waiat. It is even whispered that C'Zarcke prophesied that Waiat will claim no more brides. Dreadful times must be coming for our nation, Jakara, when the Zogo-le ignore the grievances of the great god Waiat."

"What is Beizam doing?" asked Jakara abruptly.

"Very busy," said Ormei in relief at the change of subject; "he sends and receives messenger canoes daily to Eroob, and from there messengers go to, and come from, Ugar. He is working up the people, but especially the seasoned warriors and young men, to attack the Lamars and wipe them off the seas. He says that if all the men of all the Island groups will combine and man their canoes, they will be in such numbers as to wipe off the scattered ships of the Lamars one by one."

"By Jove!" exclaimed Jakara.

"Do you really think they could do it, Jakara?" asked Ormei with great eagerness.

Jakara smiled grimly. "What if they did, Ormei? The Lamars would again come and come and come! But, next time, they would come in huge ships filled with fighting-men armed with weapons that would blow the canoes of the nations to Beig. Just as a cyclone whips the sea."

Ormei sighed. Jakara had voiced what all the people faintly believed.

"What else is Beizam doing?"

"Oh, he has surprised us all. The islands are seething with talk and all are very much excited, especially the young men, who are hurrying with the making of many new weapons throughout every village. But the old people are very doubtful. They point out that even Kebisu with chosen warriors of his own men was brutally defeated by the Lamars at Coconut."

"Yes," smiled Jakara.

"They say also that Jardin's Lamars have almost wiped out the Murralug people."

"Yes," said Jakara grimly.

"They say that every time a Lamar fighting-ship has landed on any island, the Lamars have killed many with their thunder weapons, and we could not stop them from burning our villages."

"And what does Beizam reply to those facts?" asked Jakara with interest.

"He says that the only time the Island peoples manned their canoes for battle and attacked a real Lamar fighting-ship, they drove away not only one but two such ships and their thunder weapons. The men of Tutu did that. He says, too, that the only time the Island peoples organized and fought a landing force of the Lamars, they drove them back to their ship in haste. That was—" and Ormei paused – "when Jakara with a handful of the men of Mer drove back the fighting-men of the Ulag (*Woodlark*)."

"By Jove!" exclaimed Jakara.

"Beizam says," went on Ormei, "that the Island warriors have only been beaten because they are *afraid* of the Lamars. They run and hide deep within their islands when the Lamars attack. Beizam wants all the warriors to mass in their fighting-canoes and attack the Lamars on their own fighting-ground – the sea!"

Jakara looked serious. He instantly realized that such a plan, if resolutely carried out, would at least drive the pearling-vessels from the sea for a long time – certainly until the arrival of war-ships.

"Yes?" he said at last.

"Beizam offers to organize and lead the whole great fleet, and, as Kebisu and Maros are away, he offers to lead the Tutu and Ugar men in person."

"H'm," said Jakara grimly. "Now just what would Kebisu and Maros say to that!"

"They are away in the hands of the Lamars, and many things might happen before they returned – they never would return, if Beizam won a victory over the Lamars."

Very uneasily Jakara asked, "What do the Zogo-le and C'Zarcke say to this?"

"We do not know. We seem to know nothing – which is the worst of all. The rumour is that C'Zarcke is going to await the return of Kebisu with news as to exactly what the Lamars are, how long they are going to stay on this earth, and what is their strength. He believes that the people would be simply sacrificing themselves if the Lamars are invincible, and if they are not, then we shall know all about them and can attack in confidence when Kebisu returns."

Jakara was vastly relieved. "I had no idea that Beizam's plans were so ripe and so far spread. I have had so much to think of lately. that I have given no thought to what was happening. Thank you, Ormei."

"Anything I could do for Jakara," said Ormei softly, "would be an honour and a duty. To him I owe my sweetheart's life, and – I should be Jakara's best friend if I could."

Jakara smiled warmly, and laid his hands on Ormei's shoulder.

"I am truly grateful, my friend," he said, "I need friends – very much."

CHAPTER XXXI

Plans And Counter Plans

Days dreamed by, and the south-east trades were now blowing irregularly. On some days the breeze eased to puffs that merely rippled the sea, then followed nights of calm until a day dawned to a sea as moveless as a pool. Very soon now would come the north-west, first the lull, then the change, then the lull again, then, gathering strength, the winds would roar down from New Guinea and, howling across the Strait, would tear right down the north-eastern Australian coast. And the pearling-fleet would fly before them like gulls afraid for their wings.

Day by day Jakara studied the moods of the wind, the clouding of the sky, the flights of migratory birds, the appearing of the north-west stars, the vanishing of the south-east shoals of fish, the budding of the north-west plants and shrubs. His mind grew a little easier as night after night brought nearer the day when some flying vessel must pass by. He had a light canoe all ready on the beach, even though from his Lookout he would see any sail coming towards Eroob from the direction of New Guinea hours before it could possibly pass Mer. All his thoughts and energies had long since been occupied with the getting away of Gareeb from Mer. He had found that the troubles of others gave him more anxiety than all his own since he had been on Mer. Afterwards, he and Eyes of the Sea would work out their own destiny. They were children of their environment, but Gareeb was a white girl amongst savages. Every day of light breeze and calm filled Jakara's heart with hope, for lack of wind meant that Jardine's schooner, coming from the south, must sail but slowly. A thousand times had Jakara wished hopelessly that the schooner was scheduled to call at Mer instead of Ugar. But the cunning of the Zogo-le had defeated the autocratic power of Jardine in deciding the coming and going of the schooner. Each day's delay now went to Jakara's account. It meant the slowing down of the schooner corresponding with the faster return of the pearling-fleet. If he could only get Gareeb aboard some vessel before Kebisu landed with his ominous news, all might yet be well. With anxiety creasing his face, he gazed in daily anguish of waiting from his Lookout.

But others were planning, too, forcing events swiftly. Beizam had become impatient. "The Shark" wanted a wife, and meant to have her. He told her so, in no uncertain manner. Her eyes blazed, and she laughed! In savage exasperation the chieftain seized her, and she sneered into his face:

"Fool, there is always the poison cup!" Beizam turned ashen in his secret fear.

The Pretty Lamar laughed mockingly; then her splendid eyes wooed Beizam, for she too had been impatient for just this moment.

"Beizam wants me, but he will not get me until Jakara is out of the way – which he very much wants to be," she purred.

"You know very well that C'Zarcke has forbidden me," he replied sulkily. "No man wants his spirit shrivelled when he flies in his after life to Boigu!"

"There are other ways," she said softly. "He has not forbidden you to touch the girls!"

He stared at the alluring face afire with suggestion and promise. "Tell me," he whispered doubtfully.

"Sail to Eroob. Persuade some Erubian shark-men to make a dash for Tutu and tell Eyes of the Sea about Gareeb – that they sail away any day now – that she will certainly lose Jakara."

"Then you do not think that Jakara will come back?" queried Beizam hopefully.

"Of course he will come back," she answered sharply, belying her own belief.

"Then what good will that do me?" asked the puzzled Beizam.

"It may bring you me – and other things!"

"How?"

The girl shrugged impatiently. "Because jealousy means trouble."

"But that would be Jakara's trouble. Where do I gain?"

"Fool, out of his trouble. Whichever girl wins it will mean a win for you. Eyes of the Sea would be mad enough to do anything out of spite, but if she won, well then, you have secretly desired the white figure of Gareeb!"

Beizam drew a long breath, gazing at the temptress. He knew *now* what she wanted. Another notch to his love-stick. It was woman's spite and vanity. She wanted to be prouder still of him. What a clever woman she was!

He smiled with quick understanding, for no matter which girl Jakara finally chose, he, Beizam, could also win – and with Jakara dead or married, must win this girl too.

The Pretty Lamar had won, and a smile pouted her rich red lips.

"But how do I get rid of Jakara?" he whispered keenly.

"Oh, you need not be afraid of angering C'Zarcke; others will attend to Jakara in the heat of the moment, if you do what I say. In the trouble that will be stirred up, Jakara may well lose both girls as well as himself," she whispered, and her eyes flashed the insinuation.

Beizam threw back his head and laughed delightedly. He gripped her arms with a splendid strength. "What vanity!" he chuckled. "The Beautiful Lamar will for ever be queen over every Island woman, with *two* Lamar notches to her husband's love-stick. Never has an Island girl had such an honour. You shall have those notches as a triumph of your brains and beauty, if only Bomai wills. And afterwards – afterwards, you beautiful, treacherous devil, you will marry me – quickly."

His mouth twisted in its smile, his eyes narrowed cruelly.

"Yes," said the Pretty Lamar, and stared him in the eyes.

"Then see that you are ready when next I ask. I have big schemes ahead and cannot delay for a girl."

The girl's heart sneered as she read her future in his face.

"Listen!" she said impressively; "there must be no mistake. Take no chances with Jakara the Cunning, or we lose everything; the clever Lamar might easily ruin your biggest scheme. He will fight with his brains for the Lamars, and – he is the friend of C'Zarcke. Do not send your messengers until I give you word, then post a man to watch by day from Lalour Mountain on Eroob. Eyes of the Sea will certainly come to Mer immediately she hears the news. Your lookout from big Lalour will see her many hours away. He sends up the smoke. You watch from Gelam; thus we shall know of her coming long before she even reaches Eroob. Come to me quickly when you see the smoke. Then I will tell you what next."

Beizam nodded admiringly. "Jakara has the brains of the spirit people," he said thoughtfully, "but you have the cunning of many men. C'Zarcke must have breathed on your mother ere you were born. Why not wait, though, until Kebisu arrives? There will be all the trouble you desire if he brings news of ill omen."

"Jakara will not wait for the trouble," she answered emphatically; "he will sail before it. And then," she added meaningly, "you will miss both girls."

Beizam looked steadily at the girl. "You plan, and *I* will do the work," he replied softly.

"Beizam, let us settle for ever just what is to be," said the Pretty Lamar decisively. "I have set my heart on your conquests. If you bungle, and Jakara sails with the girls, then I lose and – you take me!"

The man stared in a waiting silence. A joyous smile rippled over the girl's face.

"Do not mistake me, oh chieftain of the shark-men," she said deliberately; "remember-that poison cup!"

And the man's blood ran cold.

Time sped: a growing tension made the people nasty. There was heated talk in the villages, tinged with fear, for the Lamar ship with Kebisu aboard was nearing the Coral Sea. They knew it, though only the Zogo-le understood how and why. The people whispered of C'Zarcke's ominous brow. He seldom left the Zogo-house. There was a constant coming and going of the Mai-le priesthood travelling by night in order to dodge Lamar ships. Later, an apathy spread over the people: for if C'Zarcke could do nothing, then hope was gone.

One night Jakara awoke with a start. In the distance a mournful howl moaned over the island. He listened a while, and then lay back, warily dozing: the howl had come from distant Piad. If a man had had eyes to see through the night, he would have noticed every dog in all the villages sneaking with frightened eyes and with tail between its legs to the darkest shelter of the houses. A night of terror for the dogs, and what for human beings!

Jakara sprang up, hair on end. Two dogs howled, the long drawn wail of things that had lost their very soul. The howl was much nearer this time, apparently from the village of Babud. Noiselessly Jakara stole outside. A black night: utterly silent: not a whisper even from the palms! He grinned uneasily, thinking how tightly every door was being barricaded in every village. On noiseless feet he stole up the path and knocked at Sasowari's doorway.

"Open! It is Jakara!" he said quietly.

A relieved grunt, a shifting of wood, and he stepped inside into darkness. Sasowari quietly fastened the door, then bent over the hearth and blew on a smouldering coconut-husk. Its glow enhanced the whiteness in the face of Gareeb. Jakara smiled reassuringly.

"Everything is quite all right, Gareeb," he said; "this is only a little local affair which we can control."

The alarm eased from her eyes.

"What are they doing now?" she whispered. A long-drawn howl curdled the blood of the village from quite near.

Gareeb gasped: "Oh, Jakara, what does that dreadful noise mean?"

"They are only looking for dogs," answered Jakara.

"*They*!" Gareeb turned ashen. "I thought it was some dreadful animal! Tell me what it means; tell me everything!"

"It is the 'dogs' sacrifice, – which means that a local raiding-party has returned without securing heads. By the long-drawn note at the end of the howl, they sound to me like some of our own Crocodile clan. They cannot return to their village without at least a dog's head. It is their custom." Jakara glanced uneasily at Sasowari.

"You have not told me all. For my own safety, Jakara!"

"You are right, Gareeb. Those howlers are now keenly seeking for a child's head, an old person's head, or an able-bodied man's head. They seek the first because they are the easiest to get. But they must sound the 'dog's howl.' The people then hurry their helpless ones inside. The headhunters dare not break into a house with the door fastened and the people inside awake, but if those inside are asleep, then the hunter may enter if he can, but without waking a soul. If he can spring on a sleeping person, slash off the head, and disappear in the terror of the moment, then well and good: It is the custom, and honour is regained. But the inmates can, if they like, sham sleep, and kill the raider if possible. Great honour is the due of warrior or girl who takes the head of a 'dog's howl' raider, because in this case the honour falls like a sort of cloak over the whole clan of the killer, while a double disgrace falls on the clan of the 'dog's howl' man. So now, if these fellows should come sneaking around here, we will sham sleep and, I hope, surprise the. gentlemen. By doing that, you and Sasowari will most likely be left alone by any similar prowling gang in the future. But remember this, Gareeb; if they only secure a dog's head or a child's they may return to their homes on sufferance, but they do not regain their status of manhood until they have secured the head of a grown person; so that no one is safe on the island when he first hears the 'dog's howl,' until eventually someone has sacrificed his or her head."

Gareeb's face looked deathly. "I did not think that such beings in human form could exist;" she said at last.

"It has been a custom among the Eastern Group for thousands of years," said Jakara grimly; "the Western and Central groups have similar and worse customs."

Sasowari hissed. Instantly Jakara stretched himself out in the blackest shadows of the house. Sasowari pulled the girl down on the sleeping-mat. The women lay just where the glowing husks shed a dim light. Sasowari was snoring like a very tired old woman, but the unseen terror held Gareeb as silent as the village dogs.

Time passed, and silence swallowed it. Low down, through the matting of the wall, a little white point bored unseen. The white vanished, and black dot appeared, unrecognizable because the dot was like that of the night itself. But concentrated terror told the women that "something" was glaring at them. Something vanished: the point of the bone dagger, very slowly, quite noiselessly, bored farther through the matting: then the sharp blade swept gently down, making a slit two feet long: two black fingers gripped through on to the inner side of the matting, holding it back taut, so that the blade should make not the faintest rustle. Then Jakara became one with the shadows, with infinite quietness melting across the house-floor. A husk reddened as if blown by the breath of a spirit and was reflected in the staring eyes of Warawa: a fairy gleam kissed the blade of Lightning. Then the cut flap of the matting vanished, and the night peeped in, bringing something with it – two eyes, lit by a glare hardly animal or human, bands of white encircling those eyes, a corrugated forehead beaded with sweat, a hawk nose and black-red lips drawn back from white teeth. It glared a second at the women: then came a crash like splintered glass as Lightning drove through those teeth, taking half the jaw-bone with it: a thrashing of bushes outside as a man rolled over and over in agony: Jakara laughing in great noiseless breaths as he clung to the rigid form of Gareeb: Sasowari silent.

Jakara petted the girl with comforting whispers: "Sh-sh! Gareeb! We are safe as safe can be, but don't make a noise! They have gone, and, while they are never certain it was I, you will always be safe when the 'dog's howl' is heard in future. Never let them know! They fear most those things that they do not understand. Only by working on that trait in their character have I survived through all these years."

Gareeb sighed like one who had just about reached the limit of her endurance.

"Never leave us alone again, Jakara."

"Not until just before daylight. Then I'll sneak to my hut, and they will never know for certain what guards the home of Sasowari."

Days slipped by until there came a morning when Jakara sighted the first returning sail. There were two of them, dimly seen to the west, just like gulls' wings fading into the mists. Jakara was sorry that Gareeb saw too. To her it seemed cruel that vessels should pass the island, but so far away. She did not understand their courses, nor that the direction of the wind would prevent any canoe from overhauling them. She tried vainly to understand when Jakara carefully explained that there would inevitably be a number of vessels whose position would compel them to steer a more south-east course, which would cause them to sail miles closer to Mer. But that night she was happily excited, for she really had seen ships, and others would – *must* come! And hope sailed in dreams through her disappointed sleep.

Another worry had broken in upon Jakara's fast overcrowding troubles. He had become acutely aware of the persistent visits of the Pretty Lamar to the house of Sasowari. With an uneasy wonderment, he had gradually formed the impression that her laughing espionage was more on Sasowari than on Gareeb and himself.

The end was coming on the contrary wings of the wind, with every thrust of a schooner's bow. Kebisu and Maros were nearing Somerset. C'Zarcke knew, the Zogo-le knew, the Maid-le knew. They knew for certain, whereas Jardine, across the Strait from Somerset only guessed. The people of the Island nation knew that the Zogo-le did not *guess*, those spiritual-scientific leaders of their nation who have for centuries possessed an unexplainable power of drawing news from the air – a sense only now being dimly guessed at by the white man. And the people further sensed that the Zogo-le knew of bad news!

Jakara realized that Kebisu *must* bring back bad news, would see with his own eyes that white people were not curious spirits wandering for a playtime down to earth, but were virile human beings possessing a great land and reaching out for more; in numbers as vast as the sands of the sea when compared to the strength of the Islanders. But Jakara did not know the position of Jardine's schooner ploughing up beside the Barrier Reef, and no one told him. For Jakara had changed. He seldom left the Lamar girl. It was as if he were withdrawing from them. Once he had been like Eyes of the Sea, lived their life, loved their loves, and gloried in their hates. And this Lamar girl seldom visited among them, never joined in their nightly dances and ceremonies as a true daughter of Sasowari should do. So the Islanders hushed their voices when Jakara came by, and scowled when he passed. Gloom settled deeper on all men's thoughts.

Then a day dawned when, on distant Tutu, a girl went frantic because of one lone Lamar, while her people feared many thousands. For canoe men had sailed all night from Eroob, and Eyes of the Sea had been given her message. She would lose Jakara! He was going to sail away with another girl Lamar. And these months had been one long heartache while she awaited his coming!

Regardless of consequences, she raced down the beach and untethered a light fishing-canoe. With her own hands she hoisted the sail and steered out past the reefs into the open sea. She asked no permission, she took no food, no water. The people smiled in sympathy, and agreed that, when the girl had cried her eyes out upon the lonely sea, she would return when hungry and get over it all, afterwards seeking a nearer lover.

But Eyes of the Sea never returned. She sailed straight on into a kindly night which enveloped her in all its star-gilt loneliness; an anguished little girl, and yet a devil if needs be, ready to cry or ready to go to any length, no matter what it cost anyone – ready to attempt anything to hold the man she loved.

While he was gossiping in Sasowari's home, Jakara's hopes crashed.

Sasowari was bending over the cooking-pots, and a ray of sunlight showed him the bone in her arm. It was not a skinny arm any longer: it was merely a bone enveloped in skin. Her shoulders were bones, and her ribs were as plain and almost as dry as those of old Warawa glaring expectantly from his shroud pole. The old woman looked up into Jakara's anguished face. Her sunken eyes stared watery and glassy: her face was shrunken to mummy-colour: her mouth sagged, shreds of dank hair clung to her brow. She nodded pathetically, and then lowered her head, for Gareeb was looking.

When alone with the old woman, Jakara seized her hand. "Tell me, mother?" he whispered hoarsely.

"It is so, Jakara. I am dying. Fast. I am trying hard to hold out until Kebisu returns. Oh Jakara, I am so worn out! My spirit will slip out through these old bones at any time now: it is agony striving to hold it in."

"My God!" breathed Jakara.

She lifted clawlike fingers to fondle his hair. "There may yet be time," she whispered earnestly. "Remember – I have yet to see Gareeb!"

"Gareeb!" repeated Jakara, puzzled. "Oh yes, mother, yes! Fight to the very last of your strength until your daughter comes."

With pain in his heart he hurried away. Gareeb, from the banana-plot, saw his strained face and came towards him.

"Gareeb, we must go," he said quickly. "Be prepared at any moment. Sasowari is dying. Better we should perish in trying to battle through to Somerset, than stay here and be slaughtered when Kebisu returns."

She cast a startled look towards the house, but he seized her arm. "No, not straight away. She may – will linger a few days yet. Extreme old age! But, Gareeb, when she goes, your best protector is gone. The custom is that Beizam can claim you, because he captured you. Sasowari's nearest relation might claim you, but Beizam would have the right to purchase. I could and would claim you, but that would break the law and would mean a fight, and the people are worked up and are fanatic in their hate against us."

"Oh; God!" cried Gareeb.

"There is one other way," said Jakara hurriedly. He hesitated and gazed out to sea.

"Oh, tell me!" cried Gareeb, "everything is terrible – *nothing* could be more terrible!"

"It is not so bad as that," said Jakara. "You would have to marry me. If I claimed you for a wife, the dispute would necessarily go before C'Zarcke, since both Beizam and I are chiefs. If C'Zarcke decided against me, then nothing could save you. If the verdict were favourable – I should have to pay Beizam what he likes to ask."

"But—" said the girl. "Eyes of the Sea?"

"I don't know," Jakara said hopelessly.

The girl wrung her hands. "Oh, don't talk like that! *Think* of something. You know that can never be! Even if there were no Eyes of the Sea, you say the people are all bitter against us. C'Zarcke would decide against even that! Jakara, Jakara, what *shall* we do?"

"Listen, Gareeb! Apparently Sasowari will linger a few days at least. If so, we are saved for a certainty, for all day the wind has been blowing from the north-west. But if Sasowari goes suddenly – then we will make a bold bid for Somerset. It is only a hundred and twenty miles away, and we will try to pass the most dangerous islands at night. But, Gareeb," he gazed straight into her eyes, "it will almost certainly mean death. If we do get through," he added more brightly, "I shall have the help of Jardine in getting back and rescuing Eyes of the Sea."

They turned to stare at the Pretty Lamar running wildly towards them through the banana-garden. She clutched Jakara and panted, "Quick, quick, Beizam!" She pointed seaward to a light canoe swiftly tacking towards Eroob – "Beizam has gone for Eyes of the Sea. He swears he will take her! She has landed at Eroob on her way to see you."

Jakara seized her shoulders roughly and snarled: "Tell me now, and quick!"

"I know nothing, nothing!" cried the girl frantically. "Beizam has been watching for days from Gelam! They sent him a smoke signal from Lalour! He knew she was coming whenever a canoe could dodge the Lamar ships fishing on the reefs. He did not tell me until he came laughing down from Gelam. He sneered like a shark – because you could not stop him. Oh Jakara, Jakara, stop him! Take my canoe; it is all ready on the beach. If I cannot have you, then he will not have Eyes of the Sea."

Jakara flung her from him, and then pressed his hands to his forehead. Suddenly he hurried Gareeb out of earshot. His eyes were blazing, his face radiant.

"Gareeb, Gareeb!" he whispered excitedly. "It is the very best thing that could have happened! I will fetch Eyes of the Sea. Beizam will get there first, but Eyes of the Sea is at home on Eroob. She is almost a native girl, and Beizam must manoeuvre for hours before he gets her. I'll bring her back, and the three of us will sail together if Kebisu comes first. You are quite safe here now, even if Sasowari dies, for Beizam is not here to claim you. Wait just a little longer, Gareeb. Eroob is only thirty miles away, just a matter of hours, and – Beizam may never return! In that case the three of us can wait quietly on Mer until a ship passes. Even if Sasowari is dead, I can easily buy you from her relations. Any ship that comes will give me steel tomahawks, which are priceless here. Good-bye for just a few hours, little girl; everything is turning out wonderfully for us."

He ran down to the beach, launched the canoe, and waved to Gareeb. With a terrified heart she watched him sail into the sunset. The leading canoe was now only a blur dissolving in the night mist that was closing over the sea.

PALMS OF MER

CHAPTER XXXII

As Is Written In The Courses Of The Stars

Night fell and the sea gleamed faintly from the wilderness of stars above. Jakara knew that it was hopeless to try to overtake such an experienced sailor as Beizam. He set his mind to seize every advantage of wind and tide in lessening the distance to Eroob. He felt wretchedly uneasy, and became a prey to such a haunting dread that he found it hard to prevent himself from turning the canoe about and sailing back. A power was impressing his mind as if knock-knock-knocking, urging him to "return, return, return!" He now doubted the word of the Pretty Lamar. And yet the fact of Eyes of the Sea being on Eroob could easily have been kept from him. Since Gareeb came he had drifted far from the intimacies of the Islanders, and that they resented it, he realized fully. The hours drifting by tortured him with indecision. What if the Pretty Lamar had lied? What if Beizam had turned back under shadow of darkness? Why, Beizam might not have been in the canoe at all! And yet, if Eyes of the Sea were really at Eroob—

Someone was calling him; he was *sure* of it; he had grown so intimately into the life of the natives that he realized that, especially in these last two years, his mind had become dimly susceptible to their telepathic power. What if Gareeb – no, of course not – Sasowari were calling him? What if she were dying? For how long past had she hidden her rapid decline, to spare them anxiety? What if she were nearer death than even she had thought? Fool, how blind he had been, trying to think of everything and yet not seeing vital things happening right under his eyes! What if Sasowari really were dying? She could not! She would hang on until Kebisu came, until she saw her own Gareeb.

He struck his head with clenched fist. Idiot! He was going *native*! The real Gareeb had been drowned or killed years ago. He knew it, and now was trying to make himself believe that she would return. But Sasowari could not die until she had seen her own Gareeb; she could not!

He stared across the sea in an agony of indecision. He stood up abruptly, gazing around until finally he was looking directly back, straight back towards invisible Mer. Thoughtfully he sat down, gazing out over the dancing bows of the canoe.

How utterly strange! He could have *sworn* something had passed him, some travelling thing had slipped past to Mer. He knew that, though his eyes were keen, they had espied only the star-glaze on the waves. But some inner consciousness was struggling vainly to break through the mist shrouding his understanding. He cursed himself for not taking advantage of every aid in his present plight, whether he understood that aid or not. This was the very sort of night which the natives found most suitable for their queer second-sight sense. Atmospheric conditions were perfect. He should sit quietly in the canoe and use no physical exertion except a mere mechanical steering. He should have kept his mind an absolute blank, in a state of receptivity for any tidings purposely sent to him, or for any disturbance by mind-agencies operating in agreement or in conflict with his own anxieties. He had not done so. His mind was a tortured whirlpool of conflicting emotions and fears.

It was Kebisu's great canoe that had passed, quite a long distance off. In similar circumstances a native would have known at once. But Jakara lacked the trained mind allied to the understanding of even one of the Maid-le.

An hour later, and he sprang up again, his eyes blazing with an intensity of desire. But he saw nothing, heard nothing, while the canoe of Eyes of the Sea sped past a long way out, quite invisible.

One by one, but quickly, the stars dimmed; it seemed they had tried their hardest and now did not wish to see anything more. Jakara turned again to the bulk of Eroob, now looming from the sea. What if the Pretty Lamar had known that old Sasowari lay dying? With his brow beaded with sweat, Jakara suddenly swung the canoe round and headed straight back for Mer. With a madman's eagerness he strove to force every breath of the wind to drive him faster, faster, faster. He sobbed incoherent prayers to God for wind, wind, wind.

In Sasowari's house the coco-husks glowed. Otherwise the place was dark with a waiting silence, for the presence of Death was there. Gareeb, in helpless despair, knelt by the dying woman, who was so weak that she could not lift her bony fingers to stroke the girl's hair.

"Do not grieve, Gareeb," she croaked, "and listen carefully. Let no one know – when I am gone. To morrow, go about the garden as if I were present – as if my spirit were still in the body – but never go out of sight of the door."

She paused for breath, her fading eyes pathetic in their warning, staring up at Gareeb's ashen face. "Watch that the Pretty Lamar does not creep inside. Jakara will come back – very soon: he is coming now! You should have no need to worry – if they do not know ... I am dead."

An hour dragged by, then dimly through the walls murmured a hubbub from the village beach. A startled glaze flickered in the dying woman's eyes. "Creep out," she whispered, "watch the path – then tell me." From the shelter of the house the girl discerned dim forms hurrying into the village. They came and vanished and others came again, quick shadows of men, women, and children. Odd whispers floated with sinister suggestion to her ears. The girl did not understand that the main paths encircling the island were alive with these shadows, all converging on that beach where at any moment now Kebisu would land. "All going to a dance; it is nothing," mumbled Sasowari, when the girl whispered her report. But Sasowari did not mention Kebisu, and hopelessness iced her fluttering heart. She was past fighting now. She could only wait for the end. Strangely, even so, she seemed to be listening, watching, expecting!

Kebisu landed in the small hours of the morning. The people formed an indistinct mass under the palms. They waited breathlessly while Kebisu, followed by Maros, strode unspeaking through the laneway made for them. A thousand pairs of eyes strained in the darkness as they passed. Then a wonderful sound, the sigh of many people floating upwards to the palms. For Kebisu and Maros each wore a black feather, but the emblems were broken and fell upon the brow of the wearers. Even as the Maid-le escorted the chiefs away, there arose to the night an ominous murmuring, a frightening sound fraught with terrible possibilities – the voice of a frightened, angry people.

Up on the hill-side a shadow stole from the gloom of Sasowari's house.

Tigerish were the eyes of the Pretty Lamar.

Statues of the living and the dead were grouped inside the great Zogo-house. The Zogo-le and the Maid-le of the complete Eastern Group stood in their symbolic places by the Au-gud. The Mamooses of the allied islands were faced by the chief medicine-men, while in two crescents surrounding the Au-gud stood rigidly, each beside a mummy statue, one hundred of the Black Feathers, the seniors of the cult.

C'Zarcke waited, tragedy upon his face. The eyes of the Au-gud glared out over him as if threatening unmentionable doom to any who should harm this greatest of its priests. In this deathly waiting of the living and the dead it seemed that the soul of Bomai breathed hope and promise of everlasting life after earth's hour of trial. When Kebisu, with Maros, stood before the judges, all the arrogance was missing from both chiefs. Kebisu, his lips grim for speech, gazed into the eyes of C'Zarcke, and then flung aside his arms in resignation. Maros knelt and bowed his head. "Speak!" commanded C'Zarcke softly. "Tell us in few words what your eyes have seen, your ears have heard, your mind has learned."

"The sun of the Island nations has set," answered Kebisu sadly; "the dawn of the Lamars has come. Their numbers are as the herrings that shoal upon the sea, and they fill a land as vast as the sea. Their knowledge is too great for our minds to grasp. They command to their bidding beasts of flesh and iron and steel that have been quickened to life from the breath of the gods. Their villages they call cit-ees, and each cit-ee is greater than all Mer itself. Syd-nee is but one great cit-ee, other villages they have uncountable. Their trained fighting-men alone number more than the entire population of all the Eastern nation, and their weapons that spit thunder and fire are invincible. They spread out over the Great South Land like scurrying ants coming ever north. Their ships upon the seas and in the cit-ees are as numerous as the gulls upon the sea. Mer is doomed: Eroob and Ugar are doomed. Maubiag, and Moa, and Sabai, and Daru, and Badu, and Massig are doomed. Murralug is doomed, and Tutu and Boigu; and every Island nation and every island is doomed. The Lamars are coming, have come, and to us of the Coral Sea remains only Boigu, Isle of the Blest." And Kebisu, sinking to his knees, bowed his head beside Maros.

For tense moments silence gripped the Zogo-house. It seemed as if the mummies grinned, an understanding grin from a knowledge gained after death.

C'Zarcke sighed. His quiet voice whispered into the farthest shades of the Zogo-house. "The tidings that Kebisu confirms have been long known to the Zogo-le. Those of the west know them too, but, like us, are helpless against the numbers and superior knowledge of the Lamars. As a people upon this earth, we are doomed. But there remains to us Boigu, Isle of the Blest. As you know, our life upon earth is but a Kwod to train for the lives to come. Soon upon this earth we shall be overrun, our beliefs and ideals scattered to forgetfulness. But they cannot take our knowledge accumulated throughout the centuries by our forefathers, and they cannot intercept us from Boigu. We will take an oath then, here in the living presence of Bomai, that, when the Lamars finally come, no man shall explain to them one word of our knowledge of this earth and of the life to come, nor of anything which we know. That which we have learnt, we will take with us to Boigu, and, with the reasoning mind which cannot die, in the life after we will continue striving for the knowledge which will finally grant us power and peace and life everlasting. The great Au-gud, the Booya, and the divining instruments of every group we will hide within the hearts of mountains, and we will hand their secrets down to the descendants of the Zogo-le alone, so that, if in their turn the Lamars should eventually die out, then any Island people that may be left may reconstruct the history and knowledge of our race upon earth, and we will help them by spirit power from Boigu."

This explains why, when the missionaries landed at Eroob a very few years later, they spread over the most warlike groups of the Strait Islands with comparatively little trouble. But only now, after extensive study of the people and the lapse of years, has a missionary of great sympathy come to gain a closer understanding of the inner life of this most remarkable people.

Down on the village sands swelled a murmuring, pregnant with meaning, the birth of a people's despair. It swelled up to an angry hum very terrible in its menacing tones, the voice of an angry people growing hysterical in disaster. The younger warriors in feverish defiance whispered, then talked openly of fight. They shouted "War," and sprang together in excited groups and roared maddened defiance of the Lamars. And a thousand coco-trees flared to torches and the air shrilled to clash of weapons and spasmodic bursts of war-song. And then rolled the thunder of feet as the excitement found vent in the war-dance, and in the unprecedented emotion of national eclipse excited girls rushed the thumping squares and with thrashing limbs screamed their defiance to the cool still sky. And the roaring voices, like that of some vast animal, rolled away out over the hills of Mer, and the maddest of the mad was Beizam, for he sickened at the thought of ruling a dead people.

The Pretty Lamar clutched his trembling sword-arm and her eyes blazed with suggestion: her soft voice whispered for his ear alone: "Old Sasowari lies dying. Jakara is gone, and Gareeb the Lamar kneels helpless and forlorn!"

The man's face was transformed with frenzy. He glared at her uncomprehendingly, then whipped out his *upi* knife and snarled. She gripped him almost threateningly and hissed: "Listen, Beizam, do not spoil all at the last moment! You can join in with the warriors – later! But do not say a word to anyone. When you have finished with Gareeb, hurry to the beach; hide and await Jakara. Both he and Eyes of the Sea might come soon now. Do not dally with Eyes of the Sea; she will be alive with cunning in seeking Jakara, and you might spoil all if you seek her. You await Jakara, and I will await Eyes of the Sea – in Jakara's house!"

Even through his madness Beizam spared time to stare in amazed admiration. "No snake ever had such cunning," he said, "and if I take Eyes of the Sea when her canoe beaches, what then? Do you think now that the jealous plans of a girl count in the Councils of a people?"

The Pretty Lamar smiled: "Then you will not have the girl and me awaiting you in Jakara's house," she said. "All is not lost for you! The Lamars have not come yet! Carry on with our plan! It may sweep you on to success. Now is your time to strike for the controlling chieftainship, don't you see? Get rid of the Lamar girls and Jakara at this moment, and the people are yours. You can fight the Lamars then in your own way. But remember, Beizam; Eyes of the Sea is one of us and has many friends, and, if she screamed and got away, no one could tell what the people would do, and—"

The man seized her savagely, jerking the bamboo-knife to her neck. "Do not threaten me with the poison cup," he snarled, "or I will cut your throat as I am going to slit Gareeb's now." He flung her back against the palms, baring his teeth like a mad animal. Then he sped through the darkness towards Sasowari's house.

The Pretty Lamar sprang up, and her face was fiendish as she gazed after him. "Fool!" she whispered in an ecstasy of hate, "Jakara the Unkillable will cut your very liver out!"

She panted in her fury, then gradually grew calm and smiled – a very dreadful smile. Withdrawing her little bone dagger from the waist of her skirt she fingered the sharp point. "Yes," she breathed, "and while he is doing so I will await Eyes of the Sea in Jakara's hut – with this!"

Into the hut of Sasowari entered the angel of death. Fear crouched by his side. The old woman had withered like a mummy, with the spark of life only in her eyes, eyes blazing with terror lest the spark should die before it saw – what? Of her own strength she suddenly sat up, pushing Gareeb aside as if she were a straw, her bony arms outstretched as she screamed, "Gareeb! Oh, my own Gareeb!" For some seconds thus she stared; then she sank quietly back and died. Gareeb crouched, an icy sensation creeping along her spine, while slowly every hair in her head tingled at the roots. She felt another presence in the hut, a presence from the other world that impresses on the human being a feeling of indescribable fear. She tried to cry aloud, but no sound came. Then she looked slowly up, right into the glaring eyes of Warawa. Gareeb shrieked and crouched fumbling towards the door. It opened, as noiseless as the coming of death, and, sobbing, Gareeb passed out.

An arm, stiff with bone and knotted muscle, clutched her throat, and Gareeb's heart burst.

Eyes of the Sea sailed her canoe straight over the great *sai* and across the water, and the bows of the canoe spitted sand as it slithered up on the beach farthest away from the torch-lit trees. She leaped out and ran through the shadows, skirting the crowd, and soon tripped into the path that climbed towards Sasowari's house. She ran fiercely, imbibing the hysteria of that mad crowd down under the palms, frantic with fear that she had lost the man she loved. But her pace slackened, for uncannily she sensed that Fate had forestalled her, that, no matter what she might do, the result was taken out of her hands for ever and for ever.

She paused irresolute, peering into the foliage, then hurried on, eyes strained, ears listening, her every sense quivering, her feet ready to turn and fly. Silvery tracery presently showed where a sickly moon peered from the open into the foliage. Then the dark blob of Sasowari's house. Eyes of the Sea stood before it, and something made her look up at the Sarokag pole. She shrank within herself and forgot all hatred of her rival. In those tense minutes, as she gazed at the white girl's head, a surge of feelings broke loose within her, though why, she would never be able to understand; she only knew that she was a white girl and would never, never want to be a native any more. Sobbing, she sped along the path towards Jakara's house, wailing "Oh, Jakara, Jakara, Jakara, where are you?" A shadow sprang at her, and she screamed and writhed. An anguished voice hissed: "Be quiet, Eyes of the Sea! It is I, Ormei. Ssh! Keep quiet: do not be afraid!"

As she grew quiet, he whispered quickly and in fear, "Do not go to Jakara's house! The Pretty Lamar awaits you there! Beizam would kill you too, but he has rushed back to the people. He is fighting mad against the coming of the Lamars. They expect Jakara back from Eroob any moment.

"Then Beizam is going to kill you both," added Ormei, "in front of all the people. Do not breathe a word of me, Eyes of the Sea, or my head is gone too." He turned down the path and vanished.

Jakara, away out at sea, gazed in fearful suspense as a vivid green flame leaped up from the black bulk of Mer: it was the last time that the *booya* would flare above the Zogo-house. Then, when scarlet flames illumined the sea, he thought for one agonizing moment that Gelam had awakened from sleep. But it was only an hysterical fool who had put a torch to the village of I'Laid.

Jakara ran his canoe aground in the next bay from Maiad. He thus avoided the people whose voices made his spine creep with their terrible roar. He ran up through the trees, and the grasses switched his legs. He brushed through Oroki's banana-patch, treading tender plants underfoot. Out on the path he ran, and he whimpered to prevent himself from crying; for he *knew*. By the blackness of Sasowari's house he stopped. The head of Gareeb stared down at him from the pole, that pole which had treasured so many heads, but none before whose drooping tresses were brown.

Jakara wheeled at a cry of "Jakara, oh, Jakara!" Eyes of the Sea clung to him in abandoned grief. He kissed her in an agony of relief that she was safe, and whispered inarticulate words upon her hair, but she cried the more.

"Oh, Jakara, Jakara, take me away, take me away now! I cannot bear it. Take me quickly!"

"I must do one thing first," he whispered.

"Not Beizam!" she cried, and clutched him afresh, sobbing with frantic face. "You would never have a chance. They would rush you now like sharks. Quick, the dawn comes! It will be too late. Would you leave me to – Beizam?"

Jakara turned white. "Thank you for pricking my senses, Eyes of the Sea," he whispered. "I have been fooled already to-day – or was it yesterday? We will go now. If they catch us, they will make an end of us too – the whole island has gone mad!"

He gazed once more at the Sarokag pole, his face grown old. "Gareeb, Gareeb!" he whispered, "it is the only recompense I can make." He took the head down, and wrapped it in banana-leaves. "We will bury it at sea," he whispered to Eyes of the Sea. "Come! the big drum will boom next, and drive everyone into a maniac. Somehow I feel that C'Zarcke might set Gelam going and finish the whole island." Together they pushed off the canoe. Jakara wheeled round at a quick alarm from the girl. Beizam strode out from the bushes and stared along the shore. The twang of the bows was simultaneous, but it was Beizam who staggered to the rubble with an arrow through his heart. The bushes parted, and the Pretty Lamar, wildly lovely in the quickening light, stared across the sands. With eager fingers Jakara fitted another arrow, knowing that there stood the cause of all. The girl stepped out on to the beach, contemptuously kicked Beizam, and regally targeted her breast towards the bending bow. A shadow fell across her. With bow stretched to the fullest, Jakara gripped tight the arrow-butt, hesitating. For the last time, across the sands of sorrow, he stared into the big, calm eyes of C'Zarcke.

Turning, he leaped into the canoe. The sail filled, cool waters kissed the bow, the tip of a blood-red disk sprang above the rim of the sea. No wild alarm called from the island, but presently when the disk was a rising ball of gold, there throbbed across the waters the drums of Mer, the dread drums of Mer, now crying with despair in their deep mourning tones, sobbing to the skies the requiem of a nation.

GLOSSARY

Ad-Giz – The first gods, or ancestors.

Au-Zogo-zogo-le – Chief of priests.

Beig – A mysterious place under the sea where the spirits of the uneducated dead went to be prepared for the Isle of the Blest.

Boigu – Mythical Isle of the Blest – Does not refer to Boigu Island.

Bomai-Malu Cult – A powerful secret society; in existence for untold centuries. Bomai, Malu, Segar, and Kulka are deities that brought culture to the Islands.

Geregere-le – An order of priests having charge of the Sacred Emblems; they were among the most important members of the priesthood. Also were called the "Beizam-Boai."

Kwod – A severe training-school for youths.

Lamar – A spirit returned from the dead. Every white person was believed to be a "Lamar," possessed of supernatural powers should he be allowed to become "acclimatized" to an earthly environment. The Islanders seldom use the plural, Lamars. For a large number, "Au Lamar" is the usual word; for a small, "Kebi Lamar." "Au" means big or great; for instance, "Au-paser" – a big hill, "Au-kane" – a big sandbank, "Aukosker" – married woman with children (i.e., a woman of importance). For a group of "spirit people," the term used is "GairLamar." In the Western Group, the word "Markai" is used instead of "Lamar." The phrase is "Mura-Markail."

Lightning – The Western word is "Pani-pan."

Maid-le – A sorcerer. The subject of a Maid-le was often thrown into a hypnotic trance. "Mysteries of Maid" (sorcery) were imparted by the Maid-le to their recognized heirs.

Mamoose – Chief of chiefs: the word actually means "red hair," but came to be attached to the chief.

Sacred Grove – A dense mass of "sacred" Wongai-trees. This tree bears a rich crimson plum.

Ships – "Nar," means canoe on Mer. "Gul," is the word used by the Western people. The first ships seen were called "Lamar-Nar" and "Markai-Gul," respectively. Literally, "spirit-canoes" or "spirit-ships."

Singai – A cane loop used in carrying a head.

Tami-le – Secondary order of priests; known also as the Keparem-le. Ulag – A village so named to commemorate the raids of the *Woodlark*. Upi – A head-knife used only for one purpose.

Zogo – Something sacred or holy.

Zogo-le – The three governing priests of each main island of the Eastern Group.

Islands:
Mer – Murray Island.
Eroob – Darnley Island.
Ugar – Stephens Island.
Spirit (Maree-a-lag or Mari-a-lag) – Forbes Island.
Massig (also Kai-lag) – Yorke Island.
Tutu – Warrior Island.
Parama – Coconut Island.
Pabaju (or Gabba) – The Two Brothers Island.
Naghir – Mount Ernest Island.
Moa – Banks Island.
Waiar / Dauar – Two islets of the Murray Group.
Boigu – Talbot Island.
Sabai – Sabai Island.
Dauan – Cornwallis Island.

THE RED CHIEF

Told By the Last of his Tribe

ION IDRIESS

The 18th illustrated edition now out from ETT Imprint, Exile Bay.

> In times past there was an Aboriginal man
> called Cumbo Gunnerah
> His people called him The Red Kangaroo.
> He was a clever chief and a mighty fighter
> (this man from Gunnedah)
> Later, the white people of this place called
> him The Red Chief.

It would be hard to find a more satisfying hero than the young warrior Red Kangaroo, who by his mental and physical prowess became a chief of his tribe - the revered and powerful Red Chief of the Gunnedah district in northern New South Wales. His story is a first-rate tale of adventure but it is something more - a true story handed down from generation to generation by its hero's tribe and given by the last survivor, King Bungaree, to the white settlers of the district.

GOLD-DUST AND ASHES

The Romantic Story of the New Guinea Goldfields

ION IDRIESS

The 26th illustrated edition now out from ETT Imprint, Exile Bay.

Brisbane Courier :-"His latest book is really the romance of the Edie Creek and Bulolo diggings, situated inland from Salamau; and with the discovery of the field are associated the names of diggers as "Shark Eye Bill" (William Park), Matt Crowe, Jim Preston, Arthur Dowling, Frank and Jim Pryke... men who in pre-war years, crept across the frontier, defying the Germans and dodging the head-hunters... These men endured terrible hardships, and frequently faced grim tragedy. Mr Idriess writes of it all, and writes of it as if he had been with them.. What a romance! What a story! It is packed with adventure, studded with splendid pen-pictures of pioneer prospectors, airmen, and patrol officers, and told with a fascinating simplicity that is borne from something very close to genius."

THE YELLOW JOSS
ION IDRIESS
Foreword by Tony Grey

Sydney Morning Herald :- "The Booya is a masterpiece of the weird and terrible. But of all the tales "The Castaway" has most power and surely merits a place with similar episodes in Conrad. Mr Idriess is adept in working up the feelings of his readers to a pitch of expectancy .... Here the excitement is terrific."

The Herald (Melbourne) :- "Every one of these tales bears the impress of truth. Anybody who lets unreasoned prejudice against short stories deter them from reading this book is missing a treat."

The Sun (Sydney) :- "Idriess tells a good story. These come from another world, a primitive and violent world, where things that seem fantastic and incredible to dwellers in the Australian cities are commonplaces of life."

Queensland Times :- "He has the happy knack of being able to blend truth and fiction in such a way that even commonplace things assume an important role and have definite and impelling force."

Woman's Budget (Sydney) :- "They give a clearer insight into his varied and adventurous life than anything he has previously written."

Honi Soit (University of Sydney) :- "Rich humour enlivens the book, particularly where the exploits of one 'Scandalous' Graham are concerned."

Producers' Review (Brisbane) :- "The name of Ion Idriess has become a household word ... as a maker of short stories he has lost none of his flair for tale-telling. Indeed we prefer this style."

Now in its 11th edition, 210 pages, available from ETT Imprint.

By the same author
Available from ETT Imprint

PROSPECTING FOR GOLD
LASSETER'S LAST RIDE
FLYNN OF THE INLAND
THE DESERT COLUMN
HORRIE THE WOG DOG
THE RED CHIEF
NEMARLUK
MADMAN'S ISLAND
THE YELLOW JOSS
THE SILVER CITY
FORTY FATHOMS DEEP
GOLD-DUST AND ASHES
THE WILD WHITE MAN
OF BADU
LIGHTNING RIDGE
SHOOT TO KILL
SNIPING
GUERRILLA TACTICS

ION IDRIESS:
The Last Interview

www.ingramcontent.com/pod-product-compliance
Lightning Source LLC
Chambersburg PA
CBHW020751160426
43192CB00006B/298